THE LIBERAL HERESY

THE LIBERAL HERESY

Origins and Historical Development

MASSIMO SALVADORI

ST. MARTIN'S PRESS NEW YORK

CONTENTS

To Joyce
to whom I owe more than I can say
this book is dedicated

FOREWORD

AN HERETICAL EXPERIENCE

A civilisation was born in modern times in the midst of turmoil and suffering. Its beginnings were modest. Although resented by most people much of the time nearly everywhere, for a few generations it affected all mankind, and transformed most of it. Now, in the midst of greater turmoil and of tensions unendurable for many, limited to a small minority of independent states belonging primarily to the First World, passionately attacked at all levels from all sides, it is losing ground; this is why the book has been written.

The autonomy and responsibility of individuals, and the choices they made, were central to the civilisation: not the rights of society and the state, not guidance by rulers who know what is good for everybody. With power deriving from the freely expressed and ever-changing will of the citizens, the relationship between people and state was reversed institutionally. Contrary to what happened everywhere in the past, and happens today in Second and Third World civilisations and in illiberal states of the First, goals and policies mattered less than the way goals were pursued and decisions about policies taken.

A radical departure from the age-old orthodoxy of authoritarian and conformist societies (nearly as dominant in the world today as it once was), this civilisation has been heretical both at the level of ideas and of institutions — of spiritual and practical activities. It reduced repression, and in consequence there came expansion and advancement in all fields of endeavour. This was the credit side. Minds and expression being freer than ever before, awareness of remaining repression increased, bringing unhappiness; action being freer, tensions increased. This was the debit side.

The driving force of the new civilisation was a striving for liberty — for the right and duty to be not just a unit in the herd but oneself. It took a long time to clarify the ideas implicit in the striving, and to decide through what institutions the ideas could become a way of life. A long period elapsed before clear ideas were held by enough

people to become a political force. Once they did, they gave
direction to a movement which, successful in the revolutions of 1688,
1776 and 1789, established the institutional structure later described
as 'liberal'.

THE THEME

This book deals with the movement leading to the three revolutions,
and to many kindred ones in all continents — some successful for
long or short periods, others not — which occurred from the 1790s
to the 1970s. Early revolutionaries summed up their position in the
British Bill of Rights, the French Declaration of Rights, the
American Ten Amendments, in statutes substituting for constitutions
and in written constitutions, and in slogans such as the 'free and
equal' of the second revolution, 'liberty, equality, fraternity' of the
third. Liberalism is the movement of those who drafted Bill,
Declaration and Amendments, who approved statutes and
constitutions, who used the slogans, who replaced servile institutions
with free institutions. What they had in common mattered more in
humanity's historical scheme than what divided them. Today,
conflicts between advocates and opponents of free institutions are
what matter, not dissensions between progressive and moderate
advocates of the same institutions, or antagonisms between different
factions of opponents.

The goal of the forerunners of liberalism, and of liberals since the
term came into use in its ideological—political meaning, was
emancipation: immediate emancipation of minds from dogmas and
superstitions, and of citizens from despotism. In time, liberals hoped,
there would result emancipation from disease, ignorance, poverty,
discrimination and war. Emancipation meant an institutional
structure within which people would decide what direction to move
in, if they wanted to move. It meant means to achieve ends, not
specific ends. The institutional structure has been known as 'liberal
constitutional', if suffrage was limited, 'liberal democratic' if suffrage
was universal. (Inappropriately because of the varied meanings of
democracy, many, particularly in North America, call the
institutional structure democratic *tout court*. Unswervingly centred
on liberty, Scandinavian-type social democracy, enriched with
institutions promoting justice, belongs to the liberal family.)

The original liberties were freedom of expression (worshipping
openly according to one's conscience, saying and printing what one
wanted) and political freedom (the free election of those who make
laws and supervise their application), both being meaningful when

several requirements are fulfilled. These two and none other are liberalism's essential liberties; these and none other provide the criterion distinguishing a free society from an authoritarian one. Important, but not essential on the basis of long-standing evidence, is economic liberty, correctly understood as institutions facilitating changes in economic structures, including the passage from one economic system to another (and not to be identified, as is mistakenly done by many, with capitalism, a by-product in continual transformation of the drive for emancipation, now largely replaced by mixed welfare economies). The two essential liberties interest all and have no sectional, or class, connotation.

Within the relative security of liberal constitutional and, more recently, liberal democratic states, emancipation expressed itself in new ideas, aspirations and movements. Some strengthened the institutional structure and improved it, others aimed at destroying it. Different from the traditional authoritarian forces against which liberals had struggled, new enemies of liberty ranged from dictatorial sectors of radical revolutionarism at the end of the eighteenth century, to dictatorial sectors of today's liberation movements — which would play a liberal role if to the pursuit of specific goals of emancipation they did not add the obliteration of freedom of expression and of political liberty, and of everything making them meaningful.

One set of enemies nearly won in the early 1940s. They were held together by frenzied nationalistic conviction of their own superiority. Another set of enemies is gaining ground in all continents today. Its unifying element is hatred of capitalism — for most of its opponents a vague term covering everything they are against. Their hatred is reinforced by the conviction that they are agents of laws immanent in society, the laws in turn justifying any action one engages in. This hatred is more and more an obsession in ever-widening circles of the intelligentsia, the dynamic minority now guiding mankind. What was essential in emancipation — freedom of the mind to explore and blaze new trails, to create and to invent, freedom to share one's convictions with others, institutions centred on self-government to guarantee these freedoms, respect for others, legitimacy of opposition and dissent — is all dismissed as futile, harmful, or a dream. To eliminate malignant economic growths, the whole liberal-democratic structure and the ideas and values on which it rests, are to be eliminated. Once liberty of the mind and political liberty are lost, they may remain lost — forever. Mankind may revert in its entirety to the authoritarianism and conformity of the pre-liberal past. Whatever the wave of the future may be, it behoves one to be aware of what the liberal heresy is, and how it came about.

APOLOGIES

In other times, the title of this book might have been: 'An Introduction to the Study of Liberalism, its Nature, and its Historical Development in Modern Times as an Ideological—Political Force'. This is what the book is. As an introduction, it is necessarily incomplete; by synthesising it contains the margin of error unavoidable in all generalisations and simplifications; as a history it can be no more than a survey. On the three counts it falls short of scientific precision. In justification, it can be said that a subject alien to the consciousness of many requires an introduction and that, didactically, synthesis and survey precede analysis and detailed study of specific developments.

The index—glossary (page 230) provides brief definitions of terms to which various meanings are attached (e.g. 'imperialism') or which are not in common use (e.g. 'centrist socialism'). The use of capitals has been restricted; in some cases it is self-explanatory ('Continent', for instance, is the European continental area of Western civilisation, and 'Liberal party' is a specific party of that name). There are many names of individuals, largely in order to compensate for the often misleading simplification of general terms: the impersonal Free Democrats, for instance, does not give the idea of inner tensions, outer pressures, complexity of positions and problems personified in Heuss or Scheel. Footnotes have been dispensed with, as academically pretentious in an introductory survey.

There are a few more points. In this book, liberalism is seen in the context of global developments, not just Western ones; this changes the perspective. What among five or six hundred million Westerners is obvious and 'natural' is neither obvious nor natural among the world's four thousand millions. In the second place, while books on ideological—political positions called 'isms' mainly deal with goals, programmes and policies, a book on liberalism deals primarily with what makes goals, programmes and policies possible — that is to say with the basic institutional structure. Thirdly, little reference is made here to the economic side of liberalism or other 'isms'. This is not because of lack of awareness of economic problems and of the obsessive interest in them (this writer's doctoral thesis and much of his subsequent writing has been in the field of political economy) but because the role of economics matters less than the role of ideas (for instance, not an economic problem *per se* moves people to action, but the idea they have of the problem) and of politics, or manage-ment of society's institutional structure. Finally, as the mind is an imperfect (albeit marvellous) instrument and all faculties are limited, any phenomenon — in this book, liberalism — is perceived somewhat incorrectly; what one can, and should do, is to be as correct as possible — and to stress, unequivocably and everywhere, the freedom of thought and of expression which only can reduce inaccuracies.

San Tommaso, Capodarco, Italy
March 1977

INTRODUCTION

AIM OF THE BOOK

This book aims to describe in plain words what liberalism is for those who call themselves 'liberals' or by common consent are called 'liberals'; to summarise liberalism's historical development; to set it in the spectrum of political—ideological forces which have influenced mankind in recent generations. A sequel to this volume will deal with positive and negative elements in liberalism; with achievements and failures; with allied and hostile forces; with the prospects for liberty and free institutions.

'Liberal' and 'liberalism' have two major distinct meanings. From ancient to modern times, to be liberal has meant to be generous, broad-minded, compassionate, altruistically inclined, somewhat tolerant of different views and of new ideas, fashions, customs and trends; to prefer compromise to intransigence; possibly but not necessarily to be forward-looking in the sense of being in sympathy with change. It has meant acting on the basis of a concept which is also an attitude and which, if widely diffused, becomes the foundation of a way of life: to live and let live. Autocrats who relaxed coercion and repression have been called 'liberal'; so have wealthy people who spent freely and endowed charities, clerics indulgent towards sinners and heretics, teachers who listened to students.

Recently, during the past few generations, 'liberalism' has had a narrower meaning. It has indicated a political movement trying to reshape society; the ideas and values, the interests and aspirations that gave cohesion and direction to the movement; the institutions through which the state had to be restructured.

The driving force of liberalism as a political movement was its commitment to liberty. The commitment derived from belief that the individual possesses a capacity for choice which endows all with autonomy, and thus with responsibility; that the autonomy, or liberty, made possible the survival of the species, and was the source of the astounding progress from distant beginnings, when humans lived much like other animals, to contemporary civilisation. The ideology (i.e. the integrated system of ideas and values) of liberalism as a political force rested on four corner-stones. In the order in which they appeared as dynamic concepts accepted by enough people to influence events, these were: religious tolerance, free inquiry, self-government, market economy. Each concept was linked to various postulates; each had numerous implications and corollaries.

Parties called 'liberal', and parties with other names but with programmes identical to those of liberal ones, have existed for the last century and a half. However, what they stood for, and the goals they tried to achieve, had previously been for as long again, or a little longer, the dynamic element in the progressive movement which in time came to be identified — for several generations, and wrongly (the part is not the whole) — with modern civilisation. Tolerance was emancipation from bigotry and fanaticism; free inquiry was emancipation from intellectual dogmatism and immobility, and from what was once called 'obscurantism'; self-government was emancipation from political absolutism and arbitrary rule; market economy was emancipation from state-enforced restrictions, and from stagnation condemning the poor to remain always poor.

Continuity of liberalism, as a force moving people to action, stretches from the 1636 founding of Providence and the 1642 Great Rebellion, to the 1948 Declaration of Human Rights and the attempt in 1973—4 in four countries (Argentina, Thailand, Portugal and Greece) to establish, through free elections, self-government in its correct meaning of 'government by the citizens'. The Declaration and free elections are meaningful only for small sectors of mankind (for lack of sufficient popular support in Argentina and Thailand, the recent experiment in liberty lasted a bare three years); these small sectors are the contemporary heirs to the liberal tradition.

Movement and tradition are the theme of this book. The movement had its modest beginning (see Chapter 3) in the midst of the European religious and ethical turmoil of 400 years ago. It first acquired political significance in North Atlantic communities (see Chapter 4). Then it spread eastward and southward (see Chapters 5 and 6), finally affecting all mankind for a short while — for long enough, though, to bring about radical transformations everywhere.

There are scholars who have seen in democracy (either as organisation of individual liberty or as majority-based dictatorial power, or simply as concern for the welfare of the masses) the essential characteristic of the movement to which the contemporary world owes much of what it is. Others have stressed the expansion of knowledge; others still the application of scientific discoveries to technological inventions that revolutionised the economic process, or the Westernisation of much of mankind through political control and/or cultural impact. Today it is fashionable to stress capitalism only (and to condemn modern civilisation when liberalism was influential, on the basis of the defects, shortcomings, errors and also horrors of capitalism).

However, democracy, scientific knowledge, technological advance and the industrial revolution, Westernisation and capitalism (and other developments too numerous to list, in all fields of endeavour) were by-products of the drive for emancipation. Central in the movement that broke what Bagehot called 'the cake of custom', that woke nations and tribes from their slumber, that brought about more change than many people can endure, was commitment to the conviction summarised in a few words in the *Via Lucis* written by the seventeenth-century Czech theologian Comenius: 'for liberty man's mind . . . was made'. Because the commitment of those who formed the dynamic core of the progressive movement during its long formative period — and of those who died, from the English John Hampden in 1643 to the French Jean Antoine de Condorcet in 1794 — was first of all to liberty in all fields, not to democracy, knowledge, technology, the West, or capitalism, the term 'liberal' applies to the movement even before Liberal and kindred parties were organised.

Emphasis on liberalism as an ideological position and a political movement is not meant as minimising the importance of other forces that have absorbed much of the liberal spirit and adopted much of the liberal programme, and are deeply and sincerely committed to free institutions. World wide, two of these forces command the loyalty of more people than those who call themselves 'liberals' without further qualification.

Liberty as freedom of choice, and as individual autonomy and responsibility, divided lay and confessional conservatives against whom liberals agitated and struggled — from British Tories to traditionalists in all continents. Many conservatives stood steadfastly for 'throne and altar', or whatever equivalent slogan their war cry was. Others, in some nations a majority, came so close to the more cautious wing of liberalism (as was the case of most post-1945 Christian Democrats everywhere, and is the case now with French Gaullists and with members of the Brazilian Democratic Movement) as to become practically indistinguishable, and to merge in liberal-conservative moderatism.

The role of liberty, and the institutions through which liberty becomes part of the way of life, have divided socialist opponents of liberalism in this century. Most revisionist socialists (world wide, the majority sector of socialism at the time of the crisis caused by

Leninist action at the end of the First World War, now a minority)
came so close to the bolder wing of liberalism (Radicalism in European political terminology) as to be practically indistinguishable. In
several countries the two groups merged in liberal-socialist Labourism
(as happened in the Netherlands) and Social Democracy (as is
happening in Japan).

To debate on who influenced whom is futile. Besides liberals without qualification, today there are liberal-conservatives and liberal-
socialists (also liberal-catholics in prevalently catholic nations and
liberal-nationalists in the Third World). They differ in their policies
but not in their attachment to free institutions. Because of a
common commitment to liberty, there are only differences in degree.
The difference in kind — today just as ten generations ago — is
between the liberal and liberal-democratic state in which citizens
govern themselves and enjoy a good deal of autonomy, and the
authoritarian state in which subjects are governed and must conform.

RANDOM REFERENCES TO POLITICAL LIBERALISM TODAY

A quick perusal of recent writings gives an idea of the extent to
which liberalism is a world-wide political—ideological force.

In the United States the distinction between conservatives and
liberals overrides the distinction between Republicans and Democrats,
and is a determinant in internal and external policies. In Great
Britain a Liberal party, supported in national elections by one-fifth
of the electorate, has in recent years held about one-fiftieth of the
seats in the House of Commons. Liberal parties are influential in the
other nations of the Old Commonwealth and in some of today's
Commonwealth. At home or in exile, opponents of dictatorial
regimes are often collectively described as 'liberals'. In analysing and
classifying political forces, a distinction must be made between
supporters and adversaries of liberal democracy, the institutional
embodiment of liberal principles. In the 1970s, at one time or
another, leaders of liberal parties in the European—Mediterranean
area were heads of state or of government in Denmark, the German
Federal Republic, Lebanon, Luxembourg; in the Western hemisphere
they were heads of state or of government in Canada, Colombia,
Costa Rica, Venezuela; in eastern Asia and the Western Pacific area
in Australia, Japan, Thailand; and other states.

Again in the 1970s, the Pakistani strong man Bhutto gleefully
stated that 'liberal institutions are not prospering anywhere'. Only
a few months before her sudden authoritarian about-turn in 1975,
India's prime minister Indira Gandhi referred with sympathy, in an
interview published in December 1974, to the debt nations in the

Indian sub-continent owed to 'liberal thought'. The Yugoslav
Marshal Tito, for whom 'defiance of central party guidance smacked
of liberalism', consistently referred to his anti-authoritarian opponents
as 'anarcho-liberals', and characterised as 'liberal' Serbian autono-
mists. In a letter to the editor, an influential British newspaper was
described as 'the most liberal paper in the most liberal country in the
world'. Prominent in the *Selected Works of Mao Tse-tung* is the
article 'Combat Liberalism'. In Albania, a huge poster warned that
'liberalism is the number one enemy'. Referring to the Third World
of developing nations, an American writer observed that 'the ideas
of . . . liberalism . . . offered reformers new tools with which to
reshape their societies'. Another writer referred to the pre-Nationalist
(pre-1948) regime in the then Union of South Africa as 'liberal'. The
formation of a Centre of Independents in France was greeted as an
addition to 'the liberal family'.

For a major inter-American publication, the 1975 man of the year
was Alfonso Lopez Michelsen, leader of the Revolutionary Liberal
Movement and President of Colombia. Asked how he would describe
himself, the Soviet scientist and intellectual dissident Alexander
Sakharov replied: 'I would call myself a *liberal*.' As political activist,
the anti-*apartheid* South African writer Alan Paton for a while led a
Liberal party. To prevent the election to the Presidency of Senator
Benigno Aquino, leader of the Filipino Liberal party, his Nationalist
opponent seized dictatorial power; from his prison cell, Aquino
remained the spokesman for opposition to the dictatorship. Major
figures in opposing military dictatorships in the early 1970s in
Argentina, Greece, Peru, Thailand and Turkey were the liberals
Ricardo Balbin, George Mavros, Francisco Belaunde Terry, Sanya
Dharmasakti, Suleyman Demirel.

A DECLINING BUT STILL INFLUENTIAL 'ISM'

The demise of liberalism has been a recurrent theme for generations.
In a 1932 article, the Italian dictator Benito Mussolini stated that
liberalism had been dead since the middle of the nineteenth century.
In all continents, magazine articles of the mid-1970s have announced
that liberalism is dead or dying. A lengthy debate among Soviet
leaders on the crisis of 'capitalism' (the term used to indicate liberal
democracy, in spite of the fact that most liberal democracies have
welfare or neo-mercantilist mixed economies) ended late in 1975
with the conclusion that it was on the way out, and that communist
states and communist parties should adopt more aggressive policies.
In English-speaking nations, books published several decades ago
with the suggestive titles *Forward from Liberalism* and *Up from*

Liberalism were followed by a spate of books on the decline of liberalism, and recently by others with even more suggestive titles, such as *The Poverty of Liberalism* and *The End of Liberalism.* Evidently, whatever the value judgements, liberalism is present in the minds of adversaries as well as in those of supporters. There is no doubt that liberalism is less influential than early in the century, and that a strong authoritarian tide is gaining ground (see the following section). There is also no doubt that liberalism is still a force to be reckoned with.

Early in 1976, out of about 170 formally sovereign states, and political units likely to achieve sovereignty in the near future, over thirty (including half-a-dozen mini-states) were structured as liberal democracies. Their basic political institution is that which implements the liberals' chief tenet for the organisation of society: *election on the basis of free* (or at least tolerably free) *universal suffrage of those who make laws and are entrusted with the conduct of public affairs or with supervising those so entrusted.*

'Free' is the key word; it implies not only a choice between voting and not voting (available at times in dictatorial regimes looking for some kind of legitimacy) but — more important — a choice of candidates. The possibility for any citizen to be a candidate and for any group of citizens to nominate a candidate is essential in free universal suffrage. The elected assembly — Parliament, Congress, Diet — must exercise supreme deciding power, and not be a rubber-stamp organ as it is in authoritarian regimes in which pseudo-elections take place. The functioning of the basic institution requires freedom of expression and of association (leading to a multiplicity of parties and other political organisations). Pluralism, and consequently tension, is a main feature of the liberal-democratic way of life.

Leaving out India, readjusting after a recent authoritarian interlude, liberal democracies vary in size from gigantic Canada (the largest, nearly four million square miles) and the United States (the most populous, over two hundred million inhabitants) to minuscule San Marino and still smaller Nauru; they include the industrially advanced O.E.C.D. countries, which contribute over two-thirds of the world production of goods and services, and where standards of living are higher than in any authoritarian state. Because there is liberty, intellectual activities — in the sciences, the arts and religion — are lively, dynamic and creative. Liberal democracies embrace fewer than one-fifth of the world's population living on less than one-quarter of the planet's land area. In twenty liberal democracies free institutions are solidly entrenched; in the remaining ones they are precariously shaky.

As the only workable alternative to authoritarian rule in the contemporary world, liberal democracy is the political structure wanted not only by liberals but also by all who are close to the liberal position: labourites, social democrats, advocates of free labour organisations, constitutional conservatives, the Christian democratic wing of political catholicism, the anti-authoritarian wing of nationalism; and by smaller groups such as sections of the intelligentsia in islamic and east Asian civilisations.

Providing safeguards against the arbitrary rule of majorities and minorities, and also providing possibilities for action non-existent in authoritarian regimes, liberal democracy is supported at times (but never loved) by advocates of their own dictatorial rule: orthodox Leninists in Western Europe, Black Power groups in republics of the Western hemisphere, Arab nationalists in Israel. It is advocated in authoritarian states by spokesmen of minorities oppressed by majorities (Marxist dissident intellectuals in communist dictatorships, moslems in the Philippines, Albanians in Yugoslavia), and by spokesmen of majorities oppressed by minorities (Christians in East Europe, Lamaists in Tibet, Bantus in the Republic of South Africa, peasant masses in Haiti and Honduras). 'One man, one vote' has been the liberal slogan of Third World nationalists agitating against colonial power; as soon as they got into power, nationalists eliminated free elections. In evaluating the strength of liberal democracy, a distinction must be made between liberals and kindred groups on one side, and the many on the other side who lack the commitment to liberty but find in liberal democracy the road to survival or to power.

On the basis of electoral results and polls, in liberal democracies the liberals without a socialist, conservative or other qualification — often not a cohesive group but a weak coalition of kindred groups — represent from a third or more of the voting population (in the larger North American nations) to a small or a minuscule fraction (in the liberal democracies of eastern Asia). It is impossible to say how many liberals there are among the four-fifths of mankind living in authoritarian states. On the basis of the situation in Brazil during a recent ten-year interval between two dictatorial phases, in Czechoslovakia between liberation from Nazi occupation in 1945 and the establishment of a Stalinist dictatorship in 1948 (also in 1968), and in India before 1975, there are probably numerous liberals in the three nations. On the other hand there are no more than a handful of liberals in Middle East dictatorships and in the Soviet Union, and scarcely any in a multitude of countries from A (Albania) to Z (Zaïre). In free elections which took place in four former dictatorships, in Argentina in 1973, in Greece in 1974, in Thailand and

Portugal in 1975, between one-fifth and one-quarter of the votes went to liberal or kindred parties. However, it would be unrealistic to extrapolate from these few instances.

EXPANDING RADICAL AUTHORITARIANISM

In 1976 there were over thirty traditional authoritarian states in the world, ruled by absolute or near-absolute monarchs (eight of them in the Middle East) or by reactionary oligarchies (nearly all of these in the Western hemisphere). There were also a few straight nationalist and racist authoritarian states.

Most of the nearly one hundred states that were neither liberal democracies, nor residues of traditional authoritarianism, nor nationalist dictatorships, had radical dictatorial regimes. With a wide range of variation and an even wider range of efficiency, their structure was patterned on that of dictatorships established in Europe at the end of the First World War or soon after: a monopolistic single party and the elimination of all dissent; censorship and monopoly of communications media and of education; a command economy; an omnipotent arbitrary secret police to enforce political subservience, intellectual conformity, and economic operations. Radical authoritarian states are ruled by groups belonging to the vast dynamic movements formed by the merging of nationalism and authoritarian socialism. According to the relationship between the two components, radical dictatorships fall into three categories: national-socialist states (for instance neo-Peronist Argentina before the 1976 military takeover, Indonesia, Iraq and Uganda) in which the nationalist component predominates; national-communist states (Cuba, Mozambique, Soviet Union and Vietnam) in which the socialist component predominates; and social-nationalist states (for instance Burma, Senegal, Peru and Yugoslavia) in which the two components stay in balance and repression is at times less rigid. Nowhere in power, but influential in a number of states as a disruptive force, is anarcho-communism, the fourth major strain in the expanding anti-liberal 'ism'.

Of nearly ninety former dependencies which have achieved sovereign status since Great Britain granted independence to Egypt in 1922, only a dozen had authoritarian regimes at the moment of independence. Enthusiastic advocates of decolonisation, most liberals were convinced that leaders of newly independent states agreed with what the Mexican revolutionary Morelos wrote in 1813: 'We will not be free unless we replace the tyrannical government with a liberal one.' It was an illusion: Morelos was a liberal. From the Egyptian Zaghlul in 1922 to the Surinamese Arron in 1976, the overwhelming majority of leaders of newly independent states wanted to replace authoritarian colonial administration with their own stricter authoritarian rule. Early in 1976, in all but a few former dependencies (six in the Eastern hemisphere and the Pacific area, five in the Western hemisphere), liberal democracy had been superseded by radical dictatorships. This is further evidence that the explosive combination of nationalism and authoritarian socialism is the strongest force moving mankind today. As had happened in recent years in Afghanistan, Ethiopia, Laos, Libya, Peru and the Yemen, this explosive combination is the likely successor when surviving traditional authoritarian regimes collapse. Just as twelve centuries ago contrasts within the islamic camp did not appreciably weaken the common front presented by Islam against Christianity, so today's contrasts within the radical authoritarian camp (for instance between Iraqi national-socialists and Egyptian social-nationalists in the Middle East, between orthodox and Maoist national-communists in southern Asia and in Africa, between Castroites and Peronists in South America) do not weaken its capacity to attack liberal democracy, or diminish the authoritarian radicals' hatred of liberalism.

THREE POINTS CONCERNING APPROACH

(a) Method

The basic postulates and method of thought used in this book are those of the conceptual framework linked to the names of Locke, Mill, and Russell in treatises on the history of philosophy, described as 'empiricism'. Among the main features of this conceptual framework (as also of its variations and derivatives, such as empirio-positivism, pragmatism and neo-positivism) are: (a) stress on methods (inductive, a posteriori, combined, scientific) whose fundamental canons are observation, classification, formulation of hypotheses, verification; and (b) the legitimacy of different conclusions (i.e. of different opinions), since minds are limited and not everything can be observed or verified.

Whatever the variations, within this conceptual framework there is consent on several basic postulates:

(i) as far as possible reason should have priority over non-reason, i.e. over intuition, revelation, imagination, emotion, imitation, tradition;

(ii) a capacity for choice (or liberty, see Chapter 1) is inherent in reasoning faculties — therefore human beings are not entirely determined;

(iii) the direction action takes is influenced by what there is in the mind;

(iv) whatever is done by limited and imperfect beings is necessarily limited and imperfect, and therefore error is unavoidable and so also the gap between idea and action, between goal and realisation;

(v) openness of mind (critical thinking) and flexibility of institutions (free institutions) are essential to correct errors and to narrow gaps;

(vi) as reasoning powers exist only in the minds of individuals, what is alive and real is the individual;

(vii) the group, from the smallest to the largest, is the sum of individuals plus their innumerable interactions, and does not of itself possess mind, will, conscience.

(b) Inner Convictions versus Outer Conditions

In discussing a movement — i.e. millions of people going in the same direction — knowledge of the concepts setting its course (for the theme of this book, liberal principles, values, goals, aspirations) is derived primarily from what is empirically known. The historical evidence of what people have done, of the liberals' successful or unsuccessful actions — from the hard struggle for religious tolerance generations ago, to the setting up of welfare mixed economies in this century — matters more than what was written by theorists, however influential their writings (as in the case of Paine) or powerful their minds (as in the case of Kant).

In his book *The Rise of Liberalism*, a European theorist, H. Laski, casually and briefly mentions principles, values, goals and aspirations held by individuals, and defines liberalism primarily in terms of environmental conditions (particularly economic ones) in which the liberal movement was born, grew and declined. In his *History of Liberalism*, another European theorist, G. de Ruggiero, follows a different approach: he analyses in detail the principles, values, goals and aspirations making for the conviction held by liberals; in giving little space to environmental conditions, he minimises their role.

It is easy to say that the definition of liberalism should be in terms of inner conviction (the liberal idea or ideas) and of outer conditions. The fact is that the definition, and the understanding, of liberalism vary according to whether priority is given to conviction or to environment. For Laski, liberalism reflects the requirements of capitalistic free enterprise; for de Ruggiero it is a conviction keyed to liberty.

The perusal of widely used manuals shows that one approach or the other is used according to whether a few or many individuals are involved in a situation. When a position is held by one or a few, it is usually taken for granted that the conviction from which that position results is tied to the ideas, values, emotions and interests of the individual; it is explained and defined in terms of the inner self. (The republican Arnold of Brescia, and the abolitionist George Fox, being clearly out of step with their times, the twelfth and the seventeenth century respectively, their republicanism and abolitionism are defined in terms of their inner convictions.) When on the other hand a position is held by many, what is considered more important than the conviction is the 'nature' of human beings, or the social and phyical environment, or the more distant unknown surrounding mankind. (The republicanism of the thirteenth century, when republicans were many in European communities stretching from central Italy to northern Germany, is defined in terms not of its own concepts but of social forces; so is the abolitionism of the late eighteenth century, when abolitionists were numerous.)

The writer maintains that what is correct for a few is correct for the many, that a movement must be described and defined primarily in terms of convictions held. Liberalism is what is in the minds of liberals, especially the committed ones who are the dynamic core of the movement: it is the institutions through which liberals try to make their convictions and goals a way of life.

(c) Causation

Differences of opinion on causation are closely related to those concerning the second point, and underlying these is the unending debate on the relative roles of determining biological and environmental factors, and of freely made choice. Although the truth is not demonstrable, reasoning about any 'ism' involves leaning towards one postulate or the other.

Discarding the role of the inner self, postulating instead the overriding importance of the role of forces that reduce human beings to pawns, historians and experts in social disciplines have in recent generations built ingenious schemes so as to explain movements (the 'isms') that have carried mankind in one direction or another. It having been unfashionable since the Age of Enlightenment to call on God, gods and scriptures to provide explanations — as previously done in Western civilisations, and always in all other civilisations — secular deities have been introduced. Among the popular ones have been the Hegelian 'dialectical process' and 'peregrinations of the spirit', Comteian 'phases', Marxian 'modes of production' and 'class struggle', Darwinian and pseudo-Darwinian 'selection and survival of the fittest', the Spencerian 'law of evolution', Freudian 'neuroses', Spenglerian 'cycles', and others, from Vico's 'spirals' and Montesquieu's 'climate', to Gobineau's 'genius of the race' and Toynbee's 'challenge-and-response'.

It would be foolish to discard all of these determining factors as irrelevant; some may be considered pure inventions, most are not, and they play a role in human affairs. However, it would also be foolish to attribute too much importance to them, and totally foolish to make any of them the total explanation. After learning about human 'nature' (which is the same for all), after investigating all kinds of environmental conditions which are identical for those who act in one way and for those who act in another, after analysing societies and individuals, something is still missing from the birth, growth and nature of any 'ism'. The missing element is the response of individuals to situations and problems – the idea or ideas born in the minds of individuals and giving direction to action, the emotions creating the energy with which ideas are pursued.

The explanation of liberalism, as of any 'ism', lies in convictions (often vague and contradictory) and in arguments (not necessarily correct) supporting them, in values, interests, aspirations and goals, and not in the nature of man, or in environmental factors (or transcendental ones, if they exist), which are identical for liberals, their friends, their enemies and those who do not care.

LIBERALISM AND LIBERTY'S ESSENTIAL ROLE

Liberalism differs from all other ideological–political positions because it is not identified with specific goals, but instead aims at creating the structure within which different goals coexist, come and go. It prescribes the unchanging method for the pursuit of ever-changing goals (see Chapter 2). Individual autonomy means that individuals are responsible for establishing their own goals; freedom of expression means discussion about goals and the policies to achieve them; self-government is the procedure for the adoption of policies and the pursuit of goals, for peaceful change. Liberty is incompatible with collective single-mindedness in thought and action.

In the name of economic growth, prosperity, national independence and cohesion, of justice, peace and universal literacy, the liberals' insistence on liberty is dismissed today on a variety of grounds – as an illusion, an obstacle, a fraud, and so on. Liberals on their part can justify commitment to liberty on a variety of grounds. Relevant today is the justification that can be summarised in the following propositions:

(i) Problems created by the astounding progress of the last three centuries endanger survival – new ideas and values, and the action to which they give rise, are needed to solve the problems, and will be needed later to solve new problems created by the solution of old ones.

(ii) New ideas and values are the product of the creativity of individual minds (see Chapter 1) — only through the free play of forces can what is beneficial be separated from what is harmful.

(iii) Creativity is stifled, is easily repressed and can be suppressed by the coercion of arbitrary centralised power and censorship, the twin agents of authoritarianism. The authoritarian state is the norm of social organisation. The weakening of coercion and a consequent measure of liberty, and the possibility for creativity to express itself, have arisen, on most occasions, through conflicts disrupting society. Liberty has been with few exceptions an unwelcome accident; whatever new force was born and triumphed, it hurried to re-establish authoritarian institutions.

(iv) Liberalism consciously weakens coercion — liberals aim at introducing in the society as much liberty as is compatible with the requirements of the social order indispensable for human survival. Nowhere of course has that level of liberty been achieved — it may be achieved within the frame of basic liberal institutions, not outside it.

(v) For progress until now, possibly for survival later, what have mattered and will matter are not the goals of this or that tendency, but the institutions of the liberal — now liberal-democratic — state, enabling a variety of tendencies to take turns in trying to solve the problems facing the community.

In brief, liberty is indispensable for survival, and liberalism — a method, to which goals are subordinated — guarantees as much liberty as is realisable.

THE BIRTHPLACE OF LIBERALISM

Lists of names can give a correct idea of the extent and variety of a movement. Such lists are boring to read, however, so the paragraph that follows can be omitted.

Major intellectual forerunners of modern liberalism were Roger Williams, Locke and Voltaire, crusaders for religious tolerance and freedom of conscience; Milton and Voltaire, champions of freedom of the press, without which freedom of thought is meaningless; Locke, who upheld self-government and prepared the ground for Lincoln's 'government of the people, by the people, for the people'; Quesnay and Adam Smith, advocates of market economies; Locke and Kant, who, starting from different premises and following different roads, provided liberalism with philosophical and ethical foundations. As a comprehensive theoretical system, liberalism was formulated by,

among others, British utilitarians (Bentham, J. S. Mill), followed by
American pragmatists and continental empirio-positivists; as a
comprehensive institutional system, it was formulated by the drafters
of the 1787 American Constitution and the 1791 French Constitution. Political forerunners were the statesmen Turgot in France,
Charles Fox in Great Britain, von Humboldt in Germany, the
revolutionaries Miranda in Venezuela, Kosciuszko in Poland, La
Harpe in Switzerland. Among successful liberal statesmen there have
been Jefferson in the United States, Cavour in Italy, Seddon in New
Zealand, Cerda in Chile; and among unsuccessful ones the German
vom Stein, the Ottoman Midhat, the Russian Miliukov, the Chinese
Liang. Recent authoritative spokesmen for liberalism have been, or
are, the American Adlai Stevenson, the Indian M. Masani, the
Spaniard de Madariaga. Economic theory and policy have been
among liberalism's major weaknesses; errors in economic theory have
been corrected in this century by Irving Fisher, Lord Keynes,
J.-J. Servan-Schreiber, and in economic policies by F. D. Roosevelt,
Lord Beveridge and H. Friderichs. Promoters of liberalism through
activities in fields of private endeavour were the abolitionists
Condorcet, Grey and Greeley; militant advocates of international
co-operation and pacifism such as Bluntschli, Hugo and Lorimer;
educators like Pestalozzi, Mann and Montessori; theoreticians and
practitioners of the humanistic social gospel like Oberlin, Booth and
Niebuhr, and of humanitarian action from Priestley to Dunant and
Nansen. Rathenau, Weizmann, Hoffman, Monnet and again Keynes
have been liberals who achieved distinction in both private and public
fields of activity in this century.

As a movement, as ideas giving it direction, and as institutions
ordering a way of life, liberalism belongs to mankind. However, with
few exceptions, the names mentioned in the above paragraph indicate
that the liberal movement was born, and acquired strength, in nations
belonging to the branch of Western civilisation deeply affected by
the sixteenth-century spiritual upheaval which reached its climax in
the Reformation. Within this branch took place the seventeenth-
century intellectual revolution which expanded knowledge; the
eighteenth-century agricultural and industrial revolutions which
expanded the output of goods; the British, American and French
political revolutions which expanded responsibility, participation
and social awareness.

This branch, limited originally to a few nations of north-western
Europe, is rightly described as progressive, because it led mankind in
discoveries, in the development of science and in technological
inventions; in curbing fanaticism and in the attempt — no more than
a modest one — to replace dogmatism with reasonableness, and

intolerance with tolerance; in replacing authoritarian absolutism first
with liberal constitutionalism, substituting government from above
with government from below and hierarchical elitism with a measure
of egalitarianism, and later with liberal democracy, thus embracing
all social classes; progressive because it led in humanitarian movements, from the campaign for the abolition of slavery and serfdom to
recent campaigns for the emancipation of all held in subordinate
positions; led in trying to replace traditional repressive education with
the 'new' education (see pp. 53f.) geared to the development of the
personality of the individual.

The theological aspect of the sixteenth-century spiritual revolution
played a secondary role in the advancement of the progressive branch
of Western civilisation and the development of liberalism, except for
the radical changes it caused in the institutional structure of organised
religious bodies (see Chapter 3). Not so the ethical aspect — which
affects a way of life more than political and economic institutions do.

Millions of people, first in Europe only, later overseas, adopted
a morality based on individual autonomy and dignity, and on duty: a
morality which stressed, in small but influential sectors of the population (for instance among British nonconformists), the notion that
what is good and right is what benefits others; which — in the words
of Thomas Huxley — requires a 'mind . . . stored with . . . knowledge',
and according to which 'passions are trained to come to heel by a
vigorous will, the servant of a trained conscience'. The primacy of
duty makes this morality a member of the family of deontological
ethics, to which in ancient times stoicism belonged: the ethics that
enable people to cope with difficulties instead of running away from
them, that give strength to stand persecution and ordeals — and thus
to win. Often indifferent to religion, liberals were not decendants of
the Reformation, but it is a matter of historical evidence that their
ideas, values and institutions originated in communities in which
Reformation ethics had played a major revolutionary role. In the
measure in which these ethics are abandoned, liberalism is weakened.

1

LIBERALISM: A DEFINITION

AN 'ISM' IS IDEAS AND INSTITUTIONS

Mention of an 'ism' — from totalitarianism to its antinomy anarchism
— brings to mind images both of ideas and institutions. In reality, an
'ism' indicates an ideological—political position founded on a set of
principles, directed towards certain goals and aimed at the establishment of an institutional structure. It indicates the movement derived
from the ideological—political position: endowed with its own
identity; embracing a large, or fairly large, number of people. The set
of principles includes concepts, values and a method of thinking; the
range of concepts and values covers politics, economics, education,
ethics and other aspects of the activities of the spirit, and also the
complex web of relationships among and between individuals and
groups. The goals may be one or many, absolute or relative, concrete
or abstract, immediate or distant. The institutions have the function
of channelling activities in such a way as to give concrete expression
to concepts, values and goals. In a wide sense, an 'ism' is a way of
life — or at least an aspiration towards it.

Among English-speaking people particularly, the word 'ideology'
creates an impression of rigidity and dogmatism. This need not be so.
In these pages, ideology is used in the wide sense of a fairly cohesive
and integrated system of principles. In the area of conceptual frameworks, a flexible and critical system of thought is as much of an
intellectual ideology as a rigid and dogmatic one: empiricism, empirio-
criticism, pragmatism, empirical positivism and existentialism are
intellectual ideological systems as much as dogmatic positivism,
dialectical and non-dialectical idealism and materialism, ontologism,
the intuitive transcendentalism of most religions. A political ideology
expresses what an 'ism' — a movement — stands for, and what its goals
are. When it comes to institutional structures, sets of principles
justifying constitutionalism, parliamentarianism, liberal democracy
and the welfare state are political ideologies just as much as sets of
principles justifying the divine right of the monarchy, theocratic
absolutism, the republicanism of closed oligarchies, national-socialism
or fascism, international communism and national-communism.

A WIDE RANGE OF MEANINGS

Terminology presents difficulties. Even in the narrower ideological—political sense (see Introduction), liberal and liberalism have different meanings in different languages, and at times among different groups speaking the same language. A North American liberal is likely to shudder if told that the Liberal party of Australia or the Liberal Democratic party of Japan are liberal. European *libéristes* (integral free enterprisers) of the Austrian school of economics are convinced that they hold the key to pure liberalism, and are highly critical of the *dirigisme* of Keynesian economics. The naive American muckraker Steffens once referred to Lenin — inventor of the twentieth-century totalitarian state, more repressive than most servile states in the past — as the 'greatest of liberals'. In recent years, members of dictatorial establishments favouring a relaxation of repression, Anglican clergymen imprisoned in South Africa or expelled because of their opposition to racist *apartheid*, Soviet intellectual dissenters, committed Marxists enthusiastic about 'socialism with a human face', catholic clerics advocating theological changes and structural reforms of the Roman Church, even rural and urban guerrillas from the Andes to Mindanao, have all been referred to as 'liberals'.

The Liberal party of Australia and the Liberal Democratic party of Japan follow moderate policies (see p. 33 on moderatism), but they, the Australian one especially, can be relied upon to uphold the liberal institutional frame (see Chapter 2) which enables advocates of different policies to come into power; to that extent they are liberal. European *libéristes* had liberal goals 200 years ago, when curbing state control of economic activities was a prerequisite to the establishment of market economies; they do not have liberal goals in the twentieth century, when market economies cannot function unless private economic power is curbed. Lenin, like his disciples Stalin, Mao and Castro, and his counter-disciples Mussolini, Perón and Nasser (opponents of Leninism who in the countries they ruled enforced totalitarian institutions patterned on those introduced by Lenin in Russia), hated liberalism and everything it stood for. Liu in China and Boumedienne in Algeria opposed hard-liners Mao and Ben Bella respectively, but this did not make them liberals, nor were liberals many, or most, of the dissident officers and their civilian collaborators who in 1974 brought down inefficient authoritarian regimes in Ethiopia, Greece and Portugal. All opponents of *apartheid* are not necessarily liberals, nor are catholic clerics advocating a return to the mediaeval Age of Faith, or anti-Stalinist Marxists. There is nothing liberal in the guerrillas bent on bringing down the imperfect liberal-democratic structures of Colombia, Italy, Malaysia and Venezuela.

However, even after everything spurious has been discarded, the
range of liberal experiences remains wide.

In the same year when the cosmopolitan economist von Hayek
published his apologia for a *laissez-faire* market economy, the British
economist Beveridge, who sat in the House of Commons as a Liberal,
completed his blue-print for a mixed economy geared to welfarism.
Both were equally committed to liberalism's basic institutions. They
differed on economic policies, one being a right-wing liberal, a
moderate, the other a left-wing liberal, in British political terminology
a Radical (see pp. 33f. 'Centrifugal pull: moderatism and progressivism'). The statesman Mendès-France found it easy to pass from the
liberalism of the French Radical Socialist party, which he led, to the
social democracy of revisionist socialism; and Winston Churchill
found it easy to pass from the Liberal party, in which he had played
a major role, to the Conservative party, which in time he led; neither
had changed his convictions an iota — one consistently a left-wing,
progressive liberal close to social democrats, a Radical Socialist in
French terms, the other consistently a right-wing liberal, a moderate,
in British terms a Whig. In the United States, the term 'liberal' is
applied only to those who belong to the progressive wing of
liberalism, in Australia to those who belong to the moderate wing. In
several nations (Denmark, France, Israel, Switzerland) there is, or has
been, a party for each wing, as there was in Chile before the tragic
events of 1973, and in Thailand during the brief 1973—6 interlude
between two authoritarian phases.

Abundant evidence gives an idea of the variety of liberal experiences
and the impact of liberalism. The English revolution of 1688 and the
short-lived Ghanaian experiment in parliamentary democracy in
1969—72 were liberal; so were the *physiocrates' laissez-faire* of the
1770s and Roosevelt's New Deal of the 1930s; the closing down
of schools run by Jesuits in the eighteenth century, and the prolifer-
ation of parochial schools in the United States in the nineteenth;
the struggle against privileged religious bodies and the struggle for
persecuted religious bodies; it was liberal to support nationalists
agitating for independence, and to oppose nationalists bent on
imposing their authoritarian rule on others. Liberal, also, were
numberless wars against despots, aimed at ending political absolutism
and not at replacing one absolutism with another (for instance in the
Second World War the struggle waged by the Commonwealth against
fascist dictatorships), and anti-war movements in Great Britain at the
turn of the century and in the United States seventy years later.

European intervention in the Sudan and Zanzibar, which ended
the slave trade, and in Benin (now part of Nigeria) and Dahomey
(now renamed Benin), which ended human sacrifices, was liberal;

so was the anti-colonialist movement in Great Britain and France which contributed to the ending of British and French domination in the Sudan, Zanzibar, Benin and Dahomey, as well as in all other dependencies held by the two powers. It was liberal to intervene in Spain, in Iran and in Lebanon against fascist forces, in 1936, 1941 and 1958 respectively; and it would have been liberal to intervene in East Germany, Hungary and Czechoslovakia against post-Stalinist dictatorships in 1953, 1956 and 1968.

The word 'liberal' conjures up the names of widely different twentieth-century statesmen, from the American Woodrow Wilson, the Czech Thomas Masaryk, the German Theodor Heuss, to the Lebanese Charles Malik, the South African Jan Christian Smuts, the Venezuelan Romulo Betancourt. To envisage the diffusion and impact of liberalism, just for this century one should have present names of other statesmen: the British Lloyd George, the Canadian Mackenzie King, the French Herriot, the Hungarian Karolyi, the Indian Gokhale, the Pole Dmowski, the Russian Lvov, the Turk Kiamil, the Uruguayan Battle; also the names of liberal leaders killed this century by their authoritarian opponents: Amaya in Argentina, Amendola in Italy, Canalejas in Spain, Gaitán in Colombia, Hamaguchi in Japan, Kondomaris in Greece, Madero in Mexico, Jan Masaryk in Czechoslovakia, Rathenau in Germany, Shingariov in Russia.

THE SEARCH FOR THE COMMON DENOMINATOR

That it is impossible to define liberalism, or any 'ism', is a common-place which seems appropriate in face of the array of meanings, and experiences mentioned above. In actual fact, the definition presents no difficulty if it is preceded by, and derived from, analysis of what has been and what is (not of what should be, according to any single thinker or school of thought). As stated in the Introduction (p. 10), the correct definition of any 'ism' is that which is derived from the evidence provided by experience: by what people have done and achieved when acting together.

What has been and what is means what can be known and there-fore studied. It means the actions in which many have been involved and in which participation has made for group cohesion. It means the institutions introduced by those who have successfully worked together. The direction actions take tells us what goals the partici-pants in the actions pursue; the institutions established tell us what principles and values acted as moving forces. Goals, principles and values shared by millions participating in a movement provide the synthesis defining what that movement is.

To define an 'ism' through intellectual spokesmen, as is usually
done, provides topics for learned discussions and dissertations: in the
case of liberalism, on (among others, and at random) William von
Humboldt, Germaine de Staël, John Stuart Mill and Benedetto Croce.
If they had lived at the same time and found themselves in the same
room, these four thinkers would have quarrelled — so would four
spokesmen for constitutional conservatism such as Burke, John
Adams, von Stahl and Stolypin; four spokesmen for authoritarian
traditional conservatism such as de Maistre, von Gentz, Pope
Gregory XVI and Pobiedonostsev; four spokesmen for socialism
such as Fourier, Lavrov, Beatrice Webb and Rosa Luxemburg.

Learned discussions and dissertations inform listeners and readers
about the thinker, his or her friends, disciples, and admirers, the
school of thought to which he or she belonged, not about the
movement, the elements holding millions of people together, and
their actual aims. Complex and logically structured ideological
systems, and the institutions through which they should be realised
— such as those formulated by thinkers and thinker-statesmen from
Locke to Servan-Schreiber in the Old World, from Jefferson to
Pearson in the New World — tell us little about what holds people
together, and their actual aims. What need to be stressed, rather,
are the widely diffused and relatively simple ideas arousing
enthusiasm among their adherents, and resentment, contempt,
hatred among opponents; ideas that influenced the developments of
one or more societies and are reflected (approximately, because
action falls short of the ideas behind it) in national institutions and
policies.

THE EVIDENCE PROVIDED BY ACTING TOGETHER IN A MOVEMENT

As a movement, an 'ism' includes a large number of people who
somehow manage to work together towards certain goals; so one
must look for what they have in common that keeps them
together. Whatever the differences, British Whigs, continental
members of the cosmopolitan 'republic of letters', American
Patriots and members of masonic lodges of 200 years ago (towards
the end of liberalism's formative period) understood each other,
spoke a similar ideological language and had kindred aspirations.
They aimed at establishing an institutional order keyed to government by discussion in an assembly of freely elected representatives
of the citizens, to a market economy, to the promotion of education
and of scientific knowledge, to religious tolerance, to the priority of
law over arbitrary power and to equality before the law. Similarly,

British Liberals, New Freedom Democrats in the United States, Russian Kadets and Argentinian Radicals of two generations ago understood each other, spoke the same ideological language, had kindred aspirations. Today, Danish Radicals who led centrist coalition governments in the early 1970s, Chilean Radicals who participated in a leftist coalition, German Free Democrats vacillating between a centre—left coalition with revisionist socialists and a centre—right coalition with Christian democrats, South African Liberals repressed by a racist oligarchy, understand each other; they all speak a similar ideological language and have kindred aspirations.

Whigs, citizens of the 'republic of letters', Patriots and Masons knew what differentiated all of them from traditionalist upholders of the *ancien régime*, from lay and church-orientated conservatives, from supporters of so-called 'enlightened despots' bent on strengthening despotism. Liberals, Democrats, Kadets and Radicals knew what differentiated them during the immediate pre-1914 period, not only from traditionalists and conservatives, but also from socialists of various persuasions and from nationalists. Today's Radicals of Denmark and Chile, Free Democrats and Liberals, know what differentiates them from traditionalists, conservatives, socialists, nationalists, and also from the current explosive and widespread combinations of socialism and nationalism and of socialism and anarchism. Listing widely diffused and often repeated statements, following the aspirations, taking into account the institutions that have been established, one finds what liberalism is.

The individual autonomy and responsibility called 'freedom', the dignity of man, tolerance, free thought, free press, parliaments, constitutions, the rule of law, laws equal for all, the greatest good of the greatest number; the rights of man and careers open to talent on the eastern side of the North Atlantic, civil rights and equality of opportunity on the western side; in the economic field the desirability of the largest possible diffusion of property, 200 years ago *laissez-faire* and free trade guaranteeing a wide range of autonomy in the pursuit of economic goals, and in recent decades the welfare economy, the rights of labour, collective bargaining, social security; at the global level international co-operation, international arbitration, self-determination, collective security: these are the ideas that moved liberals to action and were the source of constitutional government based first on limited suffrage and later on universal suffrage, the source also of market economies and of the beginning of world-wide institutional structures embracing all states.

A SOCIAL ORDER FOUNDED ON INDIVIDUAL AUTONOMY

Since it was first used, derisively, by the British Tory poet Southey in 1816, the term 'liberal' has had a fairly precise meaning when applied to an ideological—political position. It was adopted from the Spanish word indicating advocates and supporters of the aborted constitution drafted in Cadiz in 1812 (the revolutionary Spaniards equally opposed to Napoleonic radical despotism and to Bourbonic traditional absolutism), in the Western hemisphere indicating Spanish-speaking Americans committed to free institutions as much as to independence. On both sides of the Atlantic for over a century and a half, and in all continents for the past three or four generations, 'liberal' has meant holding a position in the political spectrum keyed to liberty as the *autonomy of the individual*, to advocacy of *institutions* called 'free' because that liberty has been postulated or guaranteed, to *emancipation* resulting ultimately in the *obliteration of the distinction between superior and inferior*.

It is a position which has a *philosophical foundation* in the form of first principles concerning the universe, life, society, the individual human being (see the section on 'Reasonableness' on page 27); in the form also of methods of thought mentioned in the Introduction (see pp. 9f.). The liberal position has a definite *ethical connotation* focused on the dignity of the individual and on duty towards others; a *political creed* expressed in the unwritten British constitution, and in the many written constitutions from the North American ones of the 1770s and 1780s to the post-1945 liberal-democratic constitutions of countries freed by the Allies from fascist rule; it has an *economic corollary* founded on the legitimacy of private ownership of property and on preference for market economies, both limited by the responsibility of each for the welfare of all.

What the term 'liberal' expresses (individual autonomy, free institutions making for the loose social structure, philosophical foundation, ethical connotation, political creed, economic corollary) formed a synthesis 300 years ago in the minds of those belonging to a small group of English-speaking people whose influence was out of proportion to their numbers. The history of liberalism dates from that period.

LIBERTY

Implicit in the word 'liberalism' is more than a close connection with liberty; there is an interwoven tie. Any dictionary lists a variety of meanings for 'liberty'. Traditionally it has meant privilege. Today, for most, the word connotes the autonomy or independence of a

group (nation, class, community of believers, or other) to which the
individual is totally subjected. Even at a highly sophisticated level,
liberty means, for many, acceptance of the truth, or is identified
with a specific goal (see the section, 'Liberty for non-liberals',
pp. 29f.). Neither privilege, nor independence of a group, nor
acceptance of truth, nor any specific goal, are the liberal's liberty.

To a liberal, as John Locke explained in his *Essay concerning
Human Understanding*, liberty is the *capacity for choice inherent in
the reasoning faculties of human beings.* It is neither goodness nor
evil, right nor wrong, not free enterprise, the welfare economy,
justice, equality, belief or disbelief in God or any of the secular
deities mentioned earlier (pp. 11f.). *Liberty is choice*, and can be
used to good or bad purpose.

Capacity for choice means that there is an area in which human
beings are not determined, in which they are free, in which Kantian
'spontaneity' holds sway. Though never a large area, possibly in most
cases most of the time a minuscule one, its presence is sufficient to
explain the variety of experiences making for the richness of life, and
also to make for successes and failures, for progress and decline. It
cannot be proved, Kant wrote in his essays on ethics, that the human
being is endowed with 'spontaneity'; neither, he maintained, can it
be disproved. Until disproved, one is entitled to accept the postulate
that there is spontaneity, that there is liberty. Acceptance of the
postulate is essential to the liberal position; there can be acceptance
without liberalism, but there cannot be liberalism without acceptance
of the postulate. All ways of thinking that postulate determinism in
any form (and provide the conceptual frameworks within which the
minds of most of mankind operate) are reflected in authoritarian
institutions and are thus outside the area of liberalism.

In the realm of values, the basic common denominator for liberals
is the conviction that liberty comes first in whatever scale of values
people establish; that the place of other values, however high their
moral level (preservation of life, compassion, non-violence, justice,
equality) is related to the effect they have on strengthening or
weakening liberty. In the realm of institutions, liberals, and all who
whatever the label think liberally, are convinced that the foremost
problem is the political one of the proper relationship between the
individual, who has a right to his or her autonomy, and the
community which needs to curb individual autonomy in order to
maintain its own cohesion. In the context of the organised
community, the liberal's liberty is the *right, to be exercised within
limits dictated by the requirements of the social order, of each and
all to act according to their own decisions*, to make their own
choices.

The relatively small area in which choice operates is enough to free human beings from the chains of determinism. As recognised by ancient jurists, liberty makes the physical individual a person endowed with morality — the ability and duty to choose between right and wrong — and therefore with responsibility for his or her actions. Liberty gives mankind, to some extent, a chance to work out its destiny.

For liberals, creativity is a manifestation of liberty. They are convinced that, ultimately, nothing is more important than to safeguard our capacity to create, because from it depends not only progress but, in the long run, survival itself (see pp. 12f.); that no coercion should suppress it; that, thanks to liberty, mankind has changed and contemporary civilisations are more advanced than those of the past. Along with capacity to create goes ability to absorb what others have created; hence 'culture' is not the same as 'nature'. What is created is not necessarily good, true, right or useful, but on balance and in spite of disastrous setbacks, thanks to liberty mankind has widened its intellectual horizons, has improved its standards of living, has increased its sensitivity — has gone forward.

THE PROBLEM OF DIVERSITY

The evidence of diversity among human beings is everywhere around us. Sources are innumerable; liberty itself breeds diversity in everything, including what matters most in relationships among members of any community — ideas, values, interests and aspirations. It is therefore a major source of tensions and conflicts. Liberals are bound by their own convictions to approve of diversity, of pluralism, of so-called 'contradictions' — the bogey-men of all who want the uniform, conformist (and therefore authoritarian) society. Approval of diversity brings the obligation to find out how different, and antagonistic, tendencies can establish relationships that not only will maintain the social order indispensable to the survival of all, but specifically will preserve liberty itself. This is no mean task. The proper relationship between 'us' (the group or groups to which one belongs) and 'them' (the rest of the community, formed of groups holding different views, having different interests and aspirations) is always and everywhere one of the thorniest problems. Liberals simply cannot solve the problem the way non-liberals do or tend to do. Their different solution is a major and unique characteristic of liberalism.

Most non-liberals share the conviction that diversity in ideas, values, interests and aspirations is obnoxious, wrong, even evil. The cry 'unity!', underlying all efforts to achieve uniformity and conformity, is a powerful one. For traditionalists, nationalists, authoritarian socialists and combinations thereof — in brief, for the overwhelming majority of mankind — to achieve uniformity in the way people think is a desirable goal. It is uniformity of the mind they desire in the first place, not uniformity of practical and material activities. If tensions were related primarily to socio-economic differences, they would be greater among Egyptians, Indians and over one hundred other nations than among Americans; tensions instead are less: through group pressure as much as state coercion there is greater agreement among Egyptians, Indians, etc. than among Americans on basic principles and values and on ways of thinking. Castes are less disturbing than different opinions about castes.

The goal of uniformity is reached by eliminating those who do not conform, the opponents, deviationists, heretics — the procedure followed in civilisations of 5000 years ago, tried in efficient twentieth-century totalitarian states where millions were killed because they did not share the thinking of the dominant majority or minority, or else belonged to hated religious, economic and ethnic groups. In countless cases, from India thousands of years ago after the Aryan conquest, to Peru hundreds of years ago after the Spanish conquest, the alternative to elimination has been to enforce a hierarchical structure in which those whose views or whose culture differ from the views and culture of the group monopolising power are kept in a state of subjection. The alternative makes liberty a privilege, as it was in the European Middle Ages, and it is practised, or has been until recently, in states less ruthless than the totalitarian ones, in which a minority represses a majority (as in Poland and the Republic of South Africa) or a majority represses a minority (as was the case in the American Deep South before 1954 and in Cyprus before 1974).

LIBERALISM AS *EQUAL LIBERTY*

By definition, the liberal opts for diversity against uniformity, for pluralism against monism, for a society with tensions against a society without tensions — and by implication for change against stasis. Having so opted, the liberal must find a solution to the problem of diversity in ways of thought, and more generally in ways of life, which is neither abolition of diversity nor discrimination between superiors and inferiors. The solution is the equal liberty of all, of the majority (if there is one) and of minorities; of those who decide to move in one direction and those who decide to move in another; of progressives, moderates and conservatives; of welfarists, collectivists and free enterprisers; of believers, unbelievers and the indifferent; of isolationists, patriots and internationalists. The *equal liberty of all is the central concept of liberalism as a movement*. The liberal commitment is to the institutional structure enabling people to be what they decide to be as much as possible, not to this or that policy.

'Free and equal' was the liberal watchword of a new nation on the western shores of the North Atlantic Ocean 200 years ago. 'Liberty and equality' were the first three words of the revolutionary cry of old nations on the eastern shores of the North Atlantic Ocean. To the query 'what is liberalism?' the reply is simple: the movement whose ideas, values and aspirations were embodied in the British electoral Reform and the many reforms which preceded it and followed it, and had as world-shaking manifestations the American Revolution and the French Revolution.

During the last 200 years or so some progress has been made toward the realisation of equal liberty. This is clearly shown by the variety of groups intellectually, economically and politically differentiated which have appeared on the scene in liberal-constitutional and liberal-democratic states, and which today pursue their often conflicting goals in nearly two-score liberal democracies; as clearly shown too by the creativity in all fields of human endeavour and the astounding progress achieved in recent generations.

The range of opinions and the variety of movements, and the respect for the rules of peaceful coexistence, provide the measure of how much liberalism there is in any given society. Nowhere else in the world is there today the wide range of opinions and the wide variety of movements found in the United States. On the other hand, there is less respect for the rules of peaceful coexistence there than in nations of the Old Commonwealth, of north-western Europe, and a few others. It is safe to assume that, among nations which have most influenced mankind, for several generations up until recently it was in the nations of Great Britain that liberalism most affected the way of life.

FOUR OTHER KEY ELEMENTS

Liberty is operative in the measure in which individuals (a) make their decisions, and (b) can act on the basis of these decisions. It implies an inner process of which all are capable, even if not all use it. It implies outer conditions related to the structure of society, and to the availability of material and non-material means enabling the inner process to be effective in action (see Chapter 2).

Concerning the inner process, besides commitment to liberty as the highest value, and equal liberty as the norm for the correct relationship between members of the community, the liberal position includes commitment to several other principles. The more important of these are: (*a*) reasonableness as the proper way of thinking; (*b*) individualism, or the dignity of the individual, as essential feature of the ethical system; (*c*) equality (and what makes it meaningful at the material as well as the moral level); and (*d*) tolerance as criteria in the relationships between oneself and others, between 'us' and 'them'.

(a) Reasonableness

Since liberty (the capacity to make a choice, see above, p. 23) is inherent in the faculties of the mind, the liberal stresses priority of reason over non-reason, rejecting as unsound and leading to error the immediate grasping of reality implicit in intuition, revelation, imagination and emotion. The liberal also rejects all forms of dogmatic rationalism (characteristic, for instance, of current versions of idealism and materialism) and stands instead for *reasonableness*, which implies the priority of critical thought and reliance on the canons of the scientific method as the proper way to find out what is real, which also implies open-mindedness, willingness to listen to other sides and to take into account their arguments, and moderation in one's own conclusions. The liberal heeds John Stuart Mill, who in *The System of Logic* made clear that an element of doubt should always remain if the pitfalls and errors of dogmatism are to be avoided.

Besides the priority of reason over non-reason, awareness of the limitations of reason, and the use of scientific methods of thought, the philosophical foundation of liberalism includes other principles shared by most (never by all) liberals. Among them are: the unity of a dynamic, ever-changing universe regulated by its own immanent laws; evolution; the universality (at least potentially) of life; the all-important role of the mind in giving direction to action; the 'nominalistic' postulate (see Chapter 3) that the individual is live and real, not the species *per se*. Those who pride themselves on being depositories of the truth — whatever that truth may be — have no place in the liberal movement.

(b) The Dignity of the Individual

Since reason is an attribute of the individual mind, an essential liberal value is *individualism*, as the right and duty to act on the basis of one's own initiative. This on the one hand involves responsibility for what one does, and on the other the duty to maintain conditions that enable people to continue to act on the basis of their own initiative. The liberal's individualism is not selfishness or self-gratification, it is not hedonism. Because liberalism as a movement aims at achieving the equal liberty of all, and because 'I' is an infinitesimal fraction of 'all', and 'we' (I and those who agree with me) is nearly always less than the sum of 'they' (those who disagree with me), the liberal's individualism postulates self-discipline, so as not to infringe on the equal liberty of others. It is a selfless and altruistic individualism.

Stressing responsibility and duty, liberal ethics are the antithesis of hedonism. The hedonistic selfish individual may be anything from an authoritarian traditionalist to an anarchist, but not a liberal. The great modern humanitarian movement which rejects the notion that the end justifies the means, as well as the double standard justifying for oneself what one condemns in others; whose practical manifestations have included abolitionism, the elimination of torture and other cruel punishments, pacifism and internationalism, the struggle against discrimination, sickness, and poverty, is a movement that originated within liberalism and has always been closely linked to it.

(c) *Moral Equality*

For the liberal, whatever the pressure of external forces, the human being is always a person endowed with autonomy and will; thus he or she must never be considered a mindless or conscienceless pawn. No less important is the conviction that differences — whatever their origin (due to factors inherent in the individual, or external) — in no way affect the dignity of the person, in no way negate the *equality* of all.

'Equality' is a hard concept to grasp. We are surrounded by evidence of diversity, as human beings patently differ in age, sex, size, I.Q., colour, capacities, skills, interests, vitality and strength. Moreover, life in a community leads to differentiation in activities, functions and positions. Equality applies not to what comes within the range of our senses, but to what only the mind can conceive: the general concepts embracing a multitude of individual concrete realities. No effort of the mind, or technique devised by human beings, can equalise strength, vitality, senses; even at the most primitive level of existence there are differences between members of a community, and the differences increase with advancement, with rising intellectual and material levels.

Human beings are not equal at the tangible physical level; they can be equal — if the concept is developed and found correct — at the

intangible level of ideas and values. Many liberals have found a
satisfactory explanation for equality in Kant's postulate (expressed in
the categorical imperative) that those moral principles are valid
which — sharing with laws the basic feature of being the same for
all — embody the assumption that human beings are equal. Equality,
created by man, belongs to the world of 'culture' and not to that of
'nature'. Liberty is a natural right for the simple reason that nature
endows all with it. Equality is not a natural right; it is the creation of
the mind, implemented by the will [see also 'Towards equality' in
Chapter 7].

(d) Tolerance

There is no possibility of peaceful coexistence on a footing of
equality among groups possessing their own identities, and striving to
lead their lives, unless *tolerance* is widespread. Without the
development — a slow and painful one — of the idea of tolerance in
modern times, there would have been no liberalism. Now that
tolerance has been taken for granted for several generations in nations
that happened to influence most of mankind for a while, it is hard —
even today when intolerance is rapidly expanding — for citizens of
those nations to realise how repellent tolerance used to be for all, or
nearly all, and still is for most. Tolerance allows room for errors and
for lies, gives right of citizenship to heresy, even to evil; therefore it is
immoral — this is the simple belief of traditionalists, and of most old
and new radicals today. At the end of the nineteenth century, the
immorality of tolerance was stated forcefully by, among others,
Pobiedonostsev, Procurator of the Orthodox Holy Synod in Czarist
Russia, and two generations later by Vyschinsky, Chief Public
Prosecutor in Soviet Russia. For liberals, instead, tolerance is the
height of morality.

LIBERTY FOR NON-LIBERALS

Liberals are not alone in maintaining that human beings are endowed
with liberty. In today's ideological—political spectrum, many lay and
church-orientated authoritarian conservatives, many nationalists and
anti-authoritarian conservatives, democrats and socialists, and of
course the not-numerous anarchists (and those in whose convictions
anarchism plays a role, like the anarcho-syndicalists of the Old Left
and the anarcho-communists of the New Left) agree that human beings
are not entirely determined and, through their capacity for choice,
possess autonomy.

With the exception of anarchists (about whom more later), for

people belonging to the above-mentioned groups, at the practical or
political level liberty is not just the exercise of the capacity for
choice. It is a definite choice; it may be the preservation of the past,
commitment to a religious belief, the glory of the nation, orderly
processes of law and state protection of private enterprise, equality,
justice, commitment to the advancement of a class or some other
sector of the population. For Hegelians, liberty was obedience to the
absolutist state; the stronger the state, the freer the citizen, stated
neo-Hegelian thinkers half a century ago in justification of fascism.
Along that line, for many national-socialists and national-communists
liberty is the merging of the individual in the community (as concisely
put by a German-American psychologist, 'to be free from freedom').

It has been a commonplace for traditionalists in all contemporary
civilisations, and for so-called 'integral nationalists' at the turn of the
century (who merged later in fascist movements of various nations),
to consider liberty an evil to be restricted and possibly suppressed.
Others identify liberty with their main concern. For example, there
was no doubt until recently in the minds of many catholics, and there
is no doubt now in the minds of most Marxists, that to be a catholic
or a Marxist means to be free. The gist of subtle arguments in the
encyclical *Libertas*; can be summarised in four words: 'Catholicism
makes man free.' The basic idea in relation to liberty expressed in
erudite and ponderous treatises of most Marxist and near-Marxist
intellectuals can be given in three words: 'Marxism is liberty.'

Nowhere do Marxist treatises discuss the rights of empiricists,
positivists, religious believers and others who see reality through
conceptual frameworks other than dialectical materialism; of those
who prefer welfare, corporate, free enterprise, neo-mercantilist,
co-operativist economies to collectivism; of those who reject the one-
party dictatorship in favour of the free play of political forces. The
acquittal of Communist party members and anarcho-communists in
trials in the United States in recent years has been attributed by
Marxists to popular pressure, Machiavellian speculation, the inevita-
bility of revolution, or simple stupidity: Marxists simply could not
conceive that trial and acquittal were the result of the principle of
liberty under law.

THE *OPTIMUM* IS NOT THE *MAXIMUM*

To be told practically in the same breath that liberty is all-important
and that liberal and liberal-democratic structures stimulate differences,
each of which, on the basis of equal liberty, limits the freedom of
action of all others, is — to say the least — confusing (hence the wide
use of the term 'contradictions' whenever opponents criticise

liberalism). It is also evident that the pluralism implicit in liberty as
choice is disturbing for those — in most societies a large majority —
who find security in the monopolistic single truth enforced in the
authoritarian state; that freedom of expression makes citizens aware
not only of the shortcomings and defects of liberal institutional
structures but also of their unavoidable limits, and stimulates opposition to these institutional structures and to the ideas of which they
are the practical manifestation; that to express the principle of equal
liberty with the same emphasis on equality and liberty is easy, but to
grasp it with its innumerable and complex implications is not easy,
and to apply it, even partially, is extremely difficult. Reasonableness
requires that the enunciation of a principle should be accompanied by
qualifications which make the principle operative in action. To
answer critics the liberal needs to clarify his position on a simple
question: how much liberty can there be in a liberal society?

The organisation of society on the basis of a contractual agreement
(the constitution drafted and agreed upon in an assembly of freely
elected representatives of the citizens) presupposes the acceptance of
the elementary fact that an individual needs other individuals — a
community — not only to advance along the path of higher standards
of living, greater knowledge, development of the person, but simply
to survive. Liberals know that a community's efficiency is to a large
extent related to the complexity of its structure; that the more
advanced the community, the more complex the structure is bound to
be; know that structure means laws and regulations and whatever
force may be necessary to implement them. Taking all this into
account, liberals look for the principle from which derive the
institutions enabling each member of the community, each citizen of
the state, to have as much autonomy as is compatible with the
requirements of the organised community.

It is known empirically that the economists' 'law of diminishing
returns' applies to fields other than economic ones. This means that
in many fields of activity there is a point beyond which the disadvantages of whatever is done outweigh the advantages. That point
is the *optimum*: whatever the efforts made, no one can ascertain how
it can be established, in any field, except through trial and error. The
maximum — to go as far as the ideal goal prescribes — is self-destruc-
tive. A couple of examples will suffice. In the democratic process,
proportional representation is ideally an improvement over single-
constituency representation; but providing opportunities for the
excessive fragmentation of political forces, proportional representation weakens the democratic process. Self-determination is a fundamental liberal principle; but the creation of sovereign states, weak
because of their smallness, lack of cohesion, lack of resources or

other reasons, favours imperialistic expansion and thus ends self-determination. Implicit in liberalism are rejection of the maximum, of the integralism which leads to authoritarianism, and the unending search for the optimum, essential for the peaceful coexistence of different tendencies on a level of equality.

LIBERALISM AND ANARCHISM

Just a decade or so ago, there would hardly have been any need to clarify the difference between liberalism and anarchism, because the latter scarcely existed as a political force, even if it was to be found in some nations in previous generations, and if individual anarchists could be found in most free societies. Today the clarification is more than a theoretical exercise. It is a practical necessity for three main reasons: (a) for the growing number of articulate advocates of authoritarian systems, liberalism is often condemned as the ante-room to lawlessness and chaos — popularly described as 'anarchism' even if they are not relevant to theoretical anarchism; (b) anarchist and near-anarchist positions have a growing appeal for a large number of people in the anti-liberal and anti-democratic left; (c) in nations as different and as far apart as the American, the German and the Japanese, anarchists and near-anarchists have as immediate goals basic features of the liberal programme in the respective countries: greater equality, end of privilege, fairer distribution of income, internationalism, anti-racism, anti-imperialism, pacifism; their pre-empting of these basic features paralyses liberals, who find it difficult to dissociate themselves from groups which give the impression at times of being nothing more than the advanced wing of liberalism.

The anarchist admits of no limit to his autonomy. In relation to liberty, he rejects the liberal's optimum and claims the maximum. He wants to obliterate political structures, i.e. the institutions through which laws are made and enforced, and more specifically the institutions through which the community is protected against internal subversion and external aggression (police, judiciary, armed forces). In the name of total (or integral) liberty, the anarchist and near-anarchist intellectual attacks respect for laws, everything connected with procedure, 'repressive tolerance', the use of coercion to enforce laws, the discipline necessary to hold the community together which if not self-imposed must be imposed from without.

Ideologically, the difference between liberalism and anarchism often seems more in degree than in kind. In fact it is not so, for a simple reason: if there is no law (and by definition anarchists abolish laws), relations between individuals and between groups are regulated by force; any anarchist experiment is bound to end with the tyranny of the strongest. To this must be added the evidence of anarchist action at the time of the Paris *Commune* in 1871, in Russian areas in 1918–19, in Spain during the Second Republic, and in a few other instances when anarchists were strong enough to act politically: in each case they showed intolerance towards all those who did not agree with them. It must be added also that each faction within the anarchist movement tries to destroy the others. As shown by the variety of experiences in all societies in which liberalism has been influential, liberals are for the widest range of differences compatible with maintaining the social order; like the advocates of authoritarian regimes, anarchists solve the problem of the relationship between 'us' and 'them' (see p. 24) — between those who agree with me and those who disagree — through the elimination, or at least the subjugation, of 'them'.

CENTRIFUGAL PULL: MODERATISM AND PROGRESSIVISM

Without distinction between what happened thousands of years ago and what happened just yesterday, past events show that the common denominator, in the form of principles, values and goals sufficient to maintain the cohesion of a movement during a period of struggle, is not sufficient when the struggle is successfully over. Success is followed by divisions linked to the need to clarify ideas, when the moment comes to translate them into institutions and to apply them as policies. Divisions mean tensions; these can lead to secessions, at times to civil wars.

In the case of liberalism, tensions between different tendencies existing within the movement have been heightened by the fact that the principle acting as moving force was a dual one. Revolutionaries in 1688 and their sympathisers had been a relatively small (a few hundred thousand) and fairly cohesive group; their single major aspiration — checks on arbitrary government — was expressed in the Bill of Rights. A century later, reformers in Great Britain and revolutionaries in English-speaking communities overseas and on the European Continent, who were heirs to the 1688 revolution and wanted to improve on it, and their sympathisers numbered several million; and their consent was that liberty and equality were both basic to their positions.

However much they may be uttered in the same breath, liberty and equality are not the same. The problem of striking the correct balance between the two is difficult to solve — the difficulty being compounded by the dynamism implicit in movements and institutional structures founded on liberty, which continually affects the balance. From the beginning of the agitation for reform in Great Britain, and

of revolution in North America and the European Continent (the
quarter century from the late 1760s to the early 1790s), some liberals
felt the problem of equality deeply, others less.

On one side were those correctly described then or later as
'moderates': at the end of the eighteenth century, for instance, the
Grenville and other factions among British Whigs, most American
Federalists, French Feuillants; in the twentieth century German
National Liberals, renamed the People's party (whose leader Gustav
Stresemann was the major statesman of the Weimar Republic), and
the Turkish Justice party. On the other side were the progressives: at
the end of the eighteenth century the Friends of the People organised
by the British Whig Charles Grey, Jeffersonians in the United States,
Girondins in France; in the twentieth century French Radicals, the
mainstay of the Third and Fourth Republic, and Filipino Liberals. In
the nineteenth century, progressives became liberal democrats through
the advocacy of universal male suffrage, and in the twentieth century
many joined hands with liberal socialists in advocating welfare
economies. In each case they were followed at some distance, and
often reluctantly, by the moderates who chose to remain liberals
instead of merging, as many did, with conservatives.

Moderates and progressives have thus a common origin. Between
them there is agreement on basic principles and values and on the
institutional structure (see Chapter 2). There is disagreement on the
range of institutions (moderates tending to elitism, and progressives
being committed to the universalisation of fundamental institutions —
suffrage for all, education for all, property in one form or another for
all) and on policies, particularly those concerning the economy and
international relations. Moderates and progressives usually co-operated
when drafting constitutions. When the centrifugal pull was strong
each wing went its own way, to merge again when threatened by
powerful authoritarian enemies.

FRONTIERS OF LIBERALISM

However strong in 1870–1 (at the time of crucial crises) the
moderatism of the old French statesman Thiers, he could not join
hands with authoritarian and semi-authoritarian *Légitimistes*; and
however strong the progressivism of the young French liberal
democrat Gambetta, he could not join hands with the three factions
in which *communards* were divided (anarcho-socialists, Jacobins,
authoritarian socialists). There was more in common between the two
forces of which they were spokesmen than between each of the two
forces and those which were outside the liberal tradition of 1789–92.

From the union of moderates and progressives came the liberal Third Republic.

In any movement there is a twilight zone which facilitates the passage of individuals from one movement to another; it also blurs differences. The clear-cut lines dividing Whigs from Tories in Great Britain in the 1680s, and Liberals from socialists in the 1880s, do not exist in the 1970s when most Toryism is liberal conservatism and most Labourism is liberal socialism. Judging from later reactions, quite a few American liberals were surprised when, because of commitment to justice for all, they found themselves among Stalinists or, in the name of peace in 1939–41, among fascists.

Whatever the size of the twilight zone and the uncertainty about clear-cut dividing lines, there is a core of integrated ideas and institutions differentiating one movement from another. Attitudes in relation to significant events in recent decades help to establish the frontiers of liberalism in today's complex world. Most liberals were saddened by the *coup* of 26 June 1975, and rejoiced at the resignation of Ms Gandhi after the elections of March 1977; they admired Nagy's and Dubcek's attempts to reform communism in Hungary in 1956 and in Czechoslovakia in 1968; they welcomed the success of Portuguese Popular Democratic, Socialist and Social Democratic parties in the elections of 1975 and 1976; they had approved of *golpes* in Argentina in 1955 and in Venezuela in 1958; and condemned *golpes* in Brazil in 1964 and in Chile in 1973; they saw favourable omens in the election of John Kennedy to the Presidency of the United States in 1960, in the unambiguous adoption of revisionism on the part of most parties of the Socialist International, in the strengthening of socialists and Independent Republicans at the expense of communists and Gaullists in France in 1974; they saw unfavourable omens in the collapse of free institutions nearly everywhere in the Third World, in the formation of a strong coalition of dictatorial states in the United Nations, in the diffusion of dogmatism among the world intelligentsia.

These few examples suffice. The liberals' reaction was positive in all cases in which self-government (or citizens' free government) was established or strengthened, and change meant less coercion, freer expression and freer choice in deciding one's course of action. Market and mixed economies were deemed preferable to command economies, but a variety of economic systems and economic policies were held compatible with a free way of life. The frontier that liberals cannot cross without losing their identity is represented by denial of self-government and of choice in one's course of action, by censorship and enforced conformity.

2

LIBERAL INSTITUTIONS

PRIORITY OF THE POLITICAL

The final step in the making of a liberal is conviction that liberty has priority over all other concerns and aspirations; that at the community level, all members of it must equally enjoy as much liberty as is compatible with the functioning and preservation of the community itself; that reasonableness, the dignity of the individual, moral (and thus legal and political) equality and tolerance are corner-stones of any way of life founded on liberty.

Guided by these convictions, liberals aim at replacing authoritarian institutions (centred on the twins absolutism and censorship, which constitute the norm in the structure of organised society, today regulating the lives of over two-thirds of mankind) with institutions that enable individuals to have a wide range of autonomous action, to use the creativity with which all are endowed, in the measure in which they so desire — always within the limits of what is feasible without disrupting society. Liberals are also concerned about the availability of the non-material and material means which give substance and content to free choice. One may choose to send a child to a good school, but there may not be a good school; to travel during vacations, but there may not be the money for travelling. In these specific cases, the concern means emphasis on better education and on an expanding economy.

In relation to institutions and availability of means, liberals give priority to the political over the non-political. There are several reasons for this. In the first place, by protecting or restricting freedom of expression and freedom of action, the political structure of society affects all its members deeply (and therefore to classify societies on the basis of political structures is correct procedure). Second, everything in which enough people are deeply involved can become political: religious fervour becomes the political action of believers bent on making their community safe for their beliefs; commitment to a collectivist economy becomes political action aimed at using the state for the establishment (then the functioning) of collectivism;

national pride becomes political action directed at strengthening the state. Third, the collective efforts of members of a community are more effective in relation to political institutions than to others. This is demonstrated by politically successful revolutions which failed in their non-political aims: the November 1917 revolution in Russia and the September 1919 revolution in Turkey were political successes, but the former did not create the human beings endowed with a new morality dreamed of by the revolutionaries, and the latter failed in its avowed aim of eradicating attachment to religious traditionalism. The 1943 Peronist revolution in Argentina and the 1959 Castroite revolution in Cuba aimed at stimulating economic expansion through dictatorial coercion; for several years they were political successes and economic failures.

SELF-GOVERNMENT

Institutionally, liberals are committed to *self-government* as government by the citizens, either directly in an assembly of all, or indirectly through an assembly of freely elected representatives. Whatever its name — Parliament, Congress, Diet — the assembly is the liberals' pivotal element in the entire structure of society. Respect for 'parliamentary procedure' takes precedence over goals. 'Freely elected' means that anyone can be a candidate, and that voters — unless there is a rare unanimity — make a choice; they are not coerced in electing their representatives, as in one-party states where assemblies of elected deputies merely have a rubber-stamp function. Liberals are convinced that to be subjects, or even second-class citizens (as Latins were in the Roman republican commonwealth and as women are nearly everywhere even in otherwise advanced democracies), is an insult to human dignity.

The liberal is not satisfied with opposing and overthrowing a tyrant; he agrees with the German liberal poet Schiller that it is not enough to condemn individual tyrants (as it is for many people who see rule by the good dictator — the Confucians' good master — as the best thing that can happen to society); that it is tyranny itself —absolutism, dictatorship, despotism, the words vary but the content does not — which must be condemned. The liberal recognises that there is a difference between fascist dictators in the mid-1970s like the Chinese Chiang Ching-kuo, the African Amin, the Latin American Pinochet, national-communist dictators like the Asian Kim Il Sung, the European Ceausescu, the Latin American Castro, social-nationalist dictators (see p. 8) like the Burmese Ne Win, the Egyptian Sadat, the Peruvian Morales Bermudez. If a choice between them has to be made, most liberals are likely to opt for the social-nationalist variety, as it contains progressive elements lacking in the fascist variety, and is less ruthless than national-communist dictatorships. Nevertheless, liberals oppose all dictators. Today they see dictatorship as the enemy, not this or that dictator, just as generations ago absolutism was the enemy, not this or that absolute monarch or oligarchy.

SUFFRAGE

As self-government is government by discussion in an assembly of freely elected representatives, participation in self-government means suffrage to elect the representatives. For generations, the extent of the suffrage was a major element dividing liberals. The division began in the 1760s, when a group among the British Whigs (see Chapter 4) advocated universal male suffrage. They were followed some decades later by a few who in English-speaking nations and France wanted the end of sex discrimination, thus advocating genuine universal suffrage. It is easy to say that self-government is the key principle in a society composed of free citizens. But who is 'self'? 'All members of the politically organised community, of course!' is the usual but misleading answer. Even the most dogmatic democrats agree that minors, adults certified as incompetent and some categories of criminals are excluded from participation in the government of the community.

It never occurred to the democrats' idol in the eighteenth century, Rousseau, and his disciples the Jacobins, that women should have equal rights, political or other, with men. Equality of legal rights between women and men was implicit in the position of early British progressive liberals (Radicals, Benthamites, some Chartists), but not equality of political rights. Proletarians were excluded from the franchise until the most recent generations. Illiterates have often been thought ineligible for the franchise.

Not until the twentieth century has there been the democratisation of political liberalism everywhere through the advocacy and then the introduction of universal suffrage. This has been one of the thorniest problems discussed among liberals, and a major element in the division between moderates and progressives. Moreover, the long period of advocacy of restricted suffrage caused deep resentment which is still reflected everywhere in the attitude of large sectors of the public towards liberalism. The fashionable explanation for reluctance to adopt universal suffrage is the desire to safeguard privileges; it is a partial explanation only. In reality there was something more important: it was the bad, very bad, solution to the problem that majorities often prefer servile institutions to free ones.

This was true 200 years ago. To judge by the enthusiasm for dictatorial regimes today, it is even more true today.

LIBERAL CONSTITUTIONALISM

It is understandable that those for whom liberty was a privilege they enjoyed (most members of the Polish gentry before 1791, of the business community everywhere, of creoles in Latin America since independence) should have opposed universal suffrage — just as the opposition to free suffrage on the part of all today who want to monopolise political power is understandable. Less understandable for later generations was the advocacy of restricted suffrage by genuine liberals, those whose spokesmen at the end of the eighteenth century were, for instance, Kant and Jefferson, and early in the nineteenth Rivadavia and Constant.

Jefferson may have been wrong in doubting the will to liberty of a majority of his fellow Americans; not so Kant, Rivadavia and Constant in relation to their Prussian, Argentinian and French fellow countrymen respectively. The four of them, and the few millions they then represented, were convinced that a constitutional regime supported by a minority guarantees greater freedom to all than an authoritarian regime supported by the majority; that government by discussion in an assembly of freely elected representatives of citizens, laws equal for all, checks and balances to prevent abuses, freedom of conscience and of the press, considerable autonomy in all fields of endeavour, including the pursuit of economic activities, legitimacy of opposition, dissent and nonconformity, were all of benefit to those groups into which the nation happened to be divided.

Available historical evidence — in the form of comparison between English-speaking communities and most other states everywhere in the eighteenth century, between the majority-supported Napoleonic regime in France and brief periods of minority-supported constitutional regimes in France itself and in other countries shaken by the French revolution — was on their side. A liberal minority could obtain power through a revolution; it had happened in Great Britain in 1688–9, and in some Italian states in 1796–9. How could it remain in power except by restricting the suffrage?

Events that occurred in major European continental states, and elsewhere later in the nineteenth century, explain continued liberal reluctance to advocate universal suffrage, and continued antagonism in several countries between liberals and democrats. Louis Napoleon set up his dictatorship in the early 1850s with the freely given support of two-thirds of the French nation. A majority of Prussians were behind their king's, and after 1862 Bismarck's, authoritarianism. With universal suffrage, authoritarian clericalism would have been the major political force in post-unification Italy, and in all likelihood would have soon put an end to free institutions. The dictators Santa Anna in Mexico and Rosas in Argentina had greater popular support than their opponents Guerrero and Lavalle. According to travellers, Eurasian autocratic regimes had the support of the majority of their subjects. The minuscule group of Japanese progressives could influence developments in their country early in the Meiji era only as long as suffrage was restricted.

For a hundred years since the beginning of the revolutionary period 1775–1815, it seemed clear to many in most countries that universal suffrage was the road to despotism. Just as progressives at the end of the eighteenth century (British advocates of reforms, and the majority among the American Founding Fathers and the deputies of the French National Assembly) had done, at the middle of the nineteenth century liberals in continental European, Latin American and other states stood politically for *liberal constitutionalism*.

FEAR OF THE MOB AND 'BOURGEOIS' DEMOCRACY

Fear of the mob (the highly emotional crowd inclined to violence, at times with a class connotation, often without), particularly after the atrocities of the Jacobin Terror in France in 1793–4 — and, more generally, fear of 'barbarians' — was a major factor in delaying the passage from liberal constitutionalism to liberal democracy and in earning the epithet 'bourgeois' for nineteenth-century liberalism.

[Why 'barbarians'? The word came into use in a new connotation when fascism and kindred movements were winning political and military victories in quick succession in the 1920s and 1930s. Anti-totalitarian intellectuals from countries engulfed by the fascist tide saw, in events they witnessed, another instance of the collapse of civilisation which had occurred after Germanic Visigoths had asked Roman authorities in A.D. 376 for permission to settle in Roman territory, behind the shield of Roman troops and under the protection of Roman law. Permission was granted. Soon Visigoths and other tribes took advantage of their new-found security to ravage Roman provinces; within a hundred years the Western Roman empire ended. Faced with the onslaught of totalitarianism, European liberals called 'barbarians' those (in Germany, Hitlerians and Stalinists, also, among others, racist disciples of H. S. Chamberlain and intellectuals of the Frankfurt School) who take advantage of free institutions and liberal policies to destroy the institutions and put an end to the policies.]

Liberal thinkers and statesmen have always been deeply concerned about the twin problems of the mob and the 'barbarians'. 'Is freedom to be destroyed by the liberties it guarantees?' is not a rhetorical question but a real problem. For generations (for longer periods in the Eastern hemisphere and in Latin America than in North America and Australasia), the answer of advocates of liberal constitutionalism was that responsibility is the criterion for suffrage. Responsibility being the duty to act so as to benefit and strengthen that for which one is responsible, early liberals maintained that in a system founded on free institutions the right to vote and to be a candidate for office should be restricted to those who are willing to act responsibly in relation to the system; that for instance those who, in the words of the nazi leader Goebbels in 1928, arm themselves 'in the arsenal of democracy with its own weapons' in order to destroy free institutions should not have the vote. But who is to be the judge of responsibility? To this question no one ever gave a satisfactory answer.

Some Benthamites, Jeffersonians, Girondins and their contemporaries in other countries, belonging to the more advanced wing of liberalism, were agreed that the ultimate goal should be universal suffrage; that restrictions on the basis of literacy, property or other qualifications should be temporary and apply only when a majority, or a large and cohesive minority, represented a threat to free institutions. It is also correct to say that liberal constitutionalism was progressive because the minority which had the suffrage was organised democratically and could be joined automatically by anyone satisfying requirements that could be fulfilled with a modest effort; that in all liberal constitutional states there was sufficient freedom for dissent to be expressed without risk, and for initiatives to be taken even by those who did not have the right to vote. It is a fact that American liberal constitutionalism with its limited democracy, established in 1775—88, was radically different from the oligarchic regimes which between 1810 and 1824 replaced Iberian viceroys and their officials in Latin America. It is also a fact that whatever the fears, the reasons, the rationalisations and qualifications, liberal constitutionalism was oligarchic. Large sections of the population, including the majority of wage-earners and tillers of the soil, were excluded from the political process.

However, whatever can be said in its favour, or as justification, and however progressive it may have been in terms of the times, because of its oligarchic features liberal constitutionalism warranted the derisive term 'bourgeois' with which it was incorrectly branded by its opponents. The term was incorrect class-wise because the correlation — in so far as one can identify correlations — was not between liberalism and upper sections of the middle classes, deeply

divided in most nations between supporters of authoritarian
conservatism (usually the majority) and supporters of free institutions,
but between liberalism and educational levels or, more specifically,
modes of thinking, which had little to do with economic functions
and economic status; in France, for instance, a protestant peasant or
a free-thinking clerk were more likely to be on the side of liberal
revolutionaries in 1830 and in 1848 than a bourgeois.

The term 'bourgeois' continues to plague liberalism in spite of the
extension to all citizens of the liberties advocated by liberals. There
is nothing bourgeois in systems in which the liberal-democratic
institutional framework guarantees to all as much freedom of
expression and of action as is compatible with the requirements of
the social order; in which political parties count in relation to the
number of votes they receive, and those who oppose policies of
liberal parties can put their own policies into effect. Justifiable,
though erroneous during the early, constitutional phase of liberalism,
the term 'bourgeois' is unjustifiable and totally erroneous since the
democratisation of liberalism through universal suffrage. The use of
the expression 'bourgeois democracy' — a commonplace in the
ideological—political terminology of advocates of authoritarian
regimes — indicates rejection on the part of those using it, of
institutions, from self-government to freedom of expression, which
benefit all. Embracing all citizens, liberal democracy is not and
cannot be bourgeois.

THE PRIORITY OF INALIENABLE RIGHTS OVER THE WILL OF THE MAJORITY

The problem of curtailing the right to participate in the nation's
political activities had its cruel and tragic aspects when Social
Democrats who had opted for socialism's revisionist wing, and other
supporters of liberal democracy, faced the problem in 1932 in
Germany. Advocates of one or another kind of authoritarian rule had
received 57 per cent of the vote in national elections held in July of
that year, and 58 per cent in November. Which had precedence? The
will of the majority or the defence of the liberal constitution of the
Weimar republic? Many foresaw at the time that the will of the
majority would utimately mean the triumph of nazism. They also
realised that the survival of the liberal-democratic republic required
the outlawing of parties supported by a majority of citizens, and the
enforcement of severe repressive measures against leaders and
organisers of such parties, that outlawing and enforcement might
lead to civil war. In more than one nation today, citizens face the
same cruel and tragic dilemma.

It is easy today to say that democracy is not just the simplistic will of the majority. It took time to clarify ideas and to develop among liberals the awareness that, in terms of their own convictions, there is something above the will of the majority just as there is above the will of any minority. That something is the citizens' *inalienable rights*. Once the concept has been accepted, there is no longer mistrust of democracy, and universal suffrage becomes an essential element of the liberal institutional structure. In the United States, thanks largely to the position adopted since the earliest period by the Supreme Court, the priority of inalienable rights was taken for granted, in practice if not in theory, especially after the Ten Amendments were passed. Consequently the problem was hardly discussed; Americans continued to talk about majority rule, but the Supreme Court saw to it that it should be limited (as was the intent of those who drafted and approved the Constitution of 1787). This was not so in most other nations in which a liberal movement existed.

Priority of the individual's inalienable rights means that a majority is no more entitled to set up its own authoritarian rule than a minority is: that rights of majorities as well as those of minorities are limited. It means rejecting the widespread concept of a Rousseauian 'general will' endowed with unlimited power — the concept that nationalists and national-socialists (from post-1919 Italian fascists to contemporary ba'athists, Qadhafiites, neo-Peronists) share with national-communists of all persuasions; the concept used to justify dictatorial rule or to claim it. When ethnic, racial, religious, intellectual and other minorities in the United States and elsewhere demand their rights (often nothing more than the right to their identity), they are asking for the application of a basic liberal principle — the key element, perhaps, to differentiate liberal democracy from other regimes also called 'democratic', in which dictatorship is justified on the basis of majority will or concern for the welfare of the majority.

LIBERAL DEMOCRACY

Discrimination at the levels of voting, and of nominating candidates, leads to abuses that are no better than those caused by participation of authoritarian tendencies in the political process of systems based on free institutions. To make the Paris *Commune* of 1871 safe for a Jacobin version of democracy, *communards* saw to it that half of the enfranchised citizens of the city were prevented from voting. Liberal democrats and democratic socialists, in Russia in 1917 and in Czechoslovakia in 1946, accepted the communists' and fellow travellers' request that all centrist and rightist tendencies be prevented from presenting candidates. In both countries, within a short time, the one-party dictatorship had obliterated liberals, democratic socialists and all other non-communist tendencies. A similar situation had been in the making in Portugal in 1974—5, and it led to serious tensions between the military faction supported by the Communist party on one side, and on the other the liberals and social democrats of the Popular Democratic party and the revisionists of the Socialist party, upholding the rights of constitutional conservatives and of catholics to participate under their own banners in the political process.

It took time for liberals to overcome the fears, the inhibitions, the arguments and the rationalisations that had led to the restriction of suffrage. It took time to realise that one can only try; and that if one fails because of the greater strength of authoritarian tendencies, one tries again. Successful in Germany in 1848, liberals failed dismally in 1849. They tried again, with success, in 1918, and failed once more in 1933. The liberal-democratic republic established in West Germany in 1949 was still going in the late 1970s. Liberals failed in Japan in 1932. After the Second World War, with American help, they made a come-back. In most South American republics, events of the last century and a half have been centred on the struggle between conservative (and after 1945, leftist authoritarian) forces supporting dictatorial rule, and liberal forces upholding self-government, with successes and defeats alternating (see Chapter 6).

During liberalism's early constitutional phase there were always a few liberals advocating extension of the suffrage. Swiss liberals campaigned successfully for male franchise in Switzerland in the 1830s. American liberals of the Jacksonian period achieved near-universal white male suffrage in the United States. German liberals successfully called for election of a constituent assembly on the basis of near-universal male suffrage in 1848. Starting with four western American States in the late nineteenth century, and with four Scandianavian and Commonwealth nations early in the twentieth, before the First World War progress, spear-headed by liberals, had been made towards genuine universal suffrage, through elimination of political discrimination based on sex. In 1918, with a Liberal majority in the House of Commons, and a coalition government in which the Liberal party was the senior partner, Great Britain was the first major nation to achieve universal suffrage, thus definitely sanctioning the passing from liberal constitutionalism to *liberal democracy*. Today, the liberals' democracy, functioning in nearly three dozen states, is a system in which all adults participate (if they so wish) in the conduct of public affairs.

Establishment of liberal democracy is not the end of the road for liberals and liberal parties. As a method through which different goals can be achieved, it is accepted in practice by labourites and revisionist socialists, by constitutional conservatives, by catholics organised in Christian democratic parties, by liberal nationalists. As an all-embracing system tolerant of its enemies, liberal democracy enables authoritarian traditionalists (where they survive) and nationalists, and authoritarian radicals who soon appear on the scene, to agitate for their goals. A threat to free institutions is thus ever present. In the liberal-democratic state, liberals have two major functions: (a) to defend the institutional frame; and (b) to strengthen it by unequivocally pursuing the goal of equality in all fields. The two functions are implicit in the expression 'free and equal'. Because in a free society all kinds of tendencies, including authoritarian and anarchic ones, can develop, and because liberty makes for differences which can easily degenerate into inequality, there can be no respite in the exercise of either function.

THE RULE OF LAW

For liberals, self-government's twin is the *rule of law*: as Dicey puts it, 'the absolute supremacy . . . of regular laws as opposed to the influence of arbitrary power, [as the exclusion] of arbitrariness, of prerogative or even of wide discriminatory authority on the part of the government'. The rule of law subordinates all members of the community to regulations derived from the freely expressed consent of the citizens — which are equal for all. Citizens make laws; the counterpart of the right to make laws is the duty to obey them. The liberal's freedom is not the absence of laws (although the fewer the better) as it is, instead, for anarchists. Freedom requires that laws be drafted, enacted, enforced, modified and abrogated through a clear and definite procedure.

The rule of law is rejected by advocates of rightist and leftist radical dictatorships, as a harmful brake preventing dictators from making full use of their power. It is often upheld by advocates of traditional absolutist regimes, for whom, however, the law is not man-made as it is for liberals, but has transcendental (divine) origin and sanction.

In traditional authoritarian societies there has been evidence of opposition to the arbitrary action of rulers. In islamic nations, ulemas and holy men reminded emirs, sultans, even caliphs, of the Koranic law. Notables close to the throne warned Spanish and French absolute monarchs against breaking the law. Even in the best-structured authoritarian society, in China, Confucian scholars criticised Sons of Heaven for disregarding laws. Ulemas and holy men, notables and scholars, were all concerned with laws supposedly emanating from a divine source (and sanctioned by what the divine source actually is, tradition).

Republican Romans were the first (see Chapter 3) to divorce law from religion; they deprived laws of divine origin and accepted them for what they are, the product of man. Carrying further the reasoning of ancient Roman jurists, liberals maintain that laws are legitimate to the extent to which they are the expression of the citizens' freely expressed consent. Laws must be obeyed, say liberals, provided they have been willed by citizens and that there are legal channels through which they can be modified.

THE RULE OF LAW BENEFITS ALL

It is commonplace to oppose 'rule by law' to 'rule by man', legal action to arbitrary action. If members of the organised community are equal, there cannot be rule by man to enable the community to function; there must be rule by law. Opponents of liberalism contend that liberals act contradictorily in upholding respect for laws which usually limit the range of individual action. The rule of law is of course restrictive to the extent that it limits individuals in what they can do, and prescribes how to do it. Restrictions imposed on each individual are liberal, however, when they increase the range of autonomy of all other individuals. The obligation to channel actions along definite lines in order to make other actions possible is also liberal. 'The authority of them that teach hinders them that could learn' Montaigne once wrote: by limiting the teachers' authority, the students' freedom expands. Restrictions on employers and husbands have had an emancipating effect on employees and wives; restrictions on Brahmins in India and on white racists in the United States have had an emancipating effect on Indian untouchables and on American blacks. The rule of law implements the liberal principle that the equal liberty of all has priority over the greater liberty of one, or a few, or even many, which is obtained through the subjection of others — and advocated by upholders of authoritarian structures.

LIBERALISM IS NOT PERMISSIVENESS

People of good will, who often think of themselves as 'liberal', are convinced that the condoning of permissiveness is a mark of liberalism. They ignore the fact that liberal institutions are geared to reject both authoritarianism (which inevitably causes the subordination of the individual to those controlling the power structure) as harmful, and anarchism as impossible of realisation because the individual depends on integration in a group for his survival. Liberals recognise the need for regulations and controls, but insist: (*a*) on an area as wide and as clearly defined as possible within which individuals can act of their own volition; (*b*) on the subordination of the power to regulate and control to the decisions of responsible citizens, the members of legislative bodies and the judiciary; and (*c*) on a well-defined procedure for the enactment of decisions. At the same time they object to restrictions on the individual's liberty that are not needed for the preservation of a community based on the equal liberty of all; to the exercise of power by individuals and groups not responsible to the citizens; to the arbitrariness implicit in 'rule by man' — by hereditary monarch, charismatic leader, Caesarian dictator — the alternative to 'rule by law'.

Evidence shows that at all levels of political awareness and intellectual sophistication, there often occurs a process of simplification of principles, resulting in action which denies the principle itself. For many democrats in most nations, democracy is nothing but majority rule; therefore, they maintain, if the majority wants a dictatorship, it is right to replace democracy with dictatorial rule. They reject the liberal notion (see above p. 43) that majority rule is only one element in a democratic system, that it is limited by the inalienable rights of each and by the rights of minorities. The principle of national self-determination is interpreted as justifying coercion of fellow-citizens by a nationalist group, so that self-determination no longer exists. Because liberalism aims at reducing restrictions and at making those that remain less repressive, it is a mistake to deduce that it is 'liberal' to advocate abolition of all rules and the elimination of agencies charged with enforcing the rules.

LIBERALISM SHIFTS THE SOURCE OF POWER FROM ABOVE TO BELOW

Liberalism is not permissiveness any more than it is anarchy. However, the liberal road leads to the loosening of the social structure and the weakening of authority. Conscious of the requirements of the social order indispensable for the survival of each and the advancement of all, the liberal knows that there must be a limit to both the loosening and the weakening. Representative institutions, a market or mixed economy in a wide variety of manifestations, freedom of communications media and of instruction, all are means of going as far as possible along the road of political, economic and intellectual loosening. The loosening is achieved by shifting the source of authority from the top (rulers, public or private monopolists, censors) to the bottom (citizens, producer/

consumers, the public using the media and sending children to school).

For a liberal, it is essential that laws and regulations of all kinds come from below and not from above, and that there be no infringement on the procedure through which dissent is expressed and modifications are sought. As long as this is so, laws ordering children to school, young people to military or other public service, and all to pay taxes, are not illiberal. Permissiveness that leads to the deterioration of institutions enabling members of the national community to conduct their own affairs — the institutions making for self-government — is illiberal. Permissiveness is a manifestation of hedonistic ethics. Liberty requires persistence in the pursuit of one's aims (often hampered by the aims of others), patience in dealing with those with whom one disagrees, self-control on the innumerable occasions when one cannot have one's own way; persistence, patience and self-control are the reverse of hedonism and permissiveness.

UNCHANGING METHOD TO ACHIEVE EVER-CHANGING GOALS

Between a seventeenth-century debate among Englishmen, in the midst of spiritual and political turmoil, on the relative advantages of systems founded on authority and liberty (a debate which found its conclusion in the outcome of the civil war of 1688–9), and decisions taken in North America in continental Congresses and Conventions of the 1770s and 1780s, and the Declaration of Rights of 1789 and the Constitution of 1791 in France, more than a hundred years elapsed. In this period were structured the institutions that enable individuals to enjoy a maximum of liberty compatible with the order necessary for the preservation of society and the survival of its members. There have been radical modifications since. In the nine-teenth century, starting with the United States and Switzerland in the late 1820s, there was a gradual democratisation of political institutions. In the twentieth century, starting with pre-1914 nationalisations and the beginning of social-security measures in Europe, and with the New Freedom legislation in the United States, there was a gradual increase of government regulations aimed at rationalizing economic activities and at solving socio-economic problems, ultimately leading to mixed welfare economies.

Whatever the modifications, basic institutions advocated by liberals, and the spirit animating them, have remained essentially the same. They are the unchanging means through which ever-changing ends can be achieved, and through which results promoting the advancement of mankind have been obtained. Because of what liberalism is, because what matters is the development of the abilities and capabilities with which individuals are endowed rather than the continuation of any specific way of life, and because dynamism is good and stasis is harmful, liberal institutions are concerned with the way things are done more than with what is done. For a liberal, it is good and desirable that man should have new aspirations, that ends should change according to new aspirations and new situations. The unchanging method for achieving changing ends makes for the continuity of the community and the preservation of a free way of life.

NATIONAL SOVEREIGNTY

Forming a substantial movement already in the seventeenth century in Great Britain, later to the West among communities mainly derived from the British Isles, then to the East in parts of the European continent, citizens concerned with liberty — seldom numerous but sometimes influential — defined the institutions of nations which were free, not because they were independent, but because they were composed of free self-governing citizens. These institutions gave form and meaning to *national sovereignty*: meaning, in the words of Tom Paine (born in Great Britain, American revolutionary by choice, deputy to the French National Convention in 1792), that 'the nation is . . . the source of all sovereignty; nor can any individual, or any body of men, be entitled to any authority which is not expressly derived from it.'

The principle is explicit: citizens can do most things, but must not renounce their sovereignty. If they do, authority no longer derives from them. Because of this principle — together with the other, that the individual's inalienable rights can no more be taken away by majorities than by minorities — a majority, however large, is not entitled to establish its dictatorship. The version of democracy called Jacobinism cannot be liberal. No advocate of the dictatorship of the proletariat, or any other dictatorship, can be a liberal. Liberals reject the Caesarian despotism founded on majority will as vigorously as they reject despotism supported by minorities. Conservatives, socialists, nationalists, Rousseauian and Leonine democrats (see the index–glossary) can remain conservatives, socialists, nationalists or democrats whether they advocate free or authoritarian institutions. Liberals cannot reject sovereign self-government and the institutions listed below and still claim to be liberals.

INSTITUTIONAL PILLARS

Institutions through which sovereign self-government operates can be grouped under six headings:

(1) *Personal liberty* includes freedom of expression, i.e. of speech, of the press (now communications media), of teaching and preaching; freedom of assembly and of association within limits that exclude the creation of monopolistic centres of power; *habeas corpus*, trial by jury and strict enforcement of legal procedure; security of property, which is not only fixed and movable capital, and durable and non-durable consumer goods, but also labour and skills and what is acquired with labour and skills.

(2) The *equality* of citizens as moral persons requires the abolition of slavery, serfdom, peonage and all other forms of forced labour. It also requires a continual effort to curb privilege which, destroyed in one sector (for example, an aristocracy, a priestly class) is reborn in another (the business community, where there is private free enterprise, the state bureaucracy, where there is collectivism, the military, where the social structure is weak), because too many people want to give permanent tenure to their successes and want to transmit their achievements to children or followers. It requires equality before the law and access to educational opportunities; it requires, in all economic systems, limitation to the range of capital accumulation and to incomes in order to avoid the imbalance that leads to differentiation between superiors and inferiors. (No theory can establish what that range should be, it can only be established by trial and error. For a start: the Fair Deal American President Truman once stated that it should be in the ratio of one to five, and a 1972 Presidential candidate in the United States said it should be one to ten.)

(3) Personal liberty and moral equality are guaranteed by *political liberty* which means free voting, free choice of candidates, free election to office of those who make the laws and supervise their enforcement — which requires decisions reached through discussion in an assembly of freely elected representatives of the citizens.

(4) Political liberty is inseparable from *constitutional government*. By this liberals mean not just any constitution but a constitution founded on division of power between the legislative and the executive, between national and local elected authorities; founded also on responsibility of the executive, preferably to Parliament (as in Commonwealth democracies and all democracies patterned on the British one), otherwise to the nation (as in the United States and France); on the independence of the judiciary; on limitations to the majority's right to govern, so as to safeguard the rights of minorities;

on a well-defined procedure for the enactment, enforcement, revision and abrogation of laws.

(5) Political liberty also requires the *separation of state and economy*. This was once achieved in the North Atlantic area in the eighteenth century through the rejection of mercantilistic systems, the abolition of guilds and tariffs, the advocacy of a free market nationally and internationally, and free use of the means of production. Now it is achieved through curbs on private economic power, and strict parliamentary control over public economic power in order to prevent holders of economic power from exercising undue political influence.

(6) In nations where the organised religious body wields undue power (for instance many of the forty-odd ones in which catholicism is influential), and others where religious pressures are strong even if there is no cohesive organised religious body (as in most of nearly forty predominantly islamic nations), political liberty requires the *separation of church and state*.

All this means laws. Legality is hated by extremists of all colours and is often derided by pseudo-progressives who scoff at the liberals' democracy as being purely formal. It is true that laws are not sufficient to make for a way of life, that ideas, values and commitment, customs and habits, give substance to laws. It is also true that though there can be form without substance, there cannot be substance without form.

LIBERAL CONCERN WITH EDUCATION

It was noted at the beginning of this chapter that the availability of means through which free choice becomes the action of free individuals has always been a major concern for liberals. The institutions listed in the previous section protect the act of making a choice, provide citizens with the security they need to be able to make this capability an essential feature of their lives and the mainstay of their dignity. Protection in this context is also stimulation, and thus develops the variety of ideas, values, tendencies, aspirations, giving richness to the life of individuals and communities (disturbing of course to many) once in liberal-constitutional states and now, on a larger scale, in liberal democracies. To make a choice, however, is not the same as to implement it. The implementation necessitates availability of means, particularly those provided by education, and the material or economic ones of which there is acute awareness in the world today.

A major feature of liberalism is commitment to the spread of education. In a pamphlet published in 1643, *New England's First*

Fruits, Milton wrote: 'One of the . . . things we longed for, and looked after, was to advance learning, and perpetuate it to posterity.' Whatever the religious motivations and shortcomings, the 1647 decision of the General Court of Massachusetts to establish enough schools to teach most children was a revolutionary step — the first attempt at universal literacy. Several generations later, Jefferson expressed the view of all liberals when he wrote: 'A system of general education which shall reach every description of our citizens . . . as it was the earliest, so it will be the latest of all my public concerns.'

The diffusion of education is one thing; the choice of the kind of education to be given formally in schools and informally through the family, the neighbourhood, or other group, is quite another. Despite the writings of sound thinkers from Montaigne to Dewey, and of competent educators like Comenius, Pestalozzi and Froebel, for several generations often not enough thought was given by pre-liberal progressives, and later by liberals, to what education ought to be for the free individual in a free commonwealth. Nor is enough thought given today to the matter in many liberal democracies, where educators and public assume that more teachers, more schools, more equipment, are all that is needed. They do not stop to think that what is taught, and how, is of the first importance.

REPRESSIVENESS OF MOST EDUCATIONAL SYSTEMS

Formally or informally, the first function of education has always been, and still is, the socialisation of the individual: the assimilation of the young to the culture of the adults. Because of this function, even without the rod education has been, and still is in all authoritarian societies, and to a large extent remains in most liberal democracies, coercion. The goal of traditional education has not been emancipation of the individual, but the reverse. In ancient Egypt as in contemporary China, the teacher is one who teaches the 'truth' and sees to it that whoever is impervious to that 'truth' is ostracised. The wide diffusion of literacy among second-century Romans did not inspire the attachment to liberty felt by unlettered Romans of the third century B.C. Universal literacy and the expansion of higher education in radical dictatorships have fostered conformity, and hence more docile subjects.

For hundreds of years, China's efficient administrators, ruthless Ottoman officials, catholic inquisitors, were among the best-educated people in their respective nations. Germany, one of the four nations whose governments perpetrated massacres by the million in the twentieth century, had for generations been in the forefront of advancement in education. Education as indoctrination, as repression of deviationist tendencies, as suppression of individuality, as the means to achieve the triumph of conformity, held total sway in the past and holds total sway today in most nations; it can lead to universal literacy and high levels of erudition, but it is not liberal education. It probably takes a touch of lunacy or of genius to go through the 800 hours of Marxist–Leninist indoctrination in Soviet high schools and universities without succumbing and surrendering originality and autonomy.

LIBERAL 'NEW EDUCATION'

Liberals reject indoctrination. Because of their concern, ideas about education have been the subject of heated debates. As time went on, a consent developed among the more concerned liberals that education should aim primarily at the formation and development of the individual personality, socialisation and training of skills taking second place. It was not a new idea. It had been propounded by fifteenth-century humanists, among others Alberti, Bruni, Rambaldoni and Vergerio. Rambaldoni (Vittorino da Feltre) experimented with the 'new education' in the school established in 1428. The same idea was championed 500 years later by Dewey, Tagore, Montessori and Russell, some of them liberals, others not, but all fulfilling a liberal function. The idea of the new education inspired many who founded schools in liberal-constitutional and liberal-democratic states, those who reformed Commonwealth and American colleges and university colleges, and liberals — from Humboldt in Prussia in 1809 to Faure in France 160 years later — entrusted with the reform of public educational systems.

The idea of the 'new education' is simple and clear, but its implementation is difficult and creates serious problems. It brings into the schools the problems accompanying all liberalisation of institutions and of modes of life: divisions and tensions, lack of focus, doubts and uncertainty. In the context of the 'new education', instead of receiving guidance from above, each must find his or her own way.

Emancipation has a price, and for many the cost is too high. It demands stronger character than many have. It is a matter of recent evidence that large sections of the youth educated in this century in advanced liberal-democratic states proved unable to cope with the multiplicity and diversity of ideas to which they were exposed in schools and universities. It happened in France, many of the educated young in the 1920s and 1930s finding in scepticism an escape from the inability to make a choice; in Germany at the time of the Weimar

republic, when the escape took the form of the search for, and
acceptance of, simple dogmatic truths; it happened on a large scale to
the generation that reached voting age in the 1960s in the American,
Indian, and Italian nations — to mention just three major instances.

Problems and price aside, a society in which liberal education
prevails, or at least is widely diffused, as it is in the United States, is
radically different from a society in which education is assimilation
through indoctrination. Teachers, and methods of teaching, provide
significant criteria for those seeking concrete evidence of what
differentiates the free from the authoritarian way of life.

PROPERTY

Liberals agree that individual ownership of property is basic in
guaranteeing individual autonomy. Saying 'ten thousand dollars in
savings gives me independence vis-à-vis my employer, and so makes
me free', a young teacher succinctly expressed the essence of the
relationship between liberty and property. Liberals agree with
Jefferson, who once stated that it would be desirable to see the day
when all families have some property. The diffusion of property, not
its abolition, has been advocated by progressive liberals as a solution
to the perennial problem of the relationship between haves and have-
nots, between those who have too much (the ruling oligarchy, even
in the most egalitarian state) and those who do not have enough
(more numerous in relation to the total population in command
economies than in market and mixed economies). Thus, whatever
their commitment to free enterprise (see the next section), in the
nineteenth century liberals supported the co-operative movement in
Scandinavia (actually they originated it) and in Great Britain, the
Homestead and kindred Acts in North America, and in French-
speaking nations measures favouring peasant-owners, artisans and
generally small business.

Rejecting absolutes dear to dogmatists, liberals (aware of the
difference between maximum and optimum, see Chapter 1) have
agreed that not all property should be privately owned. On this
point, already Adam Smith as a theorist (see Book V in *The Wealth
of Nations*) and Jefferson in his policies three decades later as
President of the United States were clear. Even at the height of their
commitment to free enterprise, liberals in power expanded the public
sector of the economy. Their concern was that there should be as
much private ownership as necessary to fulfill the basic role of
emancipating individuals from pressures and coercion. The 'as much
. . . as necessary' varies from nation to nation; it never needs to be
all. As a rule of thumb one can state that the greater the amount of

wealth in a nation in relation to the population, the smaller the share
required to guarantee individual autonomy. During the first three
post-1945 decades, there was as much liberty in Italy as in Canada,
although in the former country a considerably larger share than in
Canada of the national wealth was owned publicly.

The liberal cannot be a collectivist because of what is implicit in
the term: the obliteration of individual autonomy in order to
strengthen the cohesion and uniformity of the collective; the
replacement of the dignity of the individual, as a major value, with
communalism; conformity instead of diversity. Because, from early
civilisations to the states ruled by national-communists today,
evidence shows that collectivism requires, or leads to, centralisation
of arbitrary power and the elimination of opposition and dissent.

Reading their works, one notes that the two foremost British
spokesmen for liberalism, Locke and J. S. Mill, had, as theorists,
reservations about the legitimacy of private ownership of what
today is called 'natural' and 'artificial' capital. They approved of it,
and justified it, because whatever the misgivings at the theoretical
level, it was evident at the practical level — at the level of life as it is
lived — that absence of private ownership of property meant absence
of autonomy in action, meant strengthening the position of those
holding political power to such an extent as to make them
independent of the citizens.

FREE ENTERPRISE

Until after the middle of the nineteenth century, liberals were
impressed by the economic system that developed spontaneously in
Great Britain when, in the wake of the successful 1688—9 Whig
revolution and the Whigs' dominant 'live and let live' attitude, many
economic restrictions and regulations were no longer enforced. Then,
for the first time in the history of civilised societies, a free market
functioned and acted as regulator of economic activities. From a
liberal point of view, the factory system, as it was called at the end of
the eighteenth century (the free-enterprise system in American
terminology, capitalism as the vague, all-embracing and emotionally
charged term generally used for a century and a half), presented two
great advantages: it enabled more people than did any other system
known at the time (or blue-prints of future systems drafted by
thinkers who knew little about the economy) to act in the economic
field on the basis of their own decisions, and it was by far the most
productive. No more licences, fees, tariffs, bureaucratic ordinances,
public or guild monopolies: this had been since the 1750s the
physiocrats' *'laissez-faire, laissez-passer'*, the slogan characterising an

entire economic system. To the extent to which *laissez-faire, laissez-passer* became policy, there was, for the times, an astounding expansion of production. Preference for command economy was then an essential feature of the conservative position, and benevolent paternalism the mark of enlightened authoritarianism.

Free enterprise had an emancipating effect for millions of entrepreneurs and would-be entrepreneurs; free trade multiplied exchanges within and among nations, and stimulated production; free movement meant that millions abandoned rural hovels where they barely subsisted and moved into urban tenements which, though squalid, were an improvement over the hovels. For the first generation of labourers who moved from the country to industrial cities, as for the tens of millions who crossed frontiers and oceans in search of a better life in foreign lands, migration meant emancipation.

Widespread awareness of its defects came several decades after the new economic system got going. Even then, to many the advantages seemed to outweigh the disadvantages. Pre-1914 liberals, not just the cautious ones but the dynamic ones who were aware of suffering, of labour resentment and of the social problem — British Radicals of the Bright and Lloyd George eras, American Progressive Democrats of the Bryan era, German Progressives of the Schulze-Delitzsch and Richter eras — advocated private initiative and free business enterprise in a free market. When liberals supported policies that made for government intervention in the market and limited free enterprise — as was the case of Swiss and French Radicals early in the century, of Australian supporters of Deakin and of New Freedom liberals during Wilson's first Presidency in the United States — the range of autonomy in economic activities remained considerable.

BEYOND THE ECONOMIC *OPTIMUM*

Whatever the fluctuations in production and excessive unevenness in distribution, the greater efficiency of free enterprise, from the point of view of economic expansion, is historically and statistically a fact. Apart from recent well-known economic 'miracles', like those of Japan, France, Taiwan and Brazil, which have occurred within the context of market economies, free enterprise was responsible for quick economic recovery in France after the ruinous Napoleonic wars and the 1870–1 war, and in West Germany and Italy after the Second World War. Lenin's New Economic Policy (N.E.P.) of 1921 was recognition of the fact — admitted by his teacher, Marx — that when capital is scarce, private initiative makes for its best utilisation. Today, Soviet collectivism requires twice the capital and three times the labour needed by American free enterprise to achieve the same rate of economic expansion. Comparing free-market economies and command economies of approximately the same level at mid-century, it is seen that in the following two decades the former performed better than the latter: West Germany did better than East Germany, Italy than Hungary, Taiwan than China, India than Indonesia, Jamaica than Cuba, the Ivory Coast than the former Gold Coast (Ghana).

At a time when progressives considered output of goods (rather than of services) all-important, liberals were lured by the mirage of future abundance — the mirage that today fascinates advocates of dictatorial systems and provides a major justification for ruthless repression and suppression. Not until recent decades have liberals realised (advocates of collectivism still have not) that the mirage was only a mirage, that wants multiply faster than the capacity to satisfy them, that scarcity is permanent.

Besides being lured for too long by the mirage of abundance for all, nineteenth-century liberal economists and statesmen were responsible for three serious economic errors.

(a) They were slow to acknowledge that market economies have a level of instability (unsatisfactorily explained through the business cycle) which is beyond the endurance of many. Unemployment and under-employment, bankruptcies and losses of savings, even hunger to some extent, are tolerable during a first depression hitting a new generation; they are less endurable during a second depression and may become quite unendurable during a third. Most Germans withstood the disastrous depression of 1919–23 stoically, but many of them could not take it any longer when another severe depression struck suddenly, early in 1930.

(b) Liberals and non-liberals alike were slow to become aware of the depletion of natural resources, despite evidence provided by several older (Chinese, Arab) and some later (Ottoman, Spanish) civilisations which transformed prosperous districts into deserts; despite evidence provided by diminishing returns, particularly in primary production, in advanced industrial nations.

(c) Liberals and non-liberals were slow to recognise the deleterious effect of pollution caused by industry, already evident at the middle of the nineteenth century in the first country to become industrialised: in Great Britain, the Thames, the Mersey and other rivers had become sewers, and smog ('pea-soup' fog in London) was choking the capital and the industrial Midlands.

Liberals were aware of the difference between optimum and maximum at the conceptual and political levels. But for too long liberal spokesmen advocated the pursuit of the economic maximum, thus delaying the application of fiscal measures, labour and social legislation, which would have kept free enterprise operating in a market economy within the range of the optimum. There would have been greater initial disadvantages (higher prices, fewer goods and services and therefore a somewhat lower standard of living in economically advanced nations), more than offset by long-term advantages, particularly the survival of a system which, whatever its defects, is less damaging to individual autonomy than its immediate mercantilistic predecessor and its major rival today, collectivism. During the last quarter of the nineteenth century, German liberals lost to Bismarck's authoritarian conservatism, which started a social-security programme badly needed by wage-earners. The British Liberal party lost heavily in popular support in the 1920s, partly (maybe largely) because of its obsession with 'free trade'. In the twentieth century, everywhere outside North America liberals lost to socialists, whose anti-capitalism appealed to large sectors of the intelligentsia identifying themselves with the long-suffering masses of wage-earners, unemployed, poor.

LIBERALS' REFORMED FREE ENTERPRISE

Less doctrinaire than others, North American liberals took the lead in advocating reforms of the free-enterprise market economy. Legislation sponsored by them goes back to the last three decades before the First World War. However slow and timid their action, they were the first to reformulate the liberal position in economic affairs. In the United States, the major aim of pre-1914 liberal policies was then to check monopolistic tendencies, and to favour the development of what later were called countervailing forces, so as to maintain some balance between labour and capital, employees and management, investments and profits, primary production and manufacturing, and so on. Outside the United States, the liberals' major concerns at that time were the development of the economic infrastructure (transportation, energy, credit) and the expansion of social services.

The German Rathenau, the British Keynes, the American Franklin Roosevelt, are names indicative of post-1919 changes in economic policies, which followed modifications in liberal economic thinking. In French-speaking nations, *libériste* denotes the free enterpriser dedicated to *laissez-faire*, *dirigiste* the free enterpriser conscious of the defects of a market economy and committed to their elimination through the action of public powers — from the central government down to municipal authorities. Most post-1919 *libéristes* joined with conservatives; most liberals were *dirigistes*. They did not want the elimination of market economies (more flexible than command economies and therefore more favourable to change and, as now well known, more responsive to needs) and private free enterprise, but they specifically wanted the elimination of the twin evils of instability of the economic system and individual economic insecurity. Legislation protecting the rights of labour, redistribution of incomes through fiscal measures and the development of public services, social security, also a modest role for public investment and for public ownership and management of enterprises, summarise the major points of liberal economic policies in the phase of limited and reformed free enterprise.

THE WELFARE ECONOMY

Other liberals soon went further, and aimed at changing the economic structure radically. In some Commonwealth and north-western European states, often in co-operation with labourites and social democrats, liberals contributed to the formulation of the principles, and the establishment of the institutions, of the welfare economy. In a welfare economy private ownership of property is guaranteed and efforts are made to widen its diffusion. Through redistribution of incomes, aimed at diminishing unevenness, the welfare economy fulfills the function of strengthening individual liberty better than do most free-enterprise systems. It leaves room for large-scale public ownership of utilities, basic industries, the economic infrastructure; full or near-full employment is pursued; output is kept at a high level, the range of incomes is narrowed considerably, and through state-directed efforts economic insecurity is abolished. In the welfare economy, government holds the market stable, but within the frame of flexible government controls it is the market which regulates investment, output and distribution of goods and services, incomes, prices. In the liberals' welfare mixed economy, private initiative and free enterprise have a role but not an exclusive one, and public authorities are responsible for the elimination of the poverty which for too long has weighed too heavily on too many.

Reformed free enterprise and the welfare economy are not the end of the road. For liberals, capitalism as the system in which capitalists have the upper hand belongs to the past, and collectivism — a more ancient system than capitalism — must not be the future, because of its tyrannical features. From a liberal viewpoint there is no end to the process of economic change along the road whose signpost reads 'free and equal'. Continuing along the road (the liberal-democratic institutional system) is more important than the building of a shelter at any given halt. It would be a disaster for mankind if the road were to become a dead-end.

3

A LONG AND DIFFICULT JOURNEY

LIBERTY AS BURDEN

Mention will be made in this chapter of several major steps taken through the centuries along the road leading to liberalism in modern times. Without them there would have been little or no advance along the way. Even with them, because of the role that choice (see p. 23) and chance play in human affairs, because of lack of awareness of liberty and antagonism to it, of inability or unwillingness to cope with liberty's problems, there never was any certainty that there would be a liberal movement and a liberal era. Past, present and future form not an unbending rod, but a chain: a single different choice in any of the innumerable factors influencing each development can alter the next and every succeeding link.

To assess the importance of the steps, they should be viewed in relation to the prevailing attitude towards liberty. As with other faculties, from imagination to ability to swim, being endowed with liberty does not mean that one is aware of it, or aware or not that one makes use of it. Whatever their level of education and intellectual achievement, millions who can and do engage in action thanks to the liberties of liberal-democratic states do not consider these liberties important. More millions go through life avoiding any kind of choice as much as possible. Neither does awareness of liberty imply that one favours it — that, specifically, one is willing to tolerate the liberty of others and to restrain the power to coerce that dominant majorities and minorities use, even when it is not formally institutionalised.

The evidence concerning liberty is clear. At all times and in all places, most people have considered responsibility for choice — Locke's 'power . . . to do or forbear doing any particular action' — a burden. The orthodox attitude, seen in all civilisations except the Greco-Roman and its Western successor for brief periods, is that the good society is the authoritarian one, politically despotic and intellectually conformist. Even in Greco-Roman and Western civilisations, many, if not most, prominent thinkers, from Plato to twentieth-century intellectuals, have considered authoritarianism the

ideal social organisation: most of the utopias in which writers have
projected their dreams describe authoritarian societies.

AUTHORITARIAN ORTHODOXY AND LIBERAL HERESY

Today, the nearly six-score authoritarian states that are members of
the United Nations represent the norm in the organisation of nations.
The combination of fanatical nationalism and dogmatic socialism,
which is the strongest force now agitating mankind (see p. 9) is a
return to the orthodox past, strengthened by modern technological
innovations. The thirty or so democracies (several of them shaky)
constituting the 'free world' are the deviation from the norm, the
heresy.

Where there is liberty there are usually divisions, quarrels, agitation
and turmoil. In 1778, Turgot expressed the hope that Americans 'may
be able to prove that man can be free and yet tranquil' but he was not
optimistic on that score. In a free society, information of wrong-doing
upsets people, discussion heightens emotions, agitation easily goes
beyond the bounds of legal action, and the ensuing repression is
visible to all. This lack of quiet terrifies the members of a national
community in the measure in which ability to cope with difficulties
without losing one's balance — i.e. character — is weak.

Lack of quiet leads majorities, irrespective of class or any other
sub-division of the national community, to greet a dictator or would-
be dictator enthusiastically, as they did in Italy in 1922, Argentina in
1943, the Sudan in 1958, Bangladesh in 1975. Subjects of traditional
and radical authoritarian regimes, at times many, as in France
in 1789, more often a handful as in the Soviet Union today, long for
liberty; but many, often most, as soon as they have it, are horrified
by what it brings. This happened to millions of Frenchmen in 1792,
of Germans in 1849 and again in 1933, of Latin Americans freed
from Spanish rule, of Chinese after the liberal revolution of 1911, of
Russians after the revolution of March 1917, of Africans when
colonial powers withdrew. With the help of the numerous and influential fault-finders among the intelligentsia of liberal democracies,
advocates of dictatorial rule (at times labeled real or guided democracy,
democratic centralism, or some other self-deceiving expression) harp
on the horrors of life in nations in which a start — no more than
that — has been made towards implementing the principle 'free and
equal'.

In the recent past, gigantic waves of totalitarianism, formed by
hundreds of millions in all continents bent on obliterating everything
connected with the liberal way of life, nearly engulfed all mankind.
More because of rivalry between two major pre-1939 totalitarian

waves — national-socialism and Stalinist national-communism — and of
errors made by dictators, than of the liberal democracies' capacity to
fight it out successfully on the battlefield, totalitarianism was effectively checked between 1942, when the tide of a war of conquest
launched by national-socialism was reversed in the Pacific, the
Mediterranean and the Volga, and 1954, when national-communism was
temporarily halted in East Asia. Much of the two waves having since
coalesced into one vast dynamic movement (with the minor differen-
tiations already mentioned, p. 8), whose appeal is growing in all
continents, totalitarianism is again gaining ground.

Considering that despotism is the norm in community organisation,
and liberty the heresy, that in the light of total experience there is
something unique in the fact that free institutions actually functioned
in a few nations (which as a result progressed rapidly, and for a while
set the tone for much of mankind); and considering that elements
which made for liberalism appeared at different times in different
places, to have an understanding of the liberal movement requires
knowledge of what prepared the ground for its birth, survival and
expansion. The birth was a manifestation of man's spontaneity, but it
could not have occurred, and there could not have been survival and
expansion, unless the ground had been favourable.

THE AWARENESS OF REASON

One of the first readings in a small book, *Liberalism*, by the historian
J. S. Schapiro, is a quotation from Socrates, who never wrote, but
whose thoughts reported by Plato have for 2400 years been the
symbol of the most significant revolution in ways of thinking.
Bertrand Russell, a libertarian socialist in the liberal tradition, begins
the history of Western philosophy with a discussion of Greek thinkers,
from the sixth century B.C. To say that the source of much or even
most of what matters today is in the Greek or Greco-Roman or
Greco-Judaic heritage may be a commonplace, but it is true: in
classical Greece awareness of reason took hold and grew, to the
extent of becoming a major feature in the Greek way of life. Without
it, there would not have been the ways of thinking that made for the
unique character of modern civilisation during the phase when
liberalism was influential. There would not have been the formulation
of empiricism, empirical positivism, instrumentalism and other
conceptual frameworks whose principles and method made it possible
to think liberally and therefore to engage in liberal action.

What happened in the sixth century B.C. was of small importance
to Greeks of the time, and hardly noticed. Attention was focused on

often tumultuous developments in hundreds of independent communities then forming the Greek world, on the active pursuit of a more prosperous life through the development of trade and industry, and on ominous changes taking place beyond eastern borders, where despotism reigned and empires came and went in quick succession.

However, as often happens in frontier settlements, in communities established a few generations earlier by Ionian Greeks on the Asian shores of the Aegean sea, traditional ways of thinking and doing had weakened and no longer held sway over the people. In these communities there was greater liberty than in those of the Old Country, some freedom of thought and sufficient affluence to provide leisure for philosophical speculation. A few, perhaps Thales of Miletus, perhaps someone else whose name has since been lost, began to use their minds consciously. The results of their reflections were communicated to disciples who, stimulated, carried the investigations further.

All use reason, but few try to discover what it is, what it is capable of, how it operates, what is the best way to use it. Conceptual frameworks used by pre-civilised and most civilised people are mainly combinations of intuition and tradition — of the immediate grasp of reality and the residue of an unconscious process of trial and error. Both intuition and tradition use methods of authority and dispense with the complex operations of the mind's reasoning faculties. The few who had consciously used reason in the sixth century B.C., and tried to improve on its operations, were not so few two and three hundred years later; a new way of thinking, founded on reason and no longer mainly on intuition and tradition, had spread among the educated minority of Greek-speaking people (a larger and intellectually more dynamic minority than in any other ancient civilisation).

THE BEGINNING OF PHILOSOPHY, HISTORY AND SCIENCE

While Greeks fought each other, and gradually lost their independence to less advanced but better organised foreigners, Greek thought soared: it was then that Anaxagoras, Plato, Aristotle, Zeno, Epicurus and countless others lived, wrote and taught; it was then that was established the Athenian Academy which lasted nearly a thousand years; it was then that were formulated some of the major ways of thinking founded on reason, critical and dogmatic alike — affirmative ones like idealism, materialism, empiricism, and negative ones like scepticism and cynicism. Then was born philosphy, in its correct meaning the discipline that aims at expanding the range of knowledge through use of reason. Then, too, within philosophy, was born logic, which concentrates on the proper use of reason.

History and science were also born at that time. Where intuition and tradition hold sway there can be chronicle, but not history, which involves reason in telling the story of what has happened; there can be chance discoveries and inventions, but not science. The 'father of history', Herodotus, really was the father, the first historian. With Euclides, Erathosthenes, Archimedes and others, science reached a level in the third century B.C. which would nowhere be surpassed until the seventeenth century (in the Greco-Roman and Western civilisations the scientific Middle Ages lasted twice as long as the political Middle Ages). In the Greek and Hellenistic world there still was plenty of superstition, magic, absurdities of all kinds sanctioned by intuition (revelation, for religious believers) and by tradition; but at least there was a tool available for getting rid of them, and for establishing the contact with the real that is indispensable for continuing progress (and that most cannot stand).

Why was there this revolution in Greece, not elsewhere? It was the manifestation of inner liberty, of spontaneity; it happened. It might not have happened. Ionian and other Greeks were no better and no worse than peoples who worshipped other gods, grew other grains, were governed by other leaders, belonged to other civilisations. In some Greek communities, the Ionian ones particularly, the institutional structure was less rigid and oppressive than was usually the case; this was the main difference between Greek and non-Greek communities, but would not have been enough by itself to give birth to the new way of thinking founded on reason. At one time or another, in Persia, India and China, there were individuals who did what Thales and Socrates did, who tried to replace intuition and tradition with the rational process, or at least to add it. However, only in the Greek, the Hellenistic, and then in the larger Greco-Roman world, did individual convictions concerning the priority of reason, and correct use of it, spread sufficiently to become a force strong enough to set the tone for a civilisation's way of life. Greek civilisation acquired its uniqueness with its consciousness of reason. Totally different from all other civilisations, it was the heresy, and was to become the major source of modern civilisation during its liberal phase.

LAW AND ROMANS

Committed to the priority of method over goals (see p. 48), liberals are concerned with clearly defined rights and duties, with the rule of law and the elimination of arbitrariness, with guarantees for personal security and autonomy, and with equality, which prevents liberty from being a privilege. Rights and duties, rule of law, guarantees, legal and therefore moral equality, are concepts slowly developed in

Roman assemblies and courts; in due course, through a centuries-long process, they were institutionalised in Roman law. The concepts and institutions survived the collapse of the Roman state in the west; they suffered an eclipse but never disappeared entirely; their revival contributed to the formulation of ideas included in the liberal synthesis, and to the all-important role attributed to legal institutions in liberal-constitutional and liberal-democratic states.

Other ancient nations in the Mediterranean and beyond shared the Romans' deep reverence for law, but the Romans created a new kind of law; they were the first to divorce it from religion, and by making it secular, they made it human (even if not necessarily humane). In the early centuries of the Roman community, the foundation on which laws were based was no different from that of other post-tribal communities: laws consisted of norms of behaviour religiously sanctioned and uncritically accepted. The separation of laws from religion was as difficult a feat as the separation now taking place — far from being achieved as yet — of ethics from religion.

A change in the Roman attitude to laws probably began in the fourth century B.C., and was completed by the second century A.D. For several generations, it had been largely a manifestation of Roman republicanism. Problems had arisen concerning the organisation of the state, also concerning relationships between different groups of the population; the problems were new and they were solved in a new way, through decisions taken in one of the three assemblies in which Romans participated and voted. A new road had been opened. Traditional legal rules sanctioned by religious authorities (such as those included in the Twelve Tables of the fifth century B.C.) had been superseded by rules sanctioned by the citizens. It amounted to a major revolution.

LAW DIVORCED FROM RELIGION

From the last century of the republic on, sophisticated Roman jurists and judges acted on the basis of the principle (an accepted even if not an explicitly formulated one) that if — as Ionian Greeks had discovered — reason characterises human beings, then laws, being man-made, should be developed according to reason. In the codification of Roman laws, completed at the middle of the sixth century, the Greek discovery of what reason is joined hands with the Roman invention of secular legal institutions, keyed to the delimitation of individual rights and of relationships among individuals as well as between individuals and society. The *Codex Justinianus*, with the Digest, the Institutes, the Novellae, has been superseded; it nevertheless remains one of the great documents in the progressive march of mankind, and it was instrumental in keeping alive heretical ideas of the Greco-Roman civilisation until the time when they could once again bear fruit.

To offset man's fallibility, Romans stressed the importance of government by law, the best guarantee of citizens' security, the best safeguard against the tyranny and cruelty of one, a few, or many. Tyrannical will and arbitrary action are curbed in so far as legal procedure is paramount. The Romans went further than any other nation until modern times in developing the concept of the person as the individual endowed with rights and duties, i.e. with morality. The person — jurists made clear — is the moral individual, just as the citizen, as a free man (or free woman now in a few advanced nations) participating in the government of the community, is the political individual. The concept of the 'citizen' developed by Romans was basic in modern times to the enactment of all liberal charters, from the British and American Bills of Rights and the French Declaration of Rights, to the Covenant of the League of Nations, the U.N. Declaration of Human Rights, and the constitutions of post-1945 liberal democracies.

Romans went furthest in their times in defining liberty, and enabled future generations to see the autonomy of the individual as the foundation of government by the citizens. Also, they were the first to conceive the equality of human beings. To conceive and to practice are two vastly different things: in practice, all the Romans achieved was the end of legal discrimination between Romans and non-Romans in their vast state; the gradual decrease of slavery in Roman territory (replaced by serfdom which, however brutal, is not the total denial of humanness that slavery is); the recognition in the *jus gentium* that all peoples have their rights, that there is no chosen people, or nation, or race. It was a great deal, for the times, eighteen to fifteen centuries ago. The idea of equality was born. It survived, to bear fruit centuries later.

'Why the Greeks?' was asked before, in relation to the discovery of reason. 'Why the Romans?' it is natural to ask now. Eighteen to fifteen centuries ago was the period of great achievements in India, and nearly as great in China and Persia. But in the Indian, Chinese and Persian civilisations the law remained what it had always been, a set of all-embracing rules sanctioned by religious tradition. They were not man-made rules. Romans were no better and no worse than their Persian neighbours, than the distant Indians, than the Chinese, about whom they knew nothing. That it was the Romans who carried out such a revolution was simply a manifestation of the creativity inherent in the human mind.

A UNIQUE RELIGION

Where the one-time Greco-Roman civilisation, shrunk and impover-
ished, had become Western civilisation, more than 800 years elapsed
between the closing of the Athenian Academy, early in the sixth
century A.D., and the rediscovery and subsequent revival of Greco-
Roman concepts and values towards the middle of the fourteenth
century. Such a period is long enough to lose entirely what had once
been achieved. During that period (when peoples whose common
bond was catholicism were on a lower plane, both material and
spiritual, than peoples in neighbouring and distant civilisations), there
were two developments which became features of the Western way
of life, and contributed to the climate in which the progressivism of
the modern era developed. One was a renewed awareness of reason,
the other a new attitude towards human beings and what surrounds
them.

The Greek-discovered role of reason, and the concern of Ancients
in the Greco-Roman world about the correct use of it, had survived in
Roman law; but they were of interest to only a few, among the
minuscule educated minority of the time. Vastly more important was
their survival in the catholic church, which, helped by the disintegration of the western Roman state and the rudimentary looseness of
successor states, had developed its own cohesive institutional structure.
The catholic church, having failed to absorb the secular power,
successfully parried the secular power's attempt to reduce it to
obedience. Through the centuries it maintained its autonomy, and
from the tenth century on strengthened its cohesion.

During that long period, catholicism was of more importance than
lords, merchants and artists in the Western way of life. Moulded
theologically and philosophically during the 200 or so years between
the time of St Ambrose and that of St Gregory Magnus, catholicism
had as major characteristic a compromise between 'paganism' (actually
Greco-Roman culture) and Pauline-Athanasian Christianity. The
compromise took the form of a partial absorption of Greco-Roman
elements, including the role of reason and concern for the correct use
of it.

In catholicism, as in all religions, and in ethical systems like
Confucianism which fill a religious role, intuition prevailed. The
authority of the *ipse dixit* restricted the use of reason, and dogma
stifled critical faculties. This notwithstanding, since the formative
period in the fifth and sixth centuries reason occupied a more
influential position in catholicism than in any other religion. More
than in the Mohammedanism of Arabs, Persians and Moors during
creative periods, when rationalism in dogmatic and non-dogmatic

versions existed but was largely a heretical or semi-heretical fringe phenomenon; more than in Confucianism, whose vague pragmatism never acquired a clearly formulated and clearly reasoned base. Scholasticism, the dominant way of thinking in catholic nations for several centuries, expressed the continuing role of reason in Western cultures. The Scholastics' efforts to demonstrate rationally theological postulates concerning God, the soul and the after-life were futile, or absurd, or both, but the efforts were made. In the mediaeval educational curriculum, logic was a major discipline. Awareness of reason survived.

THE NOMINALISTIC HERESY

The other major contribution to later developments was the appearance and survival against severe odds (including persecution and the thirteenth-century inquisitorial genocide) of something new: the clearly formulated concept that 'universals' are names. Its corollary in human affairs is that reality belongs to the individual, not to the collective. In A.D. 1100 nominalism — the conceptual framework postulating that concept — was of no greater interest to contemporaries than speculations of Ionian teachers had been in 500 B.C. Like the speculations, however, nominalism was a beginning from which in time a distinctive way of thinking derived. Adopted, sometimes deliberately but more often through imitation, by millions, it opened new horizons and became the maker of a new culture centuries later.

Within the catholic context, nominalism was heresy. Catholicism recognised individual autonomy, but only within a higher, all-embracing cohesive reality, the Church. The spelling of Church with a capital 'C' indicated that it possessed a life of its own, that it had thought and will, that it was more than the community of believers, more than just an institutional structure. In catholicism, communalism as the priority of the group over the individual prevailed, leaving small room for individual autonomy and responsibility; not enough, for instance, to have republicanism as citizens' self-government instead of monarchism.

In the eleventh century, the French cleric and teacher Roscellinus maintained that where man is concerned life belongs to individuals only. This point was made in connection with a theological dispute among Scholastics. Few, if any, at the time realised its wide implications and ramifications. Roscellinus acquired disciples, who in turn found more disciples. One man's position became a movement. At that time, the attention of ecclesiastical and secular authorities was being distracted by the growth of evangelical heresies. Consequently,

the dispute opposing Roscellinus and the better known Abelard to
St Anselm and St Bernard took second place. This helped the
religious—intellectual heresy to survive.

THE DIGNITY OF MAN

The survival of nominalism created conditions favourable to the next
step: the birth and diffusion of humanism. A revolution in ideas and
values began in Italy at the middle of the fourteenth century, in a
generation that laughed at the hollow pretensions of emperors
without empire, such as Ludwig IV and Charles IV, and of unworthy
prelates whose leaders — popes and cardinals — disported themselves
in Avignon in a palace provided by nearly independent cadets of the
kings of France. Humanism, keyed to a greater concern for man and
things on earth than for God and things in heaven, was a major
aspect of the revolution which reached its climax with the Renaissance.
Weakening the fabric of orthodoxy, it facilitated the partial success
of religious and ethical innovations brought about by Lutheran
protestantism and more radically by the Calvinist Reformation. The
humanist revolution was smothered in Italy by triumphant conformity,
enforced by the disciplined Spanish infantry on behalf of intolerant
clerics. It continued for a while in France and in parts of the Germanies.
It flourished in England two generations after it had died in Italy.

The intellectual and moral humanist revolution had begun with the
reinterpretation of writings of Greek and Roman authors, now newly
read, not through catholic lenses but as they had been written, and
also with the discovery of ancient writings containing unheard-of
ideas and long-forgotten knowledge. Freedom of the mind was the
essence of this revolution; it was more important for humanity than
wars won and lost, more than the consolidation of power in the hands
of princes and oligarchies, more than the establishment of large-scale
economic enterprises. Increasing numbers of people became dissatis-
fied with passive acceptance of what was sanctioned by tradition. New
ideas borrowed from the Ancients were soon transcended. Not just a
few philosophers, but many, who without being concerned with
philosophy were seeking truth, began to speculate on the nature of
man and on human life. The intellectual horizon widened. A
humanist's ideal took shape, an ideal that opposed fanaticism and
violence, stressed reasonableness and toleration, respect for each
individual human being. The essay on man, or rather on the dignity
of man, written by young Pico della Mirandola in 1486, was topical
then and is even more so today. Humanism was a modest movement.
Humanists were few, and far from influential, whether among the

powerful or among the masses. The Church they weakened was being weakened also by other forces, but one more step forward had been taken.

A RADICAL REVOLUTION

The period from 1517, when Luther affixed his ninety-five theses to the door of one of Wittemberg's churches, to 1536 when Calvin took up residence in Geneva, marks the passage to the modern era in what had been the Western commonwealth of catholic nations — chief heir to ancient Greece and ancient Rome, home of near-rational Scholasticism and of reasonable humanism.

There had recently been crucial, sometimes cataclysmic, events affecting the commonwealth. The East Roman or Byzantine state had come to an end, the printing press had been invented, the New World had been discovered and a sea route found to India and beyond, and firearms had come into general use. More important were the events of 1517—36 and after: the fragmentation of the catholic commonwealth, the disruption of peoples and nations as the result of bitter sectarianism, the dividing of the Western commonwealth into two branches — one composed of peoples and nations freer than before, and therefore progressive, the other of peoples and nations more servile than before and therefore soon stagnant (see pp. 14f.). By the end of the sixteenth century, new values had replaced old ones in each of the two branches, and action was guided by new ideas and new aspirations. Protestantism, Reformation and Counter-Reformation were radical revolutions which transformed life in Europe and in all areas of the world, from Peru to Cape Province, to Japan, where Europeans were present and their influence was felt.

Humanism contributed to the birth of protestantism in the sixteenth century, and a few generations later protestantism contributed to the birth of liberalism. The connection is not a direct one, however. Protestantism was a revival of faith, of commitment to God. Its concern was man's relationship to God, not relationships among men. It was keyed to the protest against corruption and unbelief among churchmen. Whatever was believed by individual reformers, and practised by minor groups like the Socinians, the mass of protestants rejected the priority of reason and tolerance of dissidents. Lutheran protestantism and the Calvinist Reformation were the successful sixteenth-century manifestations of the movement that had produced the evangelical heresies of southern France and northern Italy in the eleventh century, and also the Lollards, Utraquists and Taborites of England and central Europe in the fourteenth and fifteenth centuries. The stream protestantism belonged to was a different one from that of humanism. Still, when all is said, the fact remains that liberalism was

born among protestants, or those who had been exposed to protestantism, in nations which had embraced it (the English, the Dutch) or
(like the French) had been deeply influenced by it.

FACING GOD

At the level of ideas and institutional structures, four elements in
protestantism contributed to the formulation of the liberal position
and the formation of the liberal movement:

(1) Protestantism eliminated the intermediary of the priesthood on
earth and of heavenly spirits beyond, and put man face to face with
God. It was a heavy, at times a crushing, burden. It also meant responsibility, it enhanced dignity, it opened the road to emancipation.

(2) Protestantism gave the inner conscience priority over external
authority. Again, the burden was heavy, and dignity and responsibility
were enhanced.

(3) Specifically in the case of what were then fringe movements —
from pre-Reformation Moravian brothers and Waldensians, to
Brownists, congregationalists and baptists — the basic structural
element in the organisation of new sects was the self-government of a
congregation composed of free and equal believers, all participating
in discussion and decisions, all entitled to share in the functioning of
the community.

(4) At first only as isolated cases, from among protestants came
those committed to the most heretical value of all: religious tolerance.
From Chateillon to Roger Williams, they were hounded and ostracised
for several generations. They were repressed, but there was no
inquisitorial efficiency in protestant communities to suppress them.
A new value was born to fructify later. Compared with what it had
seceded from, protestantism was individual autonomy, responsibility
and dignity; it was equality among believers, it was emancipation.

Catholicism had meant, and still did where the Counter-Reformation
triumphed, obedience, conformism, adjustment of personal conscience
to dictates of external authority, ritual. The protestant believer, being
responsible for his actions, held his head high. At the same time, he
was humbled by the nearness of God. He valued education, because
he had to be literate to be able to read the scriptures and meditate on
them. He had to be truthful and to lead a sober life. Only God could
give absolution from sins; one's guilt remained one's guilt. Autonomy
meant that it was up to the believer to do his duty and to co-operate
with others. Duty — in practice, action beneficial to others, from
one's family to mankind, from the congregation to the state — had
precedence over self-gratification.

From Hutten's knights of 1522 to English Roundheads of 1642

and French Huguenots of 1685, protestants, excepting a few, were
not liberals, nor did they lean towards liberalism; but without their
values and ideas, without the democratic institutions of thousands of
congregations from Transylvania to New England, liberalism would
not have been possible.

THE EMANCIPATION OF MINDS

In two-thirds of what had been the catholic commonwealth, the
Reformation either made no appearance or was crushed. By their
determination and courage, protestants triumphed in areas of Germany,
then including Switzerland and the Low Countries. Elsewhere
in central and northern Europe, the determination and courage were
helped by dynastic accidents, the fortunes of near and distant wars,
the interests of groups siding with protestantism for a variety of non-
religious reasons, some noble, others sordid. In France, for centuries
the mind and heart of the Western way of life, there was a long
struggle which left its imprint on a nation that remained mostly
catholic, but not as much so as the Spanish, the Irish and the Polish.

The sheer multiplicity of conflicting absolutisms on the continent
provided some freedom. Grotius could, for instance, print in France,
and Descartes in the United Provinces, what they could not print at
home. The dynastic accident of the presence of a bizarre character on
the throne of England, for nearly forty years, led to a many-sided
conflict in Great Britain involving Anglicans, Calvinists, smaller nonconformist groups and catholics. Total victory eluded all parties
involved, with the result that from 1534 to 1688 there were
conditions of liberty at times, even if most Englishmen, Welshmen
and Scots would have preferred their own brand of authoritarianism.
These were among the conditions providing a few on either side of
the English Channel with opportunity to formulate and express new
ideas, to find followers, to launch a new movement.

Within the small minority of progressive Europeans aware of
reason and committed to the use of rational methods, familiar with
concepts developed in the Greco-Roman world and with debates
among Scholastics and post-Scholastic thinkers, inclined toward
humanism and its values, a few spontaneously developed the idea
that the chains imposed by authority (Church Fathers and Vicars of
Christ as well as Greek philosophers and Roman jurists) could be
broken. These few held that reason is susceptible of improvement;
that knowledge would increase if reason were allowed free rein,
collecting evidence and verifying conclusions; that inductive and *a
posteriori* modes of thinking are more conducive to the expansion of

knowledge and to correct understanding of the universe, life and man than are syllogistic and *a priori* modes; that there is more ahead than there is behind.

What has been taken for granted in progressive nations in recent generations (and now is becoming less and less accepted) was an innovation when that part of Bacon's *Instauratio Magna* known as the *Novum Organum* appeared in 1620, Galileo's *Dialogue* in 1632, Descartes's *Discourse* in 1636, and when the works of Grotius, Spinoza and Leibniz were published. The innovation, a new way of thinking, led to radical transformation in all aspects of life. Three centuries later its impact was felt by all peoples of the world. It was a total radical revolution.

PROGRESSIVISM AND OBSCURANTISM

The innovation met with a positive response in most communities shaken by the protestant upheaval; it had some impact on the French, and none, for a considerable time, on most catholic nations where conformity and absolutism were supreme. That Bacon became chancellor of England, and Galileo went to prison, symbolises the disparity between the two Europes, one progressive and the other stagnant. (France, whose Descartes found it safer to spend much of his adult life abroad, had elements of both.) Bacon's way of thinking, revised and improved to meet the needs of sophisticated intellectuals, simplified at the level of the general public, became the way of thinking of growing numbers of Britons, in the British Isles and overseas. From Bacon's innovation came varied and flexible empiricism and pragmatism, in time the prevailing conceptual framework of Britons and Americans of all classes.

In Italy, by contrast, few heeded Galileo either during his lifetime or later. Open-mindedness, reasonableness, dialogue as the ability to learn from others (even from those of whom one disapproves) and to persuade others, careful analysis, the gathering of evidence before making statements, induction, the use of the few basic canons of the scientific method, all remained alien to the Italian way of thinking. Whatever the intellectual level, Italians vacillated between dogmatism and cynicism, their dialogues being exchanges of monologues. Members of the intelligentsia preferred synthesis to analysis and deduction to induction, were impatient with the painstaking labour needed to assemble and elaborate evidence, delighted in unproven statements, relied on authority. Empiricism did not find many followers in France, but for 300 years Cartesian reasoned thinking, open and clear, logically structured, has been a feature of French life.

THE ADVANCE OF SCIENCE

In ancient Greece, minds freed from the chains of uncritical and authoritarian traditional thought were fascinated by speculations on ethics and metaphysics — on morality and the beyond. Scientific thought developed brilliantly during the first few generations of the Hellenistic era, but it took second place. Two thousand years later, in Great Britain, and soon too on the European continent where the new way of thinking took hold, emancipated minds were instead fascinated by the world of man and the surrounding universe. Examination prevailed over speculation, physics over metaphysics. The main tool to expand knowledge and acquire a better understanding of the world we live in was the correct method of using reason — the scientific method. There was observation, analysis, setting the evidence in order, experimentation, formulation and verification of hypotheses. The universe was investigated, then man and his world. The scientific era had begun.

Among foremost scientists, besides Galileo, there were on the European continent the German Kepler, the French Pascal, the Dutch Huyghens and Leeuwenhoek, their few teachers and their many disciples. Some of them were still tainted with superstition and dabbled in alchemy and astrology. This notwithstanding, they championed the new way of thinking. But the real revolution took place in Great Britain, where Boyle's and Hooke's 'Invisible College' became, in the freer ambiance which followed the demise of Cromwell, the Royal Society — then by far the most important institution stimulating scientific thought and research.

The Royal Society elected as member in 1671 a young man not yet thirty, Isaac Newton. His name, better known than most, symbolises the efforts of thousands and their astounding achievements. Newtonian thought, Newtonian era, Newtonian system, are expressions denoting the new world of science. At the instigation of Halley, Newton wrote the *Philosophiae Naturalis Principia Mathematica* which played in the advancement of mankind a greater role than the deeds and misdeeds of his celebrated contemporaries, the Sun King in France, the Ornament of the Throne in India, the Son of Heaven in China. The French translation of Newton's *Principia* by Madame de Châtelet led to an enthusiastic spurt of scientific activities, first in France, then elsewhere on the continent and overseas. French scientists for a while held the lead in promoting the advancement of science, then the British again, then the Germans, now the Americans.

The interest in science led those endowed with a practical turn of mind to use scientific discoveries for developing technological inventions, which in turn became the launching-pad for the rise and expansion of modern industry. There would have been no Watt in 1769, no Fulton in 1807, no Faraday in 1821, no Morse in 1832, no Siemens in 1867, no Wright brothers in 1903, no Manhattan Project in 1942, no sputnik in 1957, and no Neil Armstrong walking on the moon in 1969, without Newton. And there would have been no Newton without the favourable response of people of Great Britain to Bacon's new thought, without the emancipation of minds from the tyranny of authority and of its own dogmas, which enabled Bacon to think, if not entirely freely, at least more so than had ever been possible before.

FREEDOM OF EXPRESSION

To think freely is difficult, and is largely up to the individual; to express oneself freely is rare, and requires the weakening if not the abolition of orthodox authoritarian institutional structures. For several generations after the dawn of the modern era, freedom of expression was alien to the way of life of Great Britain, as it was at the time to the way of life of all other nations. Mediaeval British liberties had clarified the status and functions of various classes, increasing the autonomy of some and protecting others. They were progressive in so far as they curbed arbitrariness and increased the range of action of large sectors of the population. However, they were not liberal, because liberties were nothing but privileges — as they had been in Iberian catholic kingdoms and in Tuscan and Flemish city-states of the late Middle Ages, and still were in the aristocratic Polish kingdom and Venetian republic, in oligarchic Swiss cantons and Imperial cities.

In sixteenth-century and most of seventeenth-century Great Britain, liberty was restricted by the uniformity of the way of life of the group one belonged to. Labourer, yeoman, merchant and aristocrat were expected to think and behave as such. There was a minimal range of deviation within each group. It was possible to pass from one group to another, but extremely difficult. As in most nations of the Continent, even if less formally, the population was divided into estates. Though there were divisions and bitter tensions, most agreed, there as elsewhere, as they always had done everywhere, that at the level of ideas there should be uniformity of views, and that uniformity should direct activities at the practical level. Pluralism of ideas and values, and any system legitimising and organising pluralism, repelled most Britons as it did most Westerners and all non-Westerners, as it does all advocates of dictatorial rule today. English pilgrims and puritans who crossed the Atlantic were seeking their own liberty, not the liberty of others as well.

The situation changed gradually. It took about 300 years to pass from uniformity to near-complete legitimacy for all kinds of ideas, to near-complete freedom of expression. For several generations the change was favoured by the many-sided conflict between groups in the British kingdoms committed to clashing interpretations of Christianity. The conflict had an emancipating effect. At least for some it meant a lessening of coercion: a divided community cannot bring as much pressure to bear on its members as a cohesive one is able to do; and where strong opposition makes it difficult for a state to enforce its authority, some will seize the opportunity to express heretical ideas.

In the century and a half between the Act of Supremacy of 1534 and the revolution of 1688, there was no lack in Great Britain of articulate, persuasive and influential advocates of absolutism and conformity. However, the many-sided conflict also provided many with the opportunity to advance revolutionary concepts concerning the structure of society and the best method of government. A few came to the conclusion that freedom of thought and of expression (of the press, as it was to be called for 300 years) were valuable. In his *Areopagitica*, published in 1644, Milton proved to be their greatest spokesman. Some, like the deist Cherbury, ventured to express views indicating a departure from Christianity altogether, and survived. The few who heeded Milton and Cherbury were on the side that won the battles against Charles I.

FORTUITOUS SUCCESS OF LIBERALISM'S POLITICAL FOREBEARS

In the 1640s, on the European Continent, difficult and lengthy nego-tiations in the midst of heavy fighting were bringing the destructive Thirty Years' War to a close; on the populous 'closed' continent at the other extreme of the Eurasian land mass, a new dynasty took power; between Europe and China, another new dynasty was consoli-dating its autocratic stranglehold over the sparsely inhabited Russian state, stretching 5000 miles, while Osmanli Turks were victorious against the Persians, and Turkish moguls against hindu states; an empire was disintegrating in the Sudan, Japanese rulers enforced isolation and uniformity through executions, the last traces of Amerindian civilisations were being obliterated in the Western hemi-sphere. Among these events, the civil war fought in Great Britain between two relatively small sections of the population seemed a minor episode; but for the future of liberalism it was the most important.

Tension between Parliament and Crown had increased in the British realms since the early reign of James I. Through elections, dissolutions, suspensions, prorogations, through the Great Protestation of 1621, the Petition of Right of 1628, the Grand Remonstration of 1641, tension climaxed in the Great Rebellion of 1642 which pitted parliamentarian Roundheads (among whom presbyterians were the major faction) against royalist Cavaliers fighting for a king who, as a person, was a better man than most contemporary continental monarchs (and autocrats of distant empires). Without the help of specious rationalisations, Charles I wanted to introduce in the British realms and their overseas dependencies the political absolutism established, or being established, with various degrees of efficiency by Habsburg, Bourbon, Vasa and minor continental rulers. In Great Britain, however, there were committed and capable opponents of absolutism: Pym, Eliot (who died in prison), Coke, later Hampden (who died on the battle-field), Argyle, Essex and Cromwell. Religious fervour gave puritans and covenanters (the backbone of armies raised by Parliament and its allies) the strength of commitment which enables soldiers to die, and so to win, and which no economic interest can give. Thanks to a combination of factors (besides commitment and courage there were efficiency of military organisation and leadership, greater availability of funds, treachery among royalists) the parliamentary side was victorious. Within a short while intolerant Independents turned against the presbyterians, among whom were the carriers of new ideas and new values, and won. Cromwell established his own dictatorship. Fortunately for the future of liberty, death overcame him before he had completed the consolidation of his authoritarian regime.

THE GREATEST HERESY, TOLERANCE

Cromwell might have emulated Caesar. However, his successor was a Perdiccas, not an Octavian. Repressed but not yet suppressed, survivors among the carriers of new ideas and values reappeared after the Lord Protector's timely death. The victory of the Roundheads, the death of Cromwell, the divisions among the British peoples, the looseness of the institutional structure, provided the fertile ground for the few who had developed the ideal of religious tolerance against tremendous odds, and committed themselves to the extent of being willing to give up their lives for it. These few came from the ranks of the puritans, or had been close to them, but had abandoned the puritan rigid religiosity. Their position was the most heretical and the most progressive. Modern liberalism was born among those who, at a time when the religious had priority over the political and the economic, conceived the legitimacy of religious dissent.

Chateillon and Roger Williams have already been mentioned. There had been others: the Italians Fausto and Lelio Socini and their unitarian followers (soon exterminated in Italy, survivors fleeing to Hungary and Poland, finally to find shelter in the United Provinces); the Hungarian Francis David, the theologian who justified the toleration edicts of 1557, 1563 and 1571 in Transylvania; Montaigne in France, better known today than in his lifetime when prudence counselled avoidance of the limelight; and the Czech Comenius, last bishop of the Moravian brothers (the educator whose advice was sought by the founders of Harvard College). With the advocates of tolerance there was more than a radical religious break with the Roman church; there was a new way of life.

Sixteenth-century and early seventeenth-century advocates of tolerance were isolated cases. *Cuius regio, eius religio* had been the formula of the 1555 compromise in the Germanies: there could be catholics and protestants, but only in separate and politically autonomous communities. It was *apartheid*. Diversity within the community and legitimacy of religious dissent were still inconceivable. They were inconceivable for most puritans in England and in New England, and for Cavaliers and Independents during the civil wars of the 1640s. Cromwell outlawed not only catholics but also Anglicans and all non Trinitarians. After his death, peace and quiet eluded the English, the Welsh and the Scots. In the midst of political turmoil, of religious, economic and political contrasts, of restlessness everywhere, of movements forming, seceding, merging, fading away, the idea of a few became the idea of many. They were still not even a large minority, but as a result of the civil war of 1688–9, won by the Whigs (the presbyterians' political heirs) with the aid of foreign mercenaries, legitimacy of dissent and thus diversity in the activities of the mind became part of the British way of life.

It was partial tolerance. Only some of the groups into which the British were now divided religiously and intellectually could after generations of conflict and instability live their lives on a footing of equality. However, those who were discriminated against did not suffer the kind of suppression practised in nations belonging to the stagnant sections of Western civilisation, and in all non-Western civilisations. Even if lacking political rights, they could lead unharassed lives and enjoy successful careers.

The 1689 Act of Tolerance was just a beginning, but it was a revolutionary step forward. A major spokesman for the new thought, advocate of liberal constitutionalism, champion of toleration, was John Locke. The ideas he stood for were translated, at least in part, into institutions, because many of the influential people in Great Britain after the 1688–9 civil war also stood for these ideas (see Chapter 4). They set the tone for the nations of the island. The events of those two years were the prelude to revolutions in English-speaking communities which went beyond the intentions and goals of a new king and queen and their advisers. Today it is fashionable to scoff at the Whigs: the first liberals to achieve power in a nation and to give it a new direction, they gave right of citizenship to the bearers of a new way of life.

SEVEN MAJOR STEPS

The discovery of *reason*, and — centuries later — the emphasis on *reasonableness* as rejection of dogmatic rationalism with at the same time advocacy of the priority of reason over non reason; *secularisation* of law and thus of politics, through their divorce from religion; *individualism,* the ethical and political projection of the nominalists' position; the humanists' *dignity*, and the protestants' *responsibility* of the individual; *tolerance* as respect for others, leading to legitimacy of heresies, deviations and opposition, and favouring acceptance of new ideas and new movements: these were seven major steps which made possible the departure from authoritarian orthodoxy in the field of ideas and values, and were the moving force in institutional changes. They were a major part in the heritage from which liberalism sprang (a heritage excluding economic factors, which were identical for those who supported each step, for their numerous opponents, and for the many who were indifferent).

Not counting democratic conservatism, most of which today is liberalism slowed down, and democratic socialism, close to progressive liberalism (all equally committed to the liberal–democratic institutional framework and the principles underlying it), major ideological–political forces in today's world are lay and confessional traditionalism, nationalism, authoritarian socialism, anarcho-communism — and combinations thereof. The heritage of some of these forces includes, at most, three of the steps listed above; in other cases two, one, or even none (for instance in fast-disappearing confessional traditionalism); therein lies the whole difference between these forces on one side, and on the other liberalism, liberal conservatism and liberal socialism.

4

THE LIBERAL ERA:
(i) WHERE ENGLISH IS SPOKEN

A COMMON SOURCE FOR ENGLISH-SPEAKING NATIONS

The eighteenth century in Great Britain (since 1707 the official name
of the state, now inclusive of the whole island) was the Whig century.
This actually lasted for nearly 150 years, from 1688 until the
realignment of British political forces in the 1830s. Then the Whigs —
not so much a party as a movement, which included kindred and
usually quarrelling groups — divided. Those unafraid of further
changes joined with Utilitarians, Radicals, democrats, some Chartists,
and other progressives to form the Liberal party, while those who
were fearful, having concluded that enough had been achieved and
that reform should be halted or at least slowed down, moved over to
the conservative camp.

During those 150 years, in power or (half of the time) out of
power, the Whigs set the tone for the state they had reformed
institutionally after their victory in 1688–9. They set the tone for
the peoples of Great Britain. They also set the tone for those Britons
who in increasing numbers were going abroad on their own, colonis-
ing the eastern seaboard of North America, islands everywhere, then
Australia, and parts of South Africa later; trading, or just travelling;
spreading their versions of the Gospel; through their presence
checking French and Russian expansionist drives; fighting other
peoples' wars — as when they helped Corsicans against the French,
and hindus against moslems in southern India, when they led and
financed Greeks against Turks, Chileans against Spaniards.

Whig ideas and values set the tone for most of those who settled in
North America, whose way of life included a modicum of self-
government, of freedom of conscience and of the press, of market
economies. Only a modicum, but the difference between a little
liberty, as there was in Pennsylvania and Virginia, and none, as in
New Spain and Brazil, was greater than the difference between little
and more, as there would be in the former colonies after 1776. As
many as half of the Americans and Canadians of British extraction

(English, Scots and Scots-Irish, Welsh) are descended from the few hundred thousand who settled between Newfoundland and Georgia before 1800 — less than a fifth of them having arrived before the Whig revolution, the rest after. The events of 1688 in Great Britain had repercussions in North American communities. There were turmoil, confusion, irrationality and excesses — like the Salem trials. There was also the ending of authoritarian theocracies in New England, and of the authoritarian pretences of 'proprietors' south of New England.

THE WHIG CENTURY IN GREAT BRITAIN

Voltaire, soon to become the most influential writer of his time in France (then the leading Western power), went to Great Britain in 1726. He was impressed. Montesquieu, foremost political thinker of his time, went there soon after, and he was likewise deeply impressed. The list of impressed foreign visitors to the island during the Whig era is a long one. It includes Benjamin Franklin, who while in London drafted a liberal—radical political programme for his Whig friends; Hardenberg, whose far-reaching and basic reforms as Prussian chancellor were inspired by what he had seen and learnt in England; the Venezuelan patriots Miranda and Bolivar; Madame de Staël, author and Napoleon's opponent; Reshid Pasha, who took back from London, where he had been sent as ambassador, ideas he tried to incorporate in reforms aimed at modernising the Ottoman empire.

The works of Locke, Hume, Gibbon, Adam Smith, Bentham and Young were translated and avidly read, as were those of contemporary British poets and novelists. Paine was not a great thinker or an influential doer, but he was, more than Jefferson, and like his Girondist friends, an early spokesman for genuine liberal democracy: the ideas that gave him popularity for a while in the United States and France were projections of what he had learned and thought as a young anti-establishment Englishman. The work of members of the Royal Society and other British scientists set the pattern for scientific thought and research as far as St Petersburg. Romanticism, which on the continent transcended the literary field and was a powerful political force, was born in Great Britain. Parliamentary debates on a variety of topics, cabinet ministers called to give account of their actions, censure of government policies, control of public expenses, astounded foreigners, as did the quantity, quality and variety of goods produced and traded, and the multitude of ships in harbours. British technology revolutionised the economy, British engineering was admired, British machines were copied and British technicians were in great demand abroad.

Foreigners with a progressive turn of mind were impressed because they found in Great Britain what lacked (or existed to a lesser degree) elsewhere: a wide range of diversity and considerable tolerance for what was diverse, even when clearly obnoxious; greater security for persons, and for what they owned, than anywhere else; dynamism in the economy as in the arts, in politics as in science and letters; and national strength, stemming as much from the character of the people as from abundant financial means and (as then) a pre-eminent navy. Except for Americans of the United States still conscious of their links with Great Britain, and convinced that they had improved on the British model, the island north of the English Channel was a world apart, and for all who chafed under the restraints of authoritarianism, a better one. There were not many who liked the British people, but there were many who wanted to pattern their lives on the British way of life, and the institutions of their countries on British institutions.

WHIGGISM: AN ATTITUDE AND A PROGRAMME

The revolution of 1688—9 — the unexpected climax of the Great Rebellion of 1642, for liberal historians the Glorious Revolution — had few victims. There was not the blood bath that there would be after August 1792 in France and November 1917 in Russia; not the genocide that would be perpetrated in the twentieth century by (chronologically) Turks, Soviet Stalinists, German national-socialists, Chinese Maoists, Sudanese moslems, West Pakistanis, Tutsis and some of their neighbours, Khmers, no voluntary or enforced mass exodus of defeated opponents and frightened minorities, as there was in too many cases, from that of American Loyalists after 1781 to Kurds and Surinamese in 1975.

The impact of revolutions cannot be measured in terms of gallons of blood spilt and people killed. The measure of a revolution is the impact it has on a way of life. The Whigs who won in 1688—9 were a minority among the politically conscious Britons of the time, who in turn were a small minority among the few millions inhabiting the island. Varied as motivations were, Whigs agreed on commitment to Parliament, the rule of law, limitation of power for everyone and enlargement of the sphere of action within which individuals operate. They wanted an institutional framework guaranteeing security to all: strong enough to maintain order internally and to defend the country from foreign aggressors, operated by responsible (i.e. reasonable, committed and law-abiding) citizens; weak enough to leave citizens to their own devices.

For the rest, which includes most of everyone's everyday life,

Whigs believed in the principle of 'live and let live', and acted
accordingly. While they governed, and as long as they were influential
even if not in power, all sorts of restrictive regulations became dead
letters, and coercive institutions crumbled because they were no
longer in use. Eighteenth-century politically aware Britons lacked the
drive towards egalitarianism that has been a major source of progressive change in the British nation during the last 150 years, but in
terms of the situation in the island before 1688, and of the situation
nearly everywhere in the world, there was emancipation. To measure
the impact of the Whig revolution, it has to be seen in the setting of
its own time: making few victims, creating a freer climate for the
inhabitants of the island and for the colonists in overseas settlements,
it was more radical than revolutions soaked in blood. It gave rise to a
then unique way of life, something new in mankind's experience. It
made for progress. It also made — without government prodding —
for the endurance which enabled Britons to face, in wars lasting
twenty-three years, the dynamic expansionist drive, strengthened by
revolutionary fervour, of the most powerful nation in the world —
France — and finally to win, giving continental and other nations a
chance to work out their own destinies (a chance that there would
not have been if the French empire had endured; see Chapter 5).

   From 1688 until the present day, there has been more liberty in
Great Britain than would appear from a literal reading of political
and legal institutions. However, liberal constitutionalism does not
mean that liberalism prevails in the state or in the nation. It means
that the power to legislate and to conduct public affairs is in the
hands of freely elected representatives. Therefore, if liberals are a
minority of the voters, power will be in the hands of non-liberals
(for sophisticated people endowed with a monistic mentality, this is
a basic and harmful 'contradiction' in liberalism). In Great Britain,
where Tories often outnumbered Whigs in the small electorate of the
time (just as conservatives have usually outnumbered non-conserva-
tives during the twentieth-century liberal-democratic period), the
price to be paid for Whig liberal constitutionalism was Tory rule (as,
since 1922, the price to be paid for liberal democracy has been
government by non-liberals). Much of the time, the major function of
the Whigs was to make sure that Tories and Crown did not overstep
constitutional bounds — to fight the tendency (normal according to
historical evidence, and a major factor in the consolidation of
authoritarian institutions) to transform temporary tenure into
permanent tenure.

DYNAMISM AND ACHIEVEMENTS BELONGING TO CITIZENS,
NOT TO THE STATE

In conventional histories of Great Britain during the Whig era one
reads of mediocre kings and queens, of incompetent and corrupt
politicians, ministers, officials at all levels of the administration,
judges, generals and admirals; these were scarcely offset by a few
outstanding figures like Marlborough, Burke, both the Pitts and, at
the end of the era, Nelson, Canning and Wellington. From Harley to
Charles Fox (even discounting unedifying private lives) brilliance and
influence did not compensate for vices in public life. One reads of
venality and greed, of rebellions at home and overseas, of indifference
to poverty and suffering, of distant wars fought by paying someone
else to do the dying.

After the death of William III and during the reigns of a queen and
four Georges, the public side of British life was indeed seamy. Public
life mattered of course; nevertheless, it was secondary — deplorable
as it was, public life was only a fraction of national life. Whig
institutions and attitudes increased the autonomy and enlarged the
sphere of action of all Britons, not just of the Whigs. Swift made fun
of the Whig mentality, Wesley despised it and Cobbett hated it: but
these three, and countless Britons in their individual and collective
endeavours, would not have achieved what they did if Stuart or
Cromwellian absolutism had held sway over Great Britain.

What people did in their private capacity mattered more than what
went on at the public level. The appeal of deism mattered, as well as
the fact that for the first time since the fourth century one could be
a non-Christian in a European Christian nation, and lead a normal
life; the spreading of latitudinarianism mattered, the 'live and let live'
tolerance within the established churches; also the deep religiousness
of dissenters and of methodists, and the revival of sincere religious
fervour among large sections of the population and in all classes; the
intellectual curiosity and restlessness of a new breed, the scientists
(from Bradley to Hutton and Malthus), investigating nature and man
in physics, astronomy, geology, biology, new social disciplines, and
(like Cavendish, Jenner, Dalton and countless others) experimenting
in their laboratories; the astounding literary and artistic creativity;
the improvements in agricultural techniques introduced by a few
imaginative pioneers soon imitated by hundreds of thousands of
farmers which increased the output of food and capital formation;
the farm and trade surplus invested in industry (not frittered away
in conspicuous consumption, as continental aristrocrats were doing
and mediaeval merchants had done); the application of steam power
to vehicles carrying coal on rails — from which came locomotives and

railways, and to barges — from which came steamships; the macadamising of roads, the lighting of streets, the new uses of iron; the rise of a dynamic, imaginative, hard-working entrepreneurial class personified by Arkwright, Baring, Boulton, Braithwaite, Gurney, Maudslay, Rothschild, Watt, Wedgwood and Wilkinson; the growth, sustained effort and achievements, before the end of the eighteenth century, of organised humanitarian movements aimed at the abolition of slavery, at the elimination of cruelty in the penal system, at helping the poor and protecting the handicapped. The appearance of Radicalism (which in Great Britain meant the fulfilment of liberal aspirations — not their denial, as the term is now generally understood when spelled with a small 'r') mattered, and also the formulation of what will be the liberal-democratic position by Bentham and his disciples; so did the clarification by Burke and his followers of moderatism, originally the right wing of liberal constitutionalism, which in Great Britain merged with Toryism to become constitutional conservatism, and — later — progressive liberal conservatism, and which also set a guideline for moderates everywhere.

GROWING DIFFERENTIATION

Whiggism was more than the Bill of Rights, the Act of Tolerance and Parliament. It was a way of life which gradually spread until it became the way of life of most Britons, including the Tory majority of the British people, and the nonconformist, Jacobite and catholic minorities. It fostered a diversity which baffled foreigners (Americans provide the same puzzlement today), most of whom could not comprehend how such a differentiated population could have the cohesion of a nation, or what it was that held antagonistic groups together. It was a diversity which many British intellectuals found distasteful then, and ever since (fortunately for free institutions, they had little political influence).

Fundamentalists could not interfere with latitudinarians, deists and sceptics; they disliked Shaftesbury, Tindal, Hume, Gibbon and Bentham, but could not prevent the publication and sale of their works. The idle high-living hunting and fishing set looked down upon the hard-working sober-minded industrial entrepreneurs, but did not interfere with what they were doing. Slave-traders and gin-distillers would have liked to repress abolitionists and teetotallers, but could not. Owners of rotten boroughs could not stifle the agitation of those clamouring for electoral reform. Employers could not silence the voices of those who took up the cause of labour and social reform.

Liberal constitutionalism, the mark of Whiggism politically, meant that repressive interference was lessened. Consequently, as time went

on, latitudinarians, deists, sceptics, entrepreneurs, abolitionists, teetotallers, political reformers, advocates of labour legislation and
social reformers increased in numbers and influence, and in some
cases (the abolitionists by 1833, political and social reformers later)
took over entirely. The Whig state was a mansion under whose roof
lived Anglicans and their critics, the gentry and those who wanted to
abolish its privileges, selfish profit-seekers and altruistic humanitarians, exploiters and those who organised the exploited and led
them to victory, patriots who in time of war put the motherland
above all else, and their opponents who openly sided with the enemy
(with American rebels in 1776, with French revolutionaries fifteen
years later). To most foreigners, and to many Britons, it did not
make sense; there were differences, and there was no independent
superior power to hold them in line!

THE LIBERAL CENTURY IN GREAT BRITAIN

After the elections of 1830, the Whigs, composed of many factions
ranging from almost static moderatism to almost extremist radicalism,
held a majority of seats in the House of Commons. A majority of
votes did not of course by any means imply a majority of citizens, as
those who had the suffrage were then only a small percentage of the
adult male population. (It is doubtful that with universal suffrage the
Whigs would have achieved a majority in the House of Commons in
1830, or their Liberal successors at any other date.) Within a few
years, members and supporters of the parliamentary majority were
known as Liberals — the new term recently introduced into the
English language in a political connotation (see the Introduction) to
express a more dynamic progressivism than that of the Whigs.

The reforms introduced by Liberals (or by Conservatives, in the
nineteenth century forced by the electoral process to imitate their
opponents, to avoid being reduced to the status of permanent
parliamentary minority) covered most aspects of British life: central
and local administration, the armed forces and the police, the
judiciary, church—state relations, communications, health, education
at all levels, all aspects of the economy, with particular emphasis on
foreign trade, banking and labour; also social services, public utilities,
relations with overseas dependencies and with foreign powers. The
list of important decisions made by House of Commons majorities,
always after lengthy, exhaustive and none-too-friendly debates, from
the electoral reform of 1832 and the abolition of slavery in 1833, to
the social legislation of 1909—12, the beginning of self-government in
India in 1919, the granting of independence to catholic Ireland in
1921 and to Egypt in 1922, when for the last time a Liberal was

Prime Minister, is an impressive one. They amounted not to a single revolution but to several, which transformed the life of all Britons and radically modified relationships between classes and between all other sub-divisions of the peoples of Great Britain, and also between the imperial nation and peoples of overseas territories.

Liberals were spurred by their own left wing, the Radicals, a small dynamic group of enthusiasts deeply committed to a universal concept of legal, political and civil rights — to equality, and thus to militant advocacy of emancipation in all fields and for all sections of the population. Radicals were aware that emancipation is a never-ending process, that the requirements of the social order (whatever its form or structure) are inevitably a source of repression, that there can be no let-up in efforts directed at minimising repression. From that dynamic group came those who initiated the emancipation of wage-earners through the creation of trade unions and, twenty years later, of co-operatives, whose ultimate goal was the obliteration of the dichotomy between capital and labour — through agitation, strikes and parliamentary action. Mainly from the dominant Liberal wing strengthened by Radicals in the 1830s, strengthened further in the 1860s by the merging of tendencies whose spokesmen were Gladstone and Bright, came advocates of emancipation of consciences through the elimination of religious discrimination, of emancipation of minds through free universal education and free communications media, of women's emancipation through the elimination of legal discrimination and a change in mores; there came advocates of shifting the tax burden from producers to possessors of wealth, of minimum wages, workers' insurance and other social measures, of conciliation with Irish catholics and South African Boers through concessions, of self-government in overseas territories with the ultimate goal of independence, of peace through economic inter-dependence and integration. As already noted, genuine liberal democracy through universal suffrage in a major nation was first achieved in Great Britain in 1918, when Liberals were still the senior partners in a coalition government. No wonder that, as time went on, more and more moderates felt that the pace of change was too fast, and left the Liberal ranks to join the Tories.

THE LIBERAL STATE ADVANTAGES ALL, NOT LIBERALS ONLY

The Whig century had lasted 150 years, during which time spectacular changes took place in the British way of life. The Liberal century lasted a little less than a hundred years, and an even more spectacular transformation occurred.

One thinks first of the economy: of a Great Britain for several generations the workshop of the world, the major trading nation, the hub of international finance, the source of capital badly needed for development overseas, the leader in technology, the teacher of managerial efficiency, the originator of trade unionism and co-operativism, by 1914 the home of the largest and best-organised labour movement. One thinks of the passage from stage-coach to aeroplane during those years, from domestic piecework to factory mass production, from one- or two-room rural cottages to urban tenements. One thinks of factories in the industrial Midlands of England and Lowlands of Scotland, of the energy produced yearly by hundreds of millions of tons of coal mined in south Wales and around Newcastle, of iron steamships forming the largest merchant fleet, crossing all seas and all oceans. One thinks of fortunes made and lost; of millions of the poor (as badly off as the poor of other societies), of children, women and men overworked and underpaid as they had always been, and as they were everywhere else. One thinks, too, of the tensions developing in an expanding economy not because conditions were worse than before, or than elsewhere, but because freedom increased awareness and made it possible for individual aspirations to become collective action. One thinks first and foremost of the improvement that resulted from awareness and collective action.

Economic dynamism and rising standards of living were only one aspect of what the British achieved when, as the result of Liberal initiative, the institutional structure was loosened and energies were emancipated. Clearly seen in Great Britain was the essential differ-ence, at the level of practical activities, between liberalism (and in time liberal conservatism and liberal socialism as well) and all other ideological—political positions: what did not conform being protec-ted by law instead of being repressed and suppressed, the Liberal state benefited all, not just the Liberals. There had been manifesta-tions of creativity and growing differentiation within the population of the island during the Whig period; creativity and differentiation increased during the Liberal period.

To emancipate all minds from the shackles of ignorance and of dogmas there were freedom of expression and of research, of teaching and preaching, an inexpensive daily press, cheap mail services. Empiricism prevailed among the minority setting the tone for the British nations, but it did not hinder the manifestation of other conceptual frameworks, from various versions of traditional thought to idealism and dialectical materialism, to dogmatic and undogmatic positivism. State churches did not hinder the process of separation between church and state, the growth of irreligious agnosticism and atheism, the birth and diffusion of new religious beliefs. The open

society advocated by Liberals, and brought about by Liberal
political action, enabled the Irish O'Connell to formulate what two
generations later on the Continent, four generations later in Latin
America, became the Christian democratic position of anti-
authoritarian catholics. It enabled the grandson of Italian Jews to be
the first statesman of Jewish descent to lead the government of a
European great power, and allowed Jews to keep their culture while
being integrated in the British way of life. It enabled socialists to
explore social and economic alternatives through Owenism, the
Chartism of the 1830s, the Christian socialism of the 1850s, the
Fabianism of the 1880s, and finally the pre-1914 Labourism. It
enabled foreigners (some of them totally out of sympathy with
British ways and particularly with liberalism, as was the case of
Mazzini, Marx and Kropotkin) to write and publish, and from the
haven provided by British laws to lead agitation and conspiracies by
disciples and followers in their homelands. It enabled feminism to
become a powerful social and political force, pacifism and internationalism influential movements, and favoured the multiplication
of humanitarian initiatives. Scientific thought soared; in 1859 Darwin
caused a revolution no less radical than that which Newton had
caused nearly two centuries earlier. The excellence in scientific,
literary and artistic pursuits during the Liberal century was a source
of inspiration to people everywhere.

There were authoritarian residues during that century: continuing
distinction and discrimination between social classes; arrogance of
employers; educational elitism; and male superiority. Nevertheless,
the fact remains that the process of emancipation had touched more
people, that more Britons were more tolerant of each other and of
outsiders than was the case in any other nation, than is the case
today. If advancement is measured in terms of individual autonomy,
reasonableness and ability to cope with problems without losing
one's head, rather than merely in terms of consumption of calories,
metals and energy, Great Britain was for several generations the most
civilised major nation. This result came from the patient efforts of
more people than anywhere else to bring about changes while
retaining the institutions that make change possible. The 'permanent
revolution' has in recent decades been the slogan of a large group of
violent advocates of dictatorial repression; but there has been more
of a genuine permanent revolution, and for a longer time, in Great
Britain than in nations ruled by authoritarian radicals.

THE ETHICAL CORE OF THE LIBERAL CENTURY

A variety of life styles, in turn setting the tone for the nation, have
been a feature of the nearly 300-year-old permanent revolution in

Britain. The Whigs had been inclined towards hedonism. The ethics of many Liberals of the early and middle Victorian eras (particularly those coming from the nonconformist minority), keyed to duty and responsibility, were of the deontological kind. With the last pre-1914 generation mores became more relaxed; with the post-1945 generation has come mass hedonism.

It has been fashionable for some tim█ ⁄decry so-called Victorianism, to talk of hypocrisy, to call attention to unedifying exceptions — of which there were bound to be plenty in a nation of tens of millions in which conformity was not enforced. But without the neo-puritan Victorianism of those who formed the dynamic core of British Liberalism (and, at the end of the period, of Labourism, and also underlying the behaviour of many Conservatives), there would not have been, during the Liberal century and on until the Second World War, bureaucrats who were efficient and reliable because they possessed a sense of responsibility to a high degree, and were honest. There would not have been an economic expansion which at the time required reliability, honesty and hard work, as well as imagination, initiative and a thirst for profits. There would not have been the lowest level of crime ever experienced by a major nation, and the absence of vandalism — a scourge today in many democracies. There would not have been the effort which brought reforms while keeping violence at a minimum, the ability to run a vast empire with a handful of officials, the humanitarian movements (some of which, from the Salvation Army to the S.P.C.A., were the butt of jokes by Britons and, even more, by foreigners) which did more than any institutional change to lessen suffering and cruelty. Where there is character — self-discipline enabling people to cope with difficulties — there is less need to rely on outside help; where there is self-discipline there is less need for discipline enforced by external authority. Neo-puritan Victorianism, as priority of duty over self-gratification, was already weakening during the last phase of Victoria's long reign. But there remained enough of it to give the British strength to fight alone and of their own free will in 1940—1 — when the Axis of fascist powers was winning, the Soviet Union was helping Germany, and Americans were hiding their heads in the sand — so sparing mankind, at least for a while, the evil (for many the blessing) of efficient authoritarianism.

TOWARDS EQUALITY WITHIN LIBERTY

British Liberals were the first to face the difficult problem — implicit in liberalism (see pp. 33f.) — of the correct relationship between liberty and equality, and to try to cope with it reasonably. For the majority of mankind which approves of authoritarianism, liberty does not exist, or if it does, is either harmful or identified exclusively with one's own liberty. For constitutional conservatives alien to the liberal tradition, the good society is the elitist and therefore unequal one. Socialists of most persuasions fail to face the problem, and even many who are genuinely democratic act on the assumption that more equality is in itself sufficient to make for greater liberty.

Long debates among British Liberals concerning the franchise, social legislation, public education and public health showed their perception of the fact that increasing differentiation (whether of ideas, functions, skills — not just of incomes) increases pressure from those who want to reorganise society on a hierarchial basis. Those in Great Britain who kept the Liberal label were agreed that to maintain equality between different groups state action was necessary. The changing situation called for a rethinking of Liberal policies.

Whigs and early Liberals had concentrated on the elimination of restrictions and regulations. By the 1840s, as attested by Macaulay's Ten Hours Bill, it was clear that, with a different spirit and different goals, new restrictions and regulations must be introduced. John Stuart Mill as an old man during the mid-Victorian generation, H. G. Wells as a young man during the late-Victorian generation, went through the crisis of passing from a negative to a positive attitude towards action by the state: from advocacy of the abolition of old restrictions and regulations, to advocacy of new ones aimed at guaranteeing equal moral, legal and political liberty of all, and at limiting economic inequality.

In an essay written shortly before his death and left unpublished for a long time, Mill — for decades the mind and conscience of British liberalism — advocated the policies which during the Asquith premiership led to an impressive amount of social legislation. (It was tragic that a constitutional crisis distracted, and the First World War soon after diverted, Liberals' energies from the solution of British internal problems.) Based on the same policies, a third of a century later, were Liberal proposals which, implemented by a Labour administration, led to the passage from a market capitalistic economy to a mixed welfare economy, and for a while reduced the range of personal incomes considerably.

Mill's and Wells's position made common ground for many pro-gressive liberals and revisionist socialists by the turn of the century, for more after the Second World War. Dogmatic socialists inclined to authoritarianism called it the 'Lib–Lab' position — today the position of a majority of British, Australian, Caribbean, Dutch, Israeli and other Labourites, of Canadian New Democrats, of Scandinavian,

German, Japanese Social Democrats, of American progressive Democrats. In their parties, in several countries, is embodied the hope of the survival of liberalism as an idea and as a way of life.

FROM AN EMPIRE TO A COMMONWEALTH

To many, Great Britain and imperialism are synonymous. They ignore the fact that British imperialism was conditioned and limited by anti-imperialist forces active in Great Britain, that as a result it has been radically different from all 'normal' imperialisms of ancient, mediaeval and modern times, down to the Soviet one. It is primarily owing to the Liberals' influence that Great Britain is the only example of a nation holding a vast empire — the biggest that ever was — and at the same time deliberately creating conditions in dependent territories which made for the empire's disintegration and ultimate collapse: a good deal of autonomy, freedom of the press, possibility for patriots or nationalists in the dependencies to co-operate with militant, often influential, anti-imperialists in the mother country.

In power or out, British Liberals consistently championed autonomy, first as responsible self-government and then as independence for trans-oceanic territories, first home rule and then independence for catholic Ireland. Imperialism was repulsive to most Liberals (not of course to factions that ultimately merged with Conservatives), and they also made it clear that national liberty (independence) and citizens' liberty (liberal-constitutional or liberal-democratic self-government) should go together. In the 1830s the Liberal Macaulay advocated the educational and legal reforms that would prepare Indians of the subcontinent for responsible self-government; the Liberal Lord Durham prepared the report on which the policy leading to the independence of Canada in 1867 was based — the first step towards the transformation of an empire into a commonwealth of self-governing independent nations. India's Congress party (among whose founders in 1885 was the British Liberal A. Hume, and whose president in 1917 was the British liberal socialist Annie Besant) and British anti-imperialists worked together, obtaining the reforms of 1919 and 1935, and the independence of the subcontinent in 1947. N'krumah and Banda were only two of the many Africans who found among the British the help which gave success to their nationalist movements, and made them heads of independent states.

The Commonwealth is only a shadow of what Liberals had hoped for. In most Commonwealth nations, and nations that had been part of the empire and either never joined the Commonwealth or seceded from it, dictatorial absolutism reigns. Here there has been a partial failure of Liberal goals — but partial failure means that there has also been partial success.

LIBERALISM WITH A SMALL 'l' SURVIVES LIBERALISM WITH A CAPITAL 'L'

In conventional histories, the Whig—Liberal era ends with the British Liberal party's crushing electoral defeat in 1922. A party was defeated, not an idea. One might add that the party was defeated, at least partly, because the idea had triumphed. Constitutional liberals, the moderates, had been seceding from the Whigs even before the Whig—Liberals were returned to power in 1830. There was a spate of secessions from the Liberal party after Unionists opted out in 1886. Today the British Conservative party is largely a right-of-centre liberal-democratic party, and except for its right wing has lost whatever connection remained with elitist and paternalistic Tories, obsequious upholders of monarchical and ecclesiastical privilege.

The Labour party, launched in 1901, attracted an increasing number of left-of-centre liberals favouring social and labour reforms aimed at diminishing inequality, and at state participation in the economic process, but not favouring communalism and collectivism — inclined to Radicalism and not to socialism. British trade unionists, who provide most of the Labour vote, use pre-1914 socialist rhetoric, though for generations most of them have acted as Radicals; and in the late 1970s their position does not differ, where action and goals are concerned, from that of ancestors — from John Bright's era to the Lloyd George era — who provided much of the Liberal vote.

Liberalism with a capital 'L' survives in Great Britain in a party which elects few deputies but which under proportional representation would multiply them several times: Liberal candidates received from five to six million votes in the two 1974 elections, and an unknown but large number of Liberals, convinced that their candidate would not be elected, voted for candidates of other parties. Whatever the number of Liberals with a capital 'L', a majority of Britons are liberals with a small 'l', down to the generation that in its youth fought in the Second World War and in maturity governed Great Britain, completing the peaceful transition initiated during the previous generation from capitalism to a welfare economy and the peaceful transformation of an empire into a commonwealth.

When it comes to the simple and widely diffused ideas, values and attitudes on which, under conditions of freedom, social changes rest, figures can be misleading. However, one can assume in the late 1970s that — tragically, in view of the contribution of the British people to modern civilisation during its liberal phase — the illiberal minority is gaining ground. Illiberal are the more and more numerous members of the intelligentsia fascinated by what they consider successful national-communist experiments, by Third World national-socialism, and by anarcho-communism, guided in their thoughts and their actions by the commonplaces of basically repressive monistic and dogmatic socialism (see Chapter 7); illiberal too are English racists who resent the arrival of brown and black immigrants fleeing countries where independence has meant greater poverty, fewer opportunities, declining government efficiency and greater repression; also Nationalists contemptuous of self-government within a decentralised liberal state, dreaming of the wealth and power independence should bring — and which it will not.

WEST AND EAST: BEYOND WHIGGISM

Initially, both the American revolutionaries of the 1770s and 1780s, and French revolutionaries of the late 1780s and early 1790s, wanted not a departure from the English revolution of 1688 but an improvement on what the Whigs had achieved. The foundation was made of the same material: anti-authoritarian ideas, values and institutions. The aim of most Patriots (as revolutionaries were called on both sides of the Atlantic) in the two nations was, simply, in the first place to travel further than the British along that road, and in the second place to widen the road through greater awareness of equality.

Keyed to the liberty of the citizens, recognising more clearly than the Whigs had ever done the all-important role of equality (even if still limited to the field of legal and political institutions), both the American constitutional republic of 1788 and the French constitutional monarchy of 1791 (and the French republic proclaimed in September 1792, during its first six months) were liberal. The majority of Americans kept to the road first traced by progressive Englishmen of the seventeenth century, sometimes advancing along it rapidly, at other times reluctantly. Many Frenchmen — a minority which at times was a plurality — soon took another road, leading to a more efficient despotism than that of the *ancien régime* (see Chapter 5). Forerunners of today's three dozen or so liberal democracies are the victors in the events of 1776 as much as the victors in those of 1688. Many times that number of radical dictatorships (see the Introduction) have as forerunner the revolt against the liberal experiment that took place in France at the end of the summer of 1792, which quickly acquired impetus and led to the establishment of radical authoritarian regimes — civilian with the Jacobins, military with Napoleon Bonaparte.

TOWARDS 1776: MEETING HOUSES AND STOCKADES INSTEAD OF PALACES, CATHEDRALS AND FORTRESSES

Louis Hartz is one American scholar who has lucidly and exhaustively explained basic aspects of the American experience which contributed to the survival — by now for over 200 years — of free institutions in the United States, and which also contributed to the presence in the American nation of a liberal movement, seldom supported by a majority of voters, but usually strong enough to influence and contain conservative majorities and anti-constitutional minorities.

In contrast to the Spaniards, Portuguese and French in territories they occupied in the Americas, English colonists did not bring the whole fabric of the home establishment with them. The absence of palaces, cathedrals, fortresses (replaced by modest meeting houses doubling as chapels and town halls, and by wooden stockades) is the outward sign that the colonists had left aristocratic and ecclesiastical components of the establishment behind; that subjection to the Crown and all it implied was less in Philadelphia, New York and Boston than in Lima, Rio and Quebec.

Colonists in Massachussetts, Pennsylvania and other territories mainly held to the values of what were then anti-establishment fringe minorities in Great Britain. White Latin Americans were Spaniards, Portuguese or French who patterned their lives and institutions on those of the Old Country. Once settled, most Britons in America did what they could only with much difficulty have done in the Old Country; they developed a distinctive life style of their own. This made them Americans. The life style appealed to other immigrants who had come before 1776 from the continent, and facilitated their Americanisation; it appealed to most of the tens of millions of later immigrants.

1776 AND 1787: LIBERAL CONSTITUTIONALISM

Some Americans dislike the closeness of their liberals and conservatives, and their proclivity for meeting on the common ground on which majority consent is created (which, more than patriotism or any economic interest, today makes for national cohesion in the United States). There is a reason for this closeness: today's American liberalism and much of the conservatism come from the same source, the liberal constitutionalism of the Patriots of 1776 and 1787. There was no ideological difference between Americans committed to the values, principles and institutions of liberal constitutionalism 200 years ago and those elsewhere who struggled at the time to establish liberal constitutions. However, Americans were the first to undergo the process of differentiation between moderates and progressives.

In Great Britain, the Whigs, although not a party but a shifting coalition of separate groups, were held together for 150 years not only by common attitudes, commitment to a few basic institutions and their sense of identity, but also by the pressure of Toryism (pandering to monarchical and ecclesiastical privilege, and paternalistic towards subjects) and the threat of external aggression and of a Jacobite *coup*. Not even Radicals of the 1760s and 1790s seceded from the Whigs. In the United States there was a different situation. Once the war had been won and a peace treaty signed, hard-core Loyalists departed, and after years of vacillation the federal constitution was drafted and ratified. There was no strong immediate threat compelling Patriots to maintain unity.

Impressed by what happens nowadays, when independence is an obsession and little or no thought is given by its advocates to what the structure of newly independent states will be (thus facilitating takeover by militant authoritarian minorities), many see eighteenth-century American Patriots simply as nationalists. This is a misreading of the climate of the time. For many — and certainly for most of those who held positions of responsibility in the events of the time — independence was a means to the institutional structure they wanted to establish. For the future of the American nation, the structure mattered more than independence itself.

In relation to the structure, and in terms of the definition of liberalism (see Chapter 1), most Patriots were liberals. (They can be called democrats only by defining 'democracy' as the organisation of individual liberty — a definition rejected world-wide by most of those who today call themselves 'democrats'.) Had they not been liberals, they would not have approved of the principles and values implicit in the three words 'free and equal'; they would not have voted for the liberal federal constitution (which combined democratic citizens' self-government with undemocratic checks on the citizens' will), for the Ten Amendments, for liberal states' constitutions and Bills of Rights; they would not have shared approval of the writings of Locke, and admiration for Ancients who championed republicanism. The majority of Patriots believed that liberty comes first, that equality cannot be dissociated from it, and that constitutional republicanism is the organisation of the citizens' liberty. Suffrage was limited, slavery had been outlawed or was soon to be outlawed in fewer than two-thirds of the original thirteen States, discrimination negated equal opportunities, the range of economic differentiation was excessive. However, it was implicit in the constitution that suffrage could be made universal, that slavery would one day be outlawed everywhere, that citizens could use the power of the state to eliminate discrimination and to narrow the range of economic differentiation.

THE PARTING OF THE WAYS: MODERATISM AND PROGRESSIVISM

Free discussion while searching for solutions to problems facing the United States, and the need to formulate ideas and programmes in view of electoral contests, soon made for clarification of ideological—political positions and for an all-important division. On one side was the moderate right wing, to which Washington belonged (and which has been symbolised ever since, not quite accurately, by John Adams, Alexander Hamilton and John Marshall), and on the other the progressive left wing (symbolised, again somewhat inaccurately, by George Mason, Patrick Henry and, foremost, Thomas Jefferson with his collaborators and supporters, and the many Jeffersonian followers ever since). Misleadingly from the standpoint of liberalism's central concept — equal liberty — American moderates often talked of liberty, and talk of it today, without enough concern for equality (an insufficient concern puts moderates in a different category from that of rightists who have no concern, though both are usually labelled 'conservatives'). Instead, Jefferson and Jeffersonian progressives never talked of equality without due regard for liberty.

At the practical level, moderates and progressives came to be divided on the basis of demands made by groups emancipated by liberal constitutionalism, centered on ending discrimination and on improving their way of life. Excluding pro-slavery racists, dogmatically blind and impervious to argument, most Americans were soon compelled to realise that with liberty to express oneself, to organise and to agitate, the problem of equality comes to the fore and occupies the centre of the stage. American moderates were convinced that legal and moral equality was sufficient for a society of free and equal citizens. Not so the progressives.

Where to set the limits between central power and local power — between the Union and the States — was the problem that divided right-of-centre Federalists and left-of-centre Republicans in the 1780s. In terms of the time, the problem involved a good deal more than different views on Union—States relationships. Once the federal constitution had been approved, the extent of the franchise was the first major political problem pitting progressives against moderates, and family farms versus planters' estates the first major socio-economic problem. Even before male suffrage had been achieved (though only partially, on account of the persistence of the cruellest authoritarian institution, slavery) at the end of the first half-century of the republic's existence, and while a compromise between advocates of family farms and advocates of plantations had been reached, the progressives maintained that a society of free and equal citizens should have not only legal, moral and political equality, but also as much equality of economic conditions, social status and educational opportunity as may be needed to keep differences on the same level and to prevent the consolidation of a rigid hierarchical distinction between superiors and inferiors. American progressives rejected uniformity, and approved of diversity as much as moderates, perhaps more; at the same time, being opposed to hierarchy, since the earliest phase of the republic they looked to state action for eliminating the distinction between superiors and inferiors among the highly differentiated groups into which the population was divided.

The division between moderatism and progressivism is more meaningful in the United States than that between the Republican party, a coalition of moderates and rightists with a progressive wing at times large but usually small, and the Democratic party, an even more heterogeneous coalition of minorities among which the progressive wing at times occupies a pre-eminent position. The common origin of moderates and progressives is a major factor in the cohesion of the American nation.

AMERICAN LIBERALISM

The constitutional liberals of the revolutionary period had divided. Who then was the liberal? To Americans, the question seems superfluous. It is not superfluous in terms of the total development of liberalism in the world, of co-operation between kindred forces to halt authoritarian tides, of the future of free institutions. In view of the common ideological origin, an American writer of the 1950s was not incorrect in putting together, as liberals, Adlai Stevenson and Robert Taft, Arthur Schlesinger Jr and Walter Lippmann; and it was not entirely wrong to put Senators McGovern and Percy together twenty years later, and the economists Samuelson and Burns. However, on the basis not only of the common usage of the term in the United States but, more importantly, of the definition of liberalism, it is clear that Stevenson, Schlesinger, McGovern and Samuelson are liberals because the greater equality of all within the frame of free institutions is central to their ideological—political position, while Taft, Lippmann, Percy and Burns, being less concerned with equality, are conservatives — even if what they want to conserve is American liberal constitutionalism.

For 200 years, American liberalism has had a wide range of ups and downs. In the late 1970s it may be described as fairly strong in numbers and weak in commitment. Looking at their past, a rather recent one, and at their present from the vantage point of immediate concerns, aware of a myriad details, most Americans endowed with political awareness (a larger proportion of the population than in most nations, but smaller than in Commonwealth democracies and a dozen others) are struck by the antagonisms pitting one group against another on the national scene. Many, sophisticated thinkers included, are so perturbed by this that they feel at sea, are unable to envisage past and present clearly, lose the thread of continuity. In consequence they adopt a negative attitude towards the American experiment in liberal constitutionalism, which only now, and to the extent to which political discrimination on racial and sexual grounds is being eliminated, is becoming an experiment in liberal democracy. This negative attitude, a characteristic specifically of the articulate minority — the intelligentsia — feeling at sea, confused, not following the thread, contributes to the Americans' inability to communicate to new generations at home, and to foreigners everywhere, what American democracy means and what the American way of life is all about, to make and present an objective balance-sheet of their advantages and disadvantages.

For liberals all over the world this inability is regrettable. First, because, whatever the doubts and the soul-searching, there are (if not relatively to the population, in absolute numbers) more liberals in the United States than in any other nation (at a venture, one may estimate that liberals constitute one-quarter to one-third of the voting population). It is regrettable because the influence of liberals — who at times, in electorates which never included all adults, had the support of a majority (in 1830, in 1936) and at other times, helped by the electoral process, were able to govern the republic although they had received a minority of the votes cast (in 1860, in 1912) — has been felt consistently in the United States, whether they were in power or not. It is regrettable also because this is a time when human problems facing the American nation need liberal solutions through equality within a framework of free institutions. It is regrettable because the future of liberal democracy and of liberalism in the world is closely linked to what happens in the United States.

LIBERAL DEMOCRACY STRONGLY ENTRENCHED

It should be added that whatever the confusion and the decline in commitment of articulate sectors of the population, the liberal-democratic institutional framework of the United States continues to give an impression of solidity. A major factor in the solidity is of course, as stated above, the common origin of both liberals and moderates among the conservatives. Instead of a difference in kind between the two major political forces in the nation (as there is, for instance, in Japan and in Italy, where the largest plurality supports liberal democracy while the second largest opposes it), there is in the United States — as in the other larger English-speaking nations, and a dozen other democracies — mainly a difference in degree. American liberals and the conservatives of moderate persuasion differ in the economic and non-economic interests for which they are spokesmen and in policies they want to implement; at times they pull in diametrically opposed directions. In spite of this, they are closer to each other ideologically than liberals are to authoritarian and anarchic leftists often described as 'radicals', or than moderate conservatives are to racists and rightist radicals often also referred to as 'conservatives'.

Another major factor contributing to the solidity of the institutional system is the absence, so far, of an alternative. There has been no lack of suggestions, ideas and initiatives, from those put forth by monarchists in the early days of the union, to recent ones of hundreds of thousands fascinated by communalism and experimenting with collectivism, and of admirers of Castro-type dictatorial rule legitimised by mob approval. No alternative has ever appealed so far to more than a minute minority of Americans.

Even now (in spite of the decline of commitment to free institutions among the intelligentsia and the post-war generation), adding the highly fragmented Radical Right, white racists and their authoritarian separatist counterpart among coloured minorities, conservatives alienated from liberal constitutionalism, the Old and New Left and kindred groups, the sum of opponents to the American version of liberal democracy — democratic republicanism — is no more than a modest minority of the adult population. However strong at times their anti-establishment fervour, most American dissenters aim at improving the country's liberal-democratic structure and not at destroying it. This is true of most organisations concerned with improving the economic conditions and social status of wage-earners: the unions of course in the first place, and also, among others, the Social Democrats (successors of the Socialist party) and the League for Industrial Democracy. It is true of organisations committed to the elimination of racial discrimination, from the National Association for the Advancement of Colored People and the Southern Christian Leadership Conference to the Congress of Racial Equality and the Indian Rights Association. It is true of NOW (the Women's National Organisation), of Americans for Democratic Action, of the Civil Liberties Union, of many socialist intellectuals.

VARIETY MAKES FOR RICHNESS OF LIFE

At a distance enabling them to take in the American scene as a whole, outsiders (in this century Bryce, Brogan, Rappard and Revel) and Americans of recent foreign extraction (for instance, Ascoli, Brzezinski, Alistair Cooke and Eric Hoffer) see the antagonisms and also the values and institutions exercising a moderating influence. They see a system stimulating diversity which — while bringing tensions — allows a richer life to develop.

The American system embraces both egoism and altruism, exploitation and generosity, repression and permissiveness, violence and rejection of violence. The outsider can see continuity not just in internal and external policies, but in the development of the American nation and of American institutions — in the continuous process of differentiation within a unitary context. In contrast to what happened in most other nations, Americans were not hampered by forces advocating the return to an authoritarian past. But post-independence Americans owe it only to choices they themselves made if, except as an unimportant fringe phenomenon, patriotism was never superseded by frenzied authoritarian nationalism; if religious divisions, however important even today for millions of Americans, did not cause the widespread antagonism experienced where a bigoted clergy influenced fanatical masses; if violent anarcho-communists of the New Left are few, as were the violent pre-1914 anarchists and anarcho-syndicalists, and post-1919 Leninists of the Old Left.

For most people cultural uniformity has always been a desirable goal (see Chapter 1). Diversity in basic principles and values was obnoxious in the past and is so today to all who in the name of unity want to eliminate 'contradictions' (i.e. differences) and approve of the standardisation of national characteristics enforced in one-party dictatorships. Americans have shown that diversity within unity is possible. The price in tensions is of course high, but liberals agree that it is worth paying. In the eighteenth century, when church membership transcended religious belief and made for a way of life, it would not have occurred to American Patriots to advocate religious conformity; separation between church and state meant, among other things, legitimacy of different life styles within an institutional framework which respected the autonomy of all. Coexistence was sometimes difficult (as Mormons knew at the middle of the last century) but in time difficulties were overcome.

Today ethnic identity, whether or not based on race, occupies the centre of the American cultural scene. Blacks have their own culture; they treasure it, and it is gaining in distinctiveness and excellence (this does not prevent many blacks from preferring a non-black life style: it is their own choice). Most Spanish-speaking Americans are recent immigrants; stimulated by the example of the blacks, many have opted for retaining their own culture: there is no government pressure compelling them to act otherwise. The same applies to French-speaking Canadian immigrants. Except tragically for most of the eastern seaboard, there was not the total obliteration of indigenous cultures which (to mention only existing civilisations) occurred when the Chinese expanded in the Closed Continent, Arabs conquered Christian North Africa, Spaniards occupied Central and South America, Russians dispossessed Tatars and kindred peoples of their lands; there are now about three-quarters as many Indians in the United States as there were in 1620, numerous enough and suffi- ciently autonomous to revive their own cultures or to create a new one. Most catholic Irish kept their Irishness (and were a major factor in successful insurgencies of catholic Irish against the British); Jews found in the United States conditions more favourable to the survival of their culture than they had elsewhere (even than they have today in Israel); Armenians and Lithuanians are two of the many peoples preserving in the United States the national cultures now being obliterated in the Old Countries. Oblivious to the fact that a good mosaic can last for a very long time, foreigners often refer contemp- tuously to the American nation as a mosaic. Culturally it is one, held together by institutions which do not enforce conformity; its variety is also its richness.

CONCRETE PROBLEMS

Although agreeing on the liberal constitutionalism which was their common source, American liberals and conservatives could have increased the bitterness dividing them by transferring (as was done in other nations) the discussion of problems to the ideological level of the correct relationship between the liberty stressed by moderates and other conservatives, and the equality demanded by liberals. The ideological debate was omitted. Disputes concerned specific problems, some already existing during the formative period of the republic, others arising later.

A few of the important problems in the division between liberals and conservatives, in the order in which they aroused enough people to become a political issue, have been: economic development; slavery and its aftermath; status of immigrants; territorial expansion and (later) the three-cornered dissension between isolationists, imperialists and internationalists; rights of labour; regulation of the market and business; women's rights; economic insecurity, poverty, welfare, housing and medical care; relations between the white majority and coloured minorities. To these problems are now added: the status of ethnic groups other than racial; urban deterioration; crime; reform of the educational system; protection of the environment. In the fast-growing and fast-changing American system there has been no lack of problems, and thus no lack of motives for bitter antagonism between conservatives and liberals.

REGULATION OF FREE ENTERPRISE

In relation to economic development, regulation of the market and economic security, the position of American liberals has been consistent. The conservatives' economic liberty — summed up in the slogan *laissez-faire* and implying state support for business — was close to the anarchists' 'free for all' which engenders the triumph of the strong and the subjection of the weak (see Chapter 1). Liberals instead advocated legislation limiting the anarchic 'free for all' in the economy, regulating the market, restraining the owners of capital and their agents, promoting the interests of employees, more and more numerous as industry expanded. They introduced measures aimed at stimulating economic development, at checking monopolistic forces, at reducing the instability of the economy, at eliminating the insecurity weighing heavily on individuals. For liberals, the priority of human rights over property rights was a guideline for economic policies, not just a slogan.

Jefferson was a *physiocrate*, but during his eight-year Presidency public funds were used to develop transportation (then more crucial to economic expansion than anything else), and settlement of unoccupied lands was encouraged by the government. The aid given later to the building of canals and railways was a liberal measure: so were the Homestead Act, and the numerous plans that helped farmers; the Anti-Trust Act; the creation of the Federal Board; the policies of the Square, New and Fair Deals, of the New Frontier and the Great Society. Collective bargaining, unemployment compensation, old-age pensions and other social-security measures were the liberals' concerns and achievements.

As also in Canada, the liberals' awareness of economic and social problems, and their initiative in solving them, reduced the appeal of collectivism to a minimum in the United States. Awareness and initiative were major elements in obtaining the support of organised labour for the free-enterprise market economy. Already in 1902 the American Federation of Labor rejected the programme and policies of the Socialist International; seventy years later, recently reorganised American socialists rejected nationalisation of the means of produc-

tion; the Liberal party of the State of New York (genuinely liberal
in terms of the definition of liberalism) was originally established by
labour organisers and their working-class and middle-class supporters.
Thanks to the economic policies sponsored by liberals, free enterprise
has prospered in the United States within a growing web of guidelines,
regulations and controls. Paradoxically, private enterprise and the
market have remained freer than would have been the case with the
conservatives' neo-mercantilism of Hamilton's time, the guided free
enterprise of Clay's time and the post-civil war dogmatic *laissez-
faire* — the battle-cry of right-wing Americans who have severed links
with the liberal constitutionalism of the republic's Founding Fathers.

IN THE BLACK

Capitalism, profits and competition are emotion-laden words, today
particularly when applied to the American economic system, on
which some heap praise but most heap abuse. Because of the emotions
aroused, a critical approach as balanced evaluation of positive and
negative aspects is, throughout the world, out of the question for the
overwhelming majority of the intelligentsia. Scholarly analysis piles
up mountains of damaging data, most of them correct: as under a
magnifying glass each feature of Helen of Troy's face would have
looked repulsively coarse, so analysis, unless accompanied by an over-
all view of the phenomena, cannot give a correct view of an economic
or other phenomenon. In current economic literature usually little
effort is made to consider both negative and positive data, and to
weigh them accurately. Moreover, because of the abundance of data
collected and processed by an efficient and honest statistical service
and made available to all, anyone can select what fits interests and
ideologies. In view of the importance of an economy which in 1975
produced over 27 per cent of the world output of goods and services,
and which is a major element in what strength liberal democracy has
in the world today, one should be aware of the ease with which
figures can be used to damn or praise.

Corporate gross profits of 112 billion dollars in 1975 would justify
the characterisation of American free enterprise as capitalistic greed
and exploitation of workers and consumers at home, of under-
developed peoples abroad; 32 billion dollars (just over 2 per cent of
the 1975 G.N.P.) paid in dividends on shares, of which a third is
owned by labour and other pension funds, schools, hospitals and other
service institutions, would justify its characterisation as a system in
which a modest incentive makes for an extra output worth several
times the remuneration of capital, provides employees with high
wages, industry with investments (33 of the 112 billion dollars) and

the state with taxes (47 billion dollars). Gross profits of one billion dollars by one large corporation, and billions of dollars as profits on investments abroad, tell stories different from those told by the average three cents made by manufacturers out of every dollar sale after taxes, and by several times the billions invested, represented by output abroad, and by wages and taxes paid in the host country. It is depressing to know that in 1974 the median income for non-white families was 62 per cent of that for white families, that in 1976 about 30 million people lived below the poverty line and unemployment was nearly 8 per cent of the labour force; it is encouraging to know that 62 per cent is one-sixth more than the 53 per cent of 1963, and that incomes of non-white families increase faster than those of white families; that Roosevelt's one-third of a nation living in conditions of poverty is down to one-seventh, and millions of the poor are recent immigrants for whom poverty in the United States is prosperity compared with what they had been accustomed to in the Old Country; that many of the nearly 8 per cent unemployed are in no hurry to find jobs, their unemployment compensation being an addition to the salary or wage of the head of the family.

Without regard to this writer's preference for a zero-growth mixed welfare economy and for policies aimed at equalising incomes (and thus at slowing down productivity), an over-all view of the American economy brings out positive facts usually ignored by analytical observers. In inverse order of their importance, a few deserve mention:

(i) Per unit of population the American economy produces more goods and services than the economy of any other major nation; many goods and services are of higher quality and most are produced at lower cost.

(ii) The outcry against exploitation, profits, imperialism as the last phase of dying capitalism, is contradicted by the requests from those who control command economies (starting two generations ago with Soviet leaders) for American capital, technology and managerial expertise.

(iii) Large-scale famines forecast by F.A.O. experts are postponed by the productivity of American farmers and the 'green revolution' which originated in American experimental stations.

(iv) American wage-earners receive a larger share of the value produced than do wage-earners in any command economy, and their share is increasing (for instance, 76 per cent of corporate income was paid in wages, salaries and fringe benefits in 1975, instead of the 64.1 per cent in 1950); the range of median incomes for five major socio-economic groups (business proprietors and managers, professional people, white-collar workers, blue-collar workers, labourers) is smaller.

(v) The American economy played an essential role in defeating authoritarian militarism in 1918 and fascism in 1945, and in halting the onward march of national-communism until the early 1970s (enabling socialist revisionism to make headway at the same time).

(vi) Whatever the term of reference (area, availability of capital, natural resources, density of population) more people have come of their own free will to the United States than have emigrated to other countries, and the improvement in their economic conditions has been greater. Not all stayed, or liked it, but most did. Emigration to New England was emancipation for a handful of pilgrims and several thousand puritans: emigration to the United States was emancipation for millions of British, Irish and Germans at the middle of the last century, for millions of Jews, Sicilians, Scandinavians and others half a century later, for millions of West Indians and Central Americans in recent decades.

The American economic system has undergone several radical transformations, so it is misleading to apply the same term to what it was 200 years ago and 100 years ago, and what it is today. Changes have been the result of spontaneous forces but also of awareness of shortcomings, defects, errors and horrors, and of policies aimed at correcting the shortcomings, defects and errors, and at eliminating the horrors; freedom of expression stimulated awareness, and political liberty made action possible.

THE MAIN FAILURE

Slavery — the cruellest institution on American soil — and the flood of tens of millions of heterogeneous immigrants (mostly illiterate and penniless) created difficulties in the United States that were non-existent in other progressive nations such as the liberal democracies of Europe and the far-flung larger English-speaking communities of the Commonwealth.

Liberals spear-headed the agitation, which lasted well over forty years and reached its climax in a bitterly fought civil war that led to the end of slavery. The Emancipation Proclamation of 1863 was a crucial revolutionary step in the advancement of the American nation. It was nevertheless only a half-measure. Former slaves and, later, descendants of slaves, needed help in order to become responsible citizens standing on their own feet. The help they needed most was not paternalistic charity but brotherly co-operation between those who, being free, had gone ahead and those who, through cruel coercion, had been held back. The opposition of racists, supported by both rightists and moderates of the conservative majority among whites, to a generous, open-armed and warm-hearted attitude towards those who had suffered too much, was the nation's greatest error, and would become a major tragedy in the twentieth century when white hooligans (including elected officers), protected by illiberal institutions, terrorised blacks; when the inhabitants of Watts and other black ghettos revolted, sections of Detroit were looted, and sections of Washington burnt down. Racial discrimination and the subjection of blacks were worse than any depression or recession, worse than the civil war, worse than the American share in the holocausts of two world wars.

Liberals were consistently integrationists, wanting equality, as Americans, of whites, blacks and all shades of brown. However, for over two generations after emancipation they failed to do enough: they lacked the *fraternité* of the European counterpart to the American 'free and equal', or at least did not have enough of it. When, as a result of the climate created by the New and Fair Deals, the conservative opposition was overcome politically (but not yet in the minds and mores of most Americans), and the gap between the races began to shrink in the winning of public office, in education, employment, family income and property ownership, the resentment and hatred among blacks (soon imitated by other racial minorities) had justifiably reached such a pitch that many of them in turn rejected integration and advocated separatism. In the quieter mood following the emotional upheavals of the 1960s and early 1970s, there may still be a chance for integration. Failing this, only the application of the liberal principles of limited majority rule and respect for minorities can make possible the peaceful coexistence of more than one nation in the United States.

SOME SUCCESSES

American liberals have met partial failure in trying to solve the thorny problem of relationships between whites and non-whites. In other areas there have been achievements. Coming from Ireland, then from Italy, the Austrian and Russian empires, and more recently from Mexico, Quebec, the West Indies and Central America, immigrants whose cultures belonged to the stagnant branch of Western civilisation met with discrimination and arrogance. The discrimination and offensiveness, though not eliminated, have lessened enough to allow most immigrants from those areas and their descendants to feel at home in the United States and its constitutional (not yet genuinely democratic) republic. Although many are still 'hyphenated' Americans (from Irish-Americans to Cuban-Americans), most are now Americans pure and simple, and as Americans can treasure their own cultural heritage and maintain their cultural identity.

After decades of effort, most American wage-earners have gained the security and modest comfort that bourgeois living implies (the goal of pre-1914 European socialists to be reached via dictatorial collectivism). As a source of power and influence in public affairs, organised labour finds itself on a par with management.

'American women have come farther than women of any other major nation towards eliminating the double standard and male superiority. Much remains to be done to end discrimination between the sexes, but the gains already made show that the end of discrimination is in sight, that the American way of life lacks the rigidity that elsewhere hardens the 'cake of custom' and supports the arrogant superiority of one-half of the population over the other.

Just as liberals wanted, in their educational policies Americans have rejected the elitist concept with underlies all traditional educational systems and the current ones in radical dictatorships. The United States is the first nation to have achieved universality of education at the secondary level, where always in the past, and in all authoritarian societies today, the elite is separated from the masses, the ruling class from the subjects. Even on the higher level at which professional classes are formed, education has already become egalitarian to the extent that whoever has enough strength of character to overcome minor handicaps, and is qualified, can acquire a college or a university degree.

Recently, because the flow of information was free, and political liberty enabled the revulsion of many (among them a majority of American liberals) to become collective action, the American nation underwent the unique experience of losing a war through anti-war agitation at home. There was tragedy, and repercussions may be felt for a long time. However — whatever the rights and wrongs of the conflict in south-east Asia — the events of 1964—72 provide evidence of the close relationship between liberal democracy and peace. Citizens may decide that a war needs to be fought, but only where there is freedom can the decision be opposed and annulled. If liberal democracy were the norm in the world instead of the exception, the risk of armed conflicts would be nil, or nearly so. (That there has not been a single war between states with liberal-democratic regimes is meaningful.)

American liberals opposed the Mexican war and the spoliation of the Indians' lands. Liberals were instrumental in checking the expansionist drive in the Caribbean and Central America at the turn of the century, and in the withdrawal of the American military

presence from that area later. A few decades ago, they supported
self-determination for Filipinos who wanted independence; for
Puerto Ricans, most of whom chose association with the United
States; for Hawaiians, who decided to merge with the Union.

There were liberal Presidents when the decision to fight against
imperialistic states was made. The 'good neighbour policy' was
liberal, as was the help given by countless individuals and groups to
independence movements in American and non-American dependent
territories, the Marshall Plan, the Alliance for Progress, the containment
of Stalinism and then of Maoism. Wilson's Covenant of the League of
Nations in 1919 was liberal — the projection to relations between
sovereign states of the principles, values and institutions of liberal
democracy. Liberal, too, was the resurrection of the League as the
United Nations in 1945, desired by Roosevelt and effected by
Truman; and the upholding of human rights in 1977.

Thanks to freedom of communications media, Americans are
vividly aware of defects, errors and horrors in the United States.
Expatriates and would-be expatriates prefer the mean comforts of
under-developed societies (the servant, the *siesta*, the *café*) where
draft animals work the land and poorly paid artisan labour produces
hand-made objects. More numerous than those are the Americans
who (from a distance) long for the drab uniformity of Leninist and
kindred societies; who are impressed by discipline, conformity and
quiet in efficient dictatorial states. When all is said, looking at the
American scene one finds that the range of choice — whether of ideas
or religious beliefs, of goods of all kinds, and so on — is greater in the
United States than anywhere else; this means that there is greater
liberty. The fact that more and more people have the same opportunities to make choices means that inequality is becoming less.

LIBERALISM IN OTHER ENGLISH-SPEAKING NATIONS AND COMMUNITIES

Nearly fifty million people live in fourteen independent and near-
independent states and in a score or so of dependent territories (most
of them small, even minuscule) in which the population is entirely or
prevalently English-speaking; in two states of southern Africa,
English-speaking minorities form culturally cohesive and politically
influential communities. The independent and near-independent
states range in size and population from Canada — the largest and
most populous — to Grenada; the dependencies range from Belize to
Pitcairn in the Pacific Ocean. In some of these political units people
of British origin form almost the entire population. In others they are
a majority (Australia) or a large minority (Canada). In still others (for

instance Eire and Caribbean communities) there are no people of British origin, or a minuscule minority of them. In all, not more than a third of the fifty million are of English, Scots, Scots-Irish or Welsh descent. Besides the language, the common trait of all these states and dependencies is that at one time or another they had been linked to Great Britain. In the mid-1970s, except for four, the independent and near-independent English-speaking states and the English-speaking self-governing dependencies had liberal-democratic regimes. Largely because of world-wide recognition of their advanced social condition and high cultural level, Canada and Australia play a greater role in international affairs, political and non-political, and have considerably more influence than states more populous, more highly industrialised, more powerful militarily.

With the partial but all-important exception of Ireland, in the course of overseas occupation and settlement home authorities had taken it for granted that newly established settlers' communities, as soon as they became large enough to require organisation and had sufficient revenue to pay for it, should have assemblies of freely elected representatives, that in the assemblies should be represented new immigrants whatever their ethnic origin, also free men of equivalent cultural level living in the country prior to British occupation (the French-speaking communities of Quebec, Mauritius, some West Indies islands, Spanish-speaking Trinidadians, Cape Province Boers and New Zealand Maoris). Franchise, functions and powers varied (and often were unduly limited and discriminatory), but everywhere assemblies provided the ground for further develop-ment towards self-government. They were centres of agitation and channels through which inhabitants could demand and obtain an expansion of constitutional liberties, autonomy first and later (if a majority wanted it) independence. This was also the case in Ireland, in spite of the subordination of the Irish Parliament to the British for nearly half of the Whig era (1719–82). During the brief tenure of the 1782 Constitution, the Irish Parliament was instrumental in promoting Irish national identity. After the 1800 Union, the 100 or so Irish deputies elected to the House of Commons in London were a major factor in strengthening the cohesion and increasing the aware-ness of both catholic and protestant Irish communities, in achieving independence for one and autonomy for the other.

Assemblies functioned in Canadian provinces in 1791, in Cape Colony in 1833, in Australian settlements in 1842, in New Zealand in 1857. Assemblies were elected in Natal, Bermuda, Newfoundland and the West Indies. Committed to the improvement of liberal constitutionalism and not to its overthrow, most American Patriots had agreed that their constitutional republic was to be built on the foundation of the institutions developed before independence: the same happened in most other areas inhabited by English-speaking peoples. Whether there was (as in Canada) or was not (as in Jamaica) a Liberal party, whether there were many people of British descent (as in New Zealand) or practically none (as in Caribbean Nevis), continuity triumphed. It came naturally to reject authoritarianism, to build liberal-constitutional states, and in the twentieth century liberal-democratic ones, on the institutional foundation of the colonial period. Under this aspect British expansionism has been a phenomenon *sui generis*, totally different from Iberian expansionism in the Western hemisphere, Ottoman and Russian expansionism beyond Anatolia and Muscovy respectively, Chinese expansionism beyond the eighteen provinces of the 'closed' Continent.

It is possible that for many French Canadians liberalism meant nothing more than the protection given to minorities by the rule of law, limitations of power, constitutional guarantees and, most important, free elections and responsible government. Nevertheless, French-speaking Canadian leaders from separatist Papineau to Laurier and Trudeau, and most of their followers, were as committed to liberalism as English-speaking Mackenzie, Mackenzie King, Pearson and their followers. Commitment and clarity of ideas enabled the Canadian Liberal party to adopt and put into effect in the recent past an all-embracing social legislation, which greatly diminished economic insecurity despite the continuing high rate of immigration; and to adopt and put into effect in 1975 a bold plan of economic restructuring. As a result, most Canadians leaning towards social democracy, labourism, and other versions of revisionist socialism found their political home in the Liberal party. At the same time the appeal of authoritarian socialism was successfully checked. As shown by programmes, and by policies when in power, the Canadian Progressive Conservative party (the second largest in the country) functions within the tradition of liberal moderatism; this makes it less conservative than even its British counterpart, and much less conservative than the American Republican party (as already noted, a coalition including forces to the right of moderatism). The implementation of the principle of equality, particularly through federalism and educational policies, between the French-speaking minority — endowed with its distinctive cultural identity — and the English-speaking majority was the major obstacle encountered until 1976 by French-speaking separatists clamouring for independence.

In Australia, already during Deakin's premierships in the years immediately following independence, the Liberal party, committed to property rights and to state protection of private enterprise,

veered — particularly after joining hands with the Country party —
from moderatism to conservatism. It was Labourism which held the
progressive position vacated by Liberals, and pursued, often successfully, policies more liberal than those of its opponents. Whatever the
labels, liberal moderatism and liberal progressivism hold most of the
stage in Australian politics and way of life. East of the Tasmanian
Sea, the Liberal Seddon, during his long tenure as Prime Minister of
New Zealand, introduced social reforms which, in the decades
preceding the organisation of welfare economies in Scandinavian
nations, gave New Zealanders the reputation of being the most
advanced nation in social matters. Liberals also eliminated legal and
political discrimination detrimental to the minority of New
Zealanders of Polynesian descent, and proved that two communities
so different culturally that they can be considered distinct nations
can coexist peacefully in the same state on a footing of equality.

   The predominantly or largely black English-speaking communities
in and around the Caribbean probably have no more love for Great
Britain, the former colonial power, than American Patriots had in
1776. When partial or complete independence came, citizens
led by Manley Sr, Williams, Barrow, Pindling, Burnham, Price,
Compton — all of them heads of government and close to the liberal—
labour position of British Radicals — agreed that liberal democracy is
the proper structure for a progressive society. Authoritarian blandish-
ments, coming especially from admirers of Castroite national-
communism, went unheeded for several years, and attempts to set up
dictatorships in the early 1970s, made in one case by racially
motivated Leninists and in another by black racists, failed. However,
the situation was changing during the mid-1970s, when leaders like
Manley Jr and Gairy, unwilling to act democratically and to surrender
power to the opposition, convinced their followers that national
identity should be stressed through the imitation of what was being
done in much of the Third World, where absolutism was replacing
democracy.

ENGLISH-SPEAKING NATIONS AND COMMUNITIES IN WHICH
LIBERALISM HAS FAILED

In what is now Eire, where over three-quarter of the people use the
English vernacular, members of the Catholic Association during the
first half of the nineteenth century, and Home Rulers of later
generations, collaborated with Whigs and Liberals, not because of a
commitment to liberal principles, but because free institutions and
the policies of the British Liberal party provided Irish catholics with
freedom of expression and action and with greater influence in the

affairs of the United Kingdom than warranted by their numbers (soon reduced by famine and emigration to half of what they had been in the early 1840s). After independence was achieved for twenty-six counties in 1921, majority pressures in all fields of endeavour and at all levels (often stronger at the private than the public level) made life increasingly difficult for the protestant minority. Most of those belonging to that minority left the country; at the mid-1970s one-quarter of the original number remained there. For half a century, formally since the enactment of the 1937 constitution and the severance of links with the Crown, the goal of the majority was a closed, conformist, catholic society. Changes in the direction of some liberalisation began to occur in the 1970s. A liberal mentality and liberal attitudes were less weak in the small Labour party than in the two major ones.

In Ulster, for half a century (1922–72) a self-governing province of the United Kingdom, most members of the protestant majority agree that democratic liberties and opportunities should be restricted to the majority, and that discrimination against the catholic minority (as large today as it was before self-government was established) should be a permanent feature of Ulster life. Liberal voices, numerous particularly in the small Alliance party, asking for equal rights for all, have failed to convince fellow citizens moved — those in the minority no less than those in the majority — by blind sectarian passion.

In Rhodesia, liberals, who had the former Prime Minister Todd as one of their spokemen, lost out in 1965 to racists committed to the organisation of the English-speaking community as a democratically structured oligarchy arbitrarily ruling the vast Bantu majority. The oligarchy being structured democratically, there was sufficient freedom among the whites to maintain and deepen divisions which weakened the minority's hold over the state. Institutional coercion was strong enough to keep Bantus in a position of inferiority, but not to create a monolithic bloc among the whites. When, through the mediation in 1976 of the American and then of the British government, and under the prodding of rulers of neighbouring black countries, negotiations were initiated for a peaceful transfer of power from the hands of the white minority to representatives of black people, several liberal-minded whites joined clerics of various denominations, and others, in siding openly with the mediators and welcoming the transfer of power to be effected in 1978.

The republic of South Africa is the only country in which a sizeable English-speaking community (considerably larger than religious minorities discriminated against in Ulster and Eire) has in recent years lived in conditions of political inferiority. A little over one and a half million South Africans of British descent, or assimilated to the

British, (more numerous in the eastern than in the western half of the republic) were swamped in 1948 by nearly twice their number of Afrikaners, most of them obsessed nationalists and committed racists, whose main homeland since the 1830s had been areas north of the Orange river (see p. 181) and who are present also in other districts of the republic. The imprisonment, ostracism and exile of several English-speaking South Africans show that they are the voice and conscience of a persistent — even if small and for many years mostly ineffectual — liberal group opposed to *apartheid* and to the authoritarian hierarchical structure imposed by Afrikaner nationalists. The liberal group will play a role out of proportion to their number in the transformation that is likely to take place politically and socially in the republic. They may even provide for a while the central element in transitional governments to be formed when the situation is ripe for passing from a hierarchical multinational society to a less unequal one.

There are about ten million English-speaking inhabitants in Eire, Ulster, Rhodesia, the South African republic and the Caribbean communities in which liberalism is weak or even non-existent, in which free institutions either have been eliminated or are precariously shaky. More than three hundred million English-speaking people are citizens of nations in which liberalism still represents a not indifferent political force, in which, moreover, conservatism is largely liberal moderatism, and socialism is liberal progressivism.

5

THE LIBERAL ERA:
(ii) CONTINENTAL EUROPE

THE CONTINENT

As a cultural area distinct from the considerably larger geographical
one, the Continent (continental Europe) was, on the eve of the period
of liberal political ascendance and major influence in the way of life,
the territory inhabited by peoples whose civilisation was founded on
the concepts, methods of thinking, values and institutions of Western
Christianity (see Chapter 3). It included most of the large western-
most peninsula of the Eurasian land mass, extending from the Baltic
to the Black Sea, and the adjacent Scandinavian and Baltic countries.
It corresponded to what is now called West Europe (less Greece),
plus the territories of four states, and parts of the territories of two,
of what is now known as East Europe (the area detached politically
and culturally from the rest through the establishment of communist
dictatorships in 1944–8); it also included Soviet districts inhabited
until the end of the Second World War by Poles and Germans, or
once brought within the orbit of catholic Europe by mediaeval
crusading expansion.

Forests and lakes in the sparsely inhabited north, thickly wooded
swamps and Carpathian slopes in the middle, a clear-cut religious, and
thus cultural, border separating catholic from orthodox Christians in
the south (roughly following the fourth-century political border in
the Balkans between western and eastern sections of the Roman
Empire), all this early in the eighteenth century divided continental
peoples of Western civilisation from peoples whose way of life was
based on political autocracy and intellectual conformism.

Writing in 1844, the British traveller Kinglake was struck by the
radical difference in every aspect of life between those who lived on
either side of the Austrian–Ottoman border. Except for Greece, the
difference survived the disintegration of both empires. As Toynbee
explained in his *Study of History*, the autocracy and conformism
east and south of cultural Europe had been inherited from the
Byzantine civilisation, either directly or through its successors, the

Ottoman and Russian civilisations. From Greeks who later turned towards Western civilisation, to Muscovite Russians who did not, peoples east and south of the cultural border were subjects of states belonging to one or another eastern civilisation.

All through its many changes since the fifth century, and in spite of radical differentiation in the sixteenth and seventeenth (Reformed, Lutheran, Roman catholic, national catholic, as were French Gallicanism, and German Febronianism later), Western Christianity had been the major influence for the peoples of cultural continental Europe. Through the ways of thinking formulated by catholics and the system of values they created, through the use of Latin as *lingua franca*, the continuity of Roman law and the high esteem in which it was held, through humanism later, that culture included some of the important progressive features of the Greco-Roman civilisation. For over a thousand years the Roman church had enforced spiritual unity. The Holy Roman Empire, still existing in name, had been the symbol of political unity. Even after the break-up of the church, and long after the disintegration of the empire, the highly differentiated continental peoples were seen by their neighbours in the vast and (compared with Europe) thinly populated Ottoman and Russian states, and by more distant nations, as forming a unit with a distinctive way of life.

CONTINENTAL LIBERALISM

The continental version of liberalism is somewhat different from that of English-speaking nations. In this century, for example, Radicals (once, but no longer, progressive liberals) led by Chautemps in France and Lerroux in Spain, German Democrats following the liberal Naumann who was also a nationalist open to imperialistic aspirations, and Giolitti's successors in Italy who compromised with fascist totalitarianism, held the centre of the liberal stage in the four largest continental nations. The centre was not held by those deeply committed to free institutions: not by Herriot, distinguished French writer, three times Prime Minister, imprisoned by the nazis during the Second World War; not by Azaña, President of the Second Spanish republic while a civil war was being fought against a rightist authoritarian coalition; not by Heuss, whose books were burnt by nazi S.A.s in Germany in 1933, and who was later President of the German Federal Republic; not by Amendola and Gobetti, both of whom died in 1926 of wounds resulting from fascist aggression.

Liberalism's continental version, deeply divided between moderatism and progressivism, in the end almost completely taken over by moderates, has had the greater impact outside the English-speaking nations. 'Continental version' means primarily the French version, which in the 1790s inspired militant liberal revolutionaries in Poland and Italy, and Patriots in Switzerland and the Low Countries, and United Irishmen; which soon after inspired Balkan, Iberian and Latin American conspirators and insurgents, reforming ministers in Prussia and Russia, those who fought in the 1813—14 German War of Liberation, and Russian Decabrists in the early 1820s.

Things have changed, and people tend to forget that two centuries ago France, not Great Britain or the United States, was the dominant state in the cluster of Western peoples and nations. France was also the wealthiest power on earth and militarily the strongest (China, with many times more the population, came second in wealth, and in military strength all competitors were inferior on land, while on sea only the British held their own). For non-Westerners having some contact with the West (Ottoman Levantines, Russians, Persians), to visit the West meant going to France.

Even today, among the forerunners of liberalism Voltaire and Turgot are better known than the English Locke and Shrewsbury. The atheism and strong anti-clericalism prevalent among French and other continental liberals have been more influential than the tolerant Christianity and humanistic agnosticism of liberals in English-speaking nations. The dogmatic *laissez-faire* of French *physiocrates* in the eighteenth century (and of the Austrian school of economics in the twentieth) has had more disciples than Adam Smith's reasoned and reasonable *laissez-faire* and Keynesian economics. The failures of French liberals in 1793 and of French liberal-democratic republics in 1848, 1940 and 1958, of German liberals in 1849 and of the Weimar liberal republic in 1933, have made a deeper impression than the successes of American and Commonwealth constitutional and democratic liberals. Again, the Italian philosopher Croce, who knew a great deal about Germany, France and Spain but little about Great Britain and the United States, and the German statesman Stresemann, an intellectual and political descendant of William von Humboldt and vom Stein (whose minds had been fired by the French revolution), are two moderates better known throughout the world than their English-speaking progressive contemporaries Dewey and Mackenzie King.

On the Continent, in Latin America, Russia, the Middle East, the Indian subcontinent, the Far East, and now in most of Africa as well, among the four major groups into which the anti-traditionalist majority of the intelligentsia is divided (see the Introduction) resentment and hatred against liberalism are related to the image of the continental version of it. Because of that image, French progressive and moderate liberals (Left Radicals and Independent Republicans) do not use the term 'liberal'; the pre-1967 Greek Liberal party was reorganised under a different name after the collapse of the military dictatorship in 1974; Portuguese progressive liberals gave the name Popular Democratic to the party they organised in collaboration with liberal socialists after the 1974 revolution.

THE EIGHTEENTH CENTURY: PRELUDE TO THE LIBERAL ERA

On much of the continent, the eighteenth-century *ancien régime* was not as absolute as it sounded and as it is usually portrayed. There had been oases of some liberty: in cantons of the Swiss confederation like Zürich and Basle, in Norway (in spite of being a dependency of the backward Danish kingdom), in the United Provinces ruled by an open merchant oligarchy, in the aristocratic Polish and Swedish states. There had been benevolent and hence tolerant despots in German and Italian states: the Wettiner duke Charles August of Saxe-Weimar, a patron of the arts and a good administrator, the Habsburg-Lorraine grand-duke Leopold of Tuscany, concerned with economic advancement and opposed to ecclesiastical privilege.

Government inefficiency provided a certain amount of liberty, in France perhaps more than anywhere else. Inefficient censorship favoured the diffusion of new ideas, some of them progressive; starting with works of the young Voltaire in the 1720s, what in the eyes of the traditionalist majority was subversive literature could be circulated, even printed. Inefficient controls left greater freedom of action to entrepreneurs than was warranted by the authoritarian mercantilistic system. As well as inefficiency, in many states there was widespread corruption among public officials — which provided a good deal of liberty in all fields. What was once said of the Austrian regime applied to these states: absolutism tempered by corruption.

Aiming at strengthening the state and their power over it, princes and ministers described (then and ever since) as 'enlightened' introduced changes which weakened the hold of traditionalist forces, and thus unwittingly brought about a certain amount of emancipation. The ablest of all, Frederick II of Prussia, besides making intelligent use of privileged groups and subjecting them to monarchical authority, successfully strengthened the efficient authoritarian civilian and military bureaucracy organised by his father. Conversely, Joseph II in the heterogeneous Austrian state, Charles III in Spain, Gustav III in Sweden, Tanucci, Pombal and Bernstorff, reforming ministers in the Two Sicilies, Portugal and Denmark respectively, weakened traditional authoritarian forces without replacing them with new ones.

The liberty resulting from benevolence, inefficiency, corruption and reforms was of course limited. It was sufficient, however, to enable those who felt so inclined to formulate new ideas — some absurd, some reactionary, some sound and progressive — and to express them. Until the beginning of the last quarter of the eighteenth century, nowhere on the Continent was there a liberal movement, but among the numerous advocates of change there was a liberal minority.

THE AUTHORITARIAN ROAD TO PROGRESS

At the ideological–political level, members of the continental intelligentsia, fired by commitment to reason and progress, self-proclaimed citizens of the enlightened cosmopolitan republic of letters collectively described as *philosophes*, wanted reforms. They involved the obliteration of feudal residues, weighing particularly on the peasantry, which formed the mass of the population in all states, and also the elimination of clerical and aristocratic privileges. They involved freedom of conscience, diffusion of education, state responsibility for establishing secular schools, a freer press, uniform administration, a bureaucracy of civil servants responsible to the state and devoted to the common good, laws equal for all (and their codification), impartial judges, a free market, free labour, free entrepreneurial initiative, abolition of guilds, adoption of technological inventions, advancement of science and social mobility. The French 'career open to talent', a major revolutionary slogan, corresponded to the American 'equal opportunities'.

Reforms meant a wide range of emancipation. In relation to the human element expected to bring them about, among continental progressives there was a differentiation that would affect the later revolutionary movement, and make the French revolution (the most important, from an over-all perspective) a phenomenon dissimilar to the contemporary American revolution and the British reform movement. A majority of *philosophes*, and also of the not inconsiderable public reading their works, relied primarily on benevolent despots to achieve reforms. As is the case today the world over, the majority of continental progressives saw in state coercion the main channel for change leading to emancipation, lessening inequality and promoting justice. They mistrusted liberty, and in free-flowing spontaneity saw the ante-room to chaos and thus to cultural decline. Their liberty was of the kind Steffens and the Webbs admired in Stalinist Russia, and intellectuals everywhere admire today in Second and Third World dictatorships. Continental enlightened despotism, spanning the decades on either side of 1750 and reaching its peak first in one state and then in another, declining in the 1780s, was opposed to fanaticism and intolerance, and was genuinely committed to a number of civil rights; therefore it had nothing in common with today's dictatorial radicalism labelled 'democratic centralism', 'guided democracy', 'participatory democracy' or some such expression. However, enlightened despotism rejected the basic liberal institution: 'government of the people, by the people'. Progress was to be the outcome of imposition from above, not of spontaneity from below.

THE ANTI-AUTHORITARIAN ROAD

Among continental progressives there was a minority which, rejecting despotism, however benevolent and enlightened, was close to the position of British Whigs and Radicals and of American Patriots. It included *philosophes* whose goals went further than greater prosperity through the elimination of controls, greater happiness through the re-ordering of the institutional system held by a firm hand, less inequality through the abolition of privilege, and greater administrative efficiency. They wanted first of all to overturn completely the relationship between people and state, and make the citizens rulers of the state (as the word 'republicanism' meant when used then). They also wanted to enlarge the individual's range of autonomy by limiting the functions of the state.

When Paine wrote of representative government as the greatest innovation of his time, he stated in a few words how strange and heretical the idea of self-government then was. The voices of this minority within the ranks of continental progressives began to be heard in the 1730s, and became louder as time went by. They advocated constitutions enabling citizens to legislate through their representatives, guaranteeing the liberty and security of citizens through the abolition of arbitrariness, limitation of power and clear definition of the functions of public authorities. Members of the minority looked at Great Britain, about which a good deal was known, and, beginning in the 1770s, at the United States, about which little was known and much was speculated.

Among the advocates of reforms who did not rely primarily, or at all, on enlightened (not necessarily benevolent) princes and patricians' oligarchies were those who used the works of Aristotle, Cicero, Locke and Montesquieu to clarify their ideas, and sympathised with Rousseau' republicanism — though without being attracted by his mythical 'general will', and also rejecting restrictions on divisive political action as well as state monopoly of education and means of communication, implicit in the general will. Best known among them were, in France, Condorcet and the *côteries* of which Siéyès, Talleyrand and Grégoire were members; in Italy

Beccaria and his Milanese friends; in Prussia Kant in his old age and young William von Humboldt; Cornuaud and La Harpe in Switzerland. Relying on the citizens' initiative, and giving spontaneity free rein, they were liberals before the term was used.

As shown by formal and informal gatherings, by membership in masonic lodges, by associations created in the late 1780s, by agreement on contents of *cahiers*, by the number of those who joined the *Constituante* (organised in June 1789) and launched it on its revolutionary career, liberals had become sufficiently numerous in France in the 1780s and represented a sufficiently cohesive force to bring about radical changes. They were influential in most of continental Europe as well as in France. Also, however numerous and influential, in the four larger continental nations and in the minor ones to the south and east, they were a minority which never became a majority, not even (except for occasional brief periods) a plurality.

1789

There had not been an efficient head of state or chief minister in France for any length of time since the later years of Louis XIV, who died in 1715. To be kept in good running order, an authoritarian structure like the French one needed character, intelligence and firm will at the top. There had been no one of the stature of Frederick II of Prussia or of Kaunitz in Austria. At times there had been competent ministers (d'Argenson in the 1740s, Turgot in the 1770s and the Swiss Necker in the 1780s are the best known) but intrigues in the corrupt political machine centred in Versailles, and monopolising the conduct of political affairs, annulled their efforts. Inept despotism, while strong enough to hold on to power for over two generations after the death of the Sun King, had resulted in enough liberty for criticism to be expressed and for informal opposition to be organised.

The minority that prepared the ground for the 1789 revolution in France, and led it for several years, was composed of progressive sectors of the educated classes. Members of the professional classes were the most numerous, members of the upper classes the most influential (nobles, some prelates, a sprinkling of businessmen). Who they were is shown by lists of *philosophes*, subscribers to the *Encyclopédie*, *physiocrates*, members of cultural clubs, ministers and other officials futilely suggesting reforms, *habitués* of *salons*. Lacking someone who would act the difficult role of enlightened despot, authoritarian progressives lost ground.

Under the unrelenting pressure of the progressive faction of the educated classes, change became a distinct possibility when an assembly of Notables was convened early in 1787. After that, the movement for change received the further support of many in larger, somewhat less educated classes, whose thinking had not gone beyond the level at which simplification is necessary to help the mind to work, and dogmatism prevails. They could be found first of all in less sophisticated professional and semi-professional occupations, also among officials in the lower ranks of public and private employment, and among entrepreneurs — the least sophisticated of all. As soon as the movement for change took on the aspect of a revolution, i.e. within a few weeks after the first meeting of the Estates General early in May 1789, it was joined by large sections of uneducated urban and rural people.

On the basis of elections, membership in political clubs, insurgencies and counter-insurgencies, response to calls to arms, it is reckoned — very approximately — that at the end of the 1790s the eighteen million or so French adults of both sexes were divided fairly evenly between traditionalists (supporters of the authoritarian *ancien régime*) and revolutionaries. Few, even if not participating in the violent events of the time, remained indifferent to the extent of not siding with or against the revolution.

Neither social status nor economic conditions nor occupation can be taken as absolute criterion for ideological—political divisions among the French of the revolutionary period. Many simply did what other members of the family, the circle of friends and acquaintances, the neighbours, did: imitation played its usual important role. Apart from that, as happens when there is any freedom of choice, in all groups of the population — whether the basis for differentiation is economic, territorial, religious, or some other — there was a majority on one side and a minority on the other. Besides these splits in the nation, a matter of specific importance in France was the fact that revolutionaries (a considerably larger group than English Whigs and American Patriots had been at the time of their revolutions — several million, not just a few hundred thousand) were a less homogeneous body than the Whigs had been in 1688—9, and American Patriots during the formative period of the United States.

THE INTELLIGENTSIA COMES INTO ITS OWN

Of importance also was a development hardly noticed at the time: the role played by members of the intelligentsia (in the restricted meaning of those whose sole or major occupation is the using of their minds) not only in forming revolutionary tendencies but also in leading them. Ever since, the intelligentsia has more and more been the dynamic element wherever changes have occurred in the wake of the French revolution.

The development was not new in terms of the influence exercised in civilised societies by the intelligentsia, in the wider sense of educated people: the Chinese state at one end of the Eurasian land mass and the catholic church at the other were run for centuries primarily by members of the intelligentsia (scholars in one case, clerics in the other) carrying out, and usually having a hand in drafting, the instructions of absolute rulers. It was only partially a new development in terms of the ideas which gave direction to revolutionary action; many had a history going back to Greco— Roman times. It was a totally new development in terms of the way the ideas had been formulated or reformulated.

Keynes's well-known statement about the influence of ideas applies to all times and all societies. For instance, in the case of economic interests — except possibly at the level of a few primary needs — the direction action takes is given (as mentioned in the Foreword) not by the economic interest *per se* but by the idea (not necessarily a correct one) that one has of the economic interest. Moreover, whatever the relationship between object and idea of the object, in continental *ancien régimes* the widely diffused, usually simple but all-important concepts and values giving direction to the action of most were either intuitive ones originally enunciated by successful prophets and refined by their followers, or had been elaborated through the process of trial and error. Rational or not, reasonable or not, the ideas giving direction to the action of French revolutionaries had instead been formulated through a conscious process. Their sources could be traced to individual minds (of Montesquieu, Voltaire, Rousseau and others) or to the minds of kindred individuals (the *encyclopédistes*, the *physiocrates*).

Of course, the process which resulted in the ideas of the 1688 and 1776 English and American revolutionaries had been equally conscious. There was, however, a difference. Among the 1688 and 1776 leaders there were intellectuals of great stature or influence, or both, but most of them, besides being educated and consciously using their minds in formulating ideas, had had experience in two major fields of practical activity: the running of institutions which enable society to function, and the running of economic activities. They were practitioners of the difficult art of organising services and producing goods. Among the influential French leaders many, on the contrary, had had experience with ideas only; until the revolution came they had operated solely at the theoretical level, not at all at the practical one. They were intelligentsia pure and simple.

In view of fashionable commonplaces, it may be added that it came naturally to many who later wrote about the French revolution to describe it only in terms of classes and economic interests. Such description was the projection first of all of the fact that at the end of the eighteenth century most continental nations were still clearly divided into estates or classes; second, of the commonplace that societies had been run by warrior, priestly, merchant or other elites; and then of the popularity of economics among the intelligentsia. Writers now fashionable did not take into account that all French classes split in 1789 and have remained split; that only under conditions of freedom do economic interests become paramount; that even when they become paramount they do not inspire the heroism which characterised French revolutionaries and anti-revolutionaries. Class loyalty and economic interests played important roles, but they were secondary in relation to the commitment of half the French nation to the authoritarian way of life of the past, of the other half to a new way of life.

THE RADICALS' REVOLT AGAINST LIBERALISM

In 1789 there were both moderates and progressives among liberal revolutionaries. A third tendency, composed of various groups among which the Jacobins later emerged, appeared shortly after the agitation had become a revolution. This tendency requires special attention, as it has influenced mankind ever since, and now has the upper hand (see the section on 'Expanding radical authoritarianism' in the Introduction).

Liberals stayed on the crest of the revolutionary wave for nearly four years. During that brief period, through the Declaration of Rights of 1789 and the Constitution of 1791, the reform of the French administration, the establishment of a system of public education, the abolition of ecclesiastical privilege, the formulation of economic policies, the formation of political parties, they set precedents which for several generations guided all continental liberals, and those (never numerous) who elsewhere, from the Argentine and Mexico to Russia and Japan, took inspiration from them.

The cleavage between moderates and progressives followed the lines of what had occurred in the United States in the 1780s. While the reorganisation of the French institutional structure was being discussed, those who had been the prime movers in the agitation of 1787–9 separated into right-of-centre Feuillants (moderates) and left-of-centre Girondists (progressives), to use terms popular in 1791–2. The scientist Bailly, the poet Chénier, and Lafayette were in the first group dominant in the National Assembly organised in June 1789 and acting as a constituent assembly; it aimed at creating an institutional system patterned after and improving on the British one. Brissot, Vergniaud and Roland were in the second group, which, except for the federal element, looked primarily to the American system, had a dominant voice in the Legislative Assembly elected in 1791 and courageously opposed dictatorial tendencies among members of the Convention elected in 1792. Mirabeau, writer and statesman, the major figure in the National Assembly, died before having to make a clear-cut choice. Although intellectually and temperamentally he was close to the first group, had he survived he might have sided politically with the second, like Condorcet, Pétion and Paine.

In the fourth year of the revolution, Jacobinism became a household word. What in England had happened on a small scale in the wake of the Great Rebellion of 1642, with Levellers, Diggers and other groups, soon to fizzle out, what in the United States might (and probably would not) have developed if Shay's rebellion and other small dissidences had not been crushed or absorbed (and had had time to formulate an ideological position), happened in France on a large scale. In 1793—4 half a million members of Jacobin and kindred clubs (familiar today through the names of Marat, Danton, Robespierre, Saint-Just, Hébert, Babeuf — except for Marat, insignificant figures or even absent when the revolutionary storm was gathering), and several times that number of sympathisers, used the liberty that liberal revolutionaries had brought to France to claim and gain greater liberty for themselves by destroying the liberty of others. To explain the presence of this large group in France and its near absence in Great Britain and the United States, one can bring in the usual *dei ex machina*, from the once fashionable 'spirit of the times' and 'conspiracy' of this or that mysterious group, to the now fashionable 'class structure' of the French nation, and 'class struggle'. One *deus* is as good as another. What did count was the fact that Jacobins were numerous, highly motivated and deeply committed.

JACOBINS

Commitment to 'revolution' as the total obliteration of everything obnoxious, an attitude centred on dogmatism and extremism, advocacy of violence against all opponents — these were the three major elements that characterised French Jacobinism of the 1790s more than any specific programme for the structuring of democracy (in reality there were a variety of programmes). Commitment, attitude and advocacy mean that the Jacobins' main emphasis was on method; just as method made the liberals' democracy the organisation of individual liberties, so it made the Jacobins' democracy the dictatorship eliminating individual liberties. When mentioning Jacobinism in other contexts than that of the 1790s (for instance in relation to the 1970s 'revolutionaries' on all continents), the reference is to the commitment, attitude, advocacy and dictatorship. With their dogmatism, extremism and violence, with the self-appointed committees ruling France in 1793–4, Jacobins set a pattern which is consciously imitated throughout the world today.

Whatever their differences, revolutionaries of the first (Feuillants) and second (Girondists) waves were committed to free institutions guaranteeing the liberty of all: 'we' and also 'they', who have different goals, interests and aspirations. Not so the Jacobins.

Like Feuillants and Girondists, Jacobins rejected the divine right of princes, the sanctity of tradition, the priority of non-reason over reason. However, their rationalism being of the dogmatic variety and having as corollary a moral duty to enforce truth, Jacobins agreed with supporters of the *ancien régime* in rejecting the idea of equality between 'us' and 'them' (see Chapter 1). They were not satisfied with an institutional structure enabling them to hold to their position and to have a share in running public affairs; they wanted their position to be everyone's. They believed that all members of the community should have the same ideas, values and aspirations. This made them committed advocates of a new absolutism and a new conformism.

Like the traditionalists, Jacobins started from an anti-nominalist position: the people (or the nation – in the revolutionary rhetoric of the time they were synonymous) were an entity endowed with life, thought, functions, mission and will. Rousseau's 'general will' came in handy. Communalism was the Jacobins' key value. What was related to individualism – from humanistic dignity and the protestants' responsibility of the individual to humanitarian compassion for individual suffering, from the right of each to control his own life to the duties which are the counterpart of that right, and legal and political institutions geared to individual responsibility – was for them meaningless.

For Jacobins, liberty meant the liberty of the whole – the people or nation – not that of the citizens. (Substituting proletariat for people, this is the position of today's national-communists and anarcho-communists; identifying people with nation or race, it is the position of national-socialists and social-nationalists.) The whole must be undifferentiated; the greater the equality of its component parts, the citizens, the healthier and stronger would the nation be. Anything weakening cohesion – divisions and differences of any kind – was damaging. Worse, it was evil. This kind of equality was not the liberals' equal status of individuals who freely choose the direction in which they wish to go, and therefore are diverse, it was uniformity.

When Jacobins said 'democracy', they meant a majority which becomes a totality through elimination of all minorities: a national community of citizens thinking alike and sharing an identical way of life. When they said 'republic', they meant a cohesive body of citizens acting as one unit, not the self-government of citizens who, being free, go in different directions. Lincoln's government 'for the people' would have been alright for the Jacobins provided power was in the hands of those who knew what was good for the people, but 'government of the people, by the people' was in practice an absurdity denied by Nature and by Reason.

Whoever held differing views was an enemy of the revolution, an agent of the *ancien régime* and foreign powers. Terror, implementing a sacred duty, was the highest expression of morality and would take care of enemies. From the Jacobin point of view (as from that of twentieth-century Stalinists and Hitlerians) there was no cruelty in terror, only rightful elimination of evil for the good of the people. Many of the Jacobins about whom most is known were good people, individually: just as Dominican and Franciscan friars entrusted with inquisitorial duties had been, as were Chinese officials entrusted at the end of the third century B.C., and again in the 1970s, with the elimination of Confucians and Confucianism — of opposition to a new set of autocratic rulers.

Jacobinism was simplicity itself. Conviction that the people are one, that uniformity is the greatest good, ruthless violence the proper method for eliminating those who bring divisions among the people, reaches its culmination in a totalitarian dictatorship of the few who are so convinced of the rightness of their position that they do not trouble to ask the many what they want, and cannot envisage a society in which people make free choices.

AN OLD IDEOLOGY IN MODERN CLOTHING

There was nothing new in the Jacobins' fanatical commitment to absolute conformity of ideas and values, and to violence as a means to achieve it, nor in the use of cold-blooded cruelty which was more inhuman than the unpremeditated cruelty of so-called savages and barbarians. Fanaticism, conformism, violence and cruelty have characterised fourth-century Christians and eighth-century Moors in the Mediterranean world, eleventh- and nineteenth-century moslems in India and the Sudan respectively, late sixteenth-century Counter-Reformation catholics and early seventeenth-century Japanese traditionalists — to give a few examples of successful obliteration of opponents, heretics and deviationists. What was new was the Jacobins' successful attempt to resurrect traditional values and ways in a modern setting, and to justify them in terms of progress. Eighteenth-century Western progressives — whether supporters or opponents of enlightened despotism — had seen fanaticism, conformism, violence and cruelty as horrible features of a past which should be abandoned, but with the Jacobins they became features of the future. That future is now gaining ground with the growing approval of dictatorial coercion and terrorism.

Primarily as the result of internal dissension (Danton sent Hébert to the guillotine, Robespierre sent Danton, and Tallien sent Robespierre), Jacobins lost power in France in the summer of 1794. However, they survived as a dynamic ideological–political force. Many soon found a comfortable home in Bonapartism, the first efficient modern totalitarian dictatorship. During the first post-Napoleonic generation, Jacobinism — idealised as pure democracy — appealed to continental democrats whose spokesmen were the Pole Lelewel, the German Blum, the Hungarian Kossuth, the Italian Garibaldi (who, less sophisticated than the others, clearly equated democracy with dictatorship). They and others were enthusiastic about intransigence and forgetful about terror. Their revolutions failed. The violent explosion of a socialist movement imbued with Jacobinism in June 1848 (mainly in Paris but also in some provincial cities), led three-quarters of the French electorate — the majority of the people of France! — to vote in December of that year for another Bonaparte (with disastrous results for France and some of the many nations with which the dictatorial Second Empire became involved, from the Vietnamese to the Mexicans). The eruption of the Parisian *communards* in 1871, important ever since as a powerful myth, was only a fringe event. Late in the nineteenth century, Jacobinism was an important component in the position of socialists advocating the dictatorship of the proletariat, but on the Continent (and in English-speaking nations) it was checked until the end of the First World War by other socialists imbued with liberal values .

JACOBINISM AS THE SOURCE OF TWENTIETH-CENTURY TOTALITARIANISM

In nations of Western civilisation, Jacobinism as fanaticism, violence and dictatorship was for four generations no more than an obnoxious rash which would clear in time. It was no passing rash outside Western areas, among four-fifths or so of mankind. Since its success in Russia two generations ago Jacobinism has been rampant, and it may take its revenge even in France for the defeats suffered in 1794, 1848 and 1871. Starting with the Russian Pestel and his friends in the 1820s, Jacobinism appealed in this century to democrats like the Chinese Sun Yat-sen in his post-liberal phase, the Indonesian ideologue of 'guided democracy', Sukarno, the Egyptian Nasser before he discovered socialism, the Cuban Castro before his conversion to Leninism.

Many people who in recent generations vaguely thought of themselves as 'radicals', given a chance would have acted as Jacobins. Russian Bolsheviks were not vague radicals; in 1917, and before, they saw themselves politically and ideologically as successors to French Jacobins. In prison and in exile their leaders had thought a good deal about the French revolution; they identified with Jacobins and wanted to avoid the errors which they thought had led to the failure of Robespierre and his friends. They succeeded. In the chaos created by a war which had caused too much suffering, and by upheavals they had not started and had had little to do with (see Chapter 6), the disciplined band of a few thousand Russian Bolsheviks seized power in Petrograd and Moscow. Within ten years they were in undisputed control of all resources of the largest state in the world. That was the first step (and a corner had been turned in the development of mankind).

The second step soon followed. In the wake of the fear created by Bolshevik victories, in Europe, Asia and the Americas fascist national-socialists were astoundingly successful in the 1920s and 1930s, until defeated on the battlefield. They, as much as the Bolsheviks, shared the Jacobins' commitment to absolute conformity, subordination of the individual to the organised community, glorification of violence, belief in the purifying value of terror, dictatorial power. Enemies and at the same time imitators of the Bolsheviks, fascists had a love—hate relationship with communists. The years from 1944 to 1949 saw the equally astounding success of the Stalinists, an improved version of the 1917 Bolsheviks.

Then came the third step in the growing diffusion of Jacobin mentality and its dictatorial authoritarianism. Observers have been impressed by the breaking-up of Stalinism into various national-communist segments in the 1950s. However, more important than the fragmentation was the ideological and institutional similarity of the segments, and the power of attraction each of them had. At the same time most non-European national-socialists, from Brazilian *integralistas* to Iraqi ba'athists, veered from an anti-communist to a pro-communist position. As things stand in the mid-1970s, anarcho-communists dream of doing what Saint-Just did and Babeuf failed to do, and all combinations of nationalism and socialism are variations

of a single powerful authoritarian movement. Whether they rule
China, Cuba, South Yemen, Uganda or Yugoslavia, whether they are
active in India with Naxalites and in Japan with the Red Army, in
Ulster with Provos and in Italy with the Black Order, in Palestine
with Black September terrorists and in Zanzibar with black racists,
in Uruguay with Tupamaros and in Argentina with Montoneros,
whether leaders and followers have heard of the Jacobins or not,
national-socialists, social-nationalists and national communists share
the Jacobins' passions, simple convictions and unsophisticated
conclusions.

IN THE WAKE OF 1789

The liberal phase of the revolution in France ended soon after the
Parisian massacres of August 1792. It had lasted long enough to
destroy the old order for ever, and to have an emancipating effect in
France and beyond. From emancipation came the powerful
emotional wave of nationalism in 1792, and the fanatical Jacobinism
of 1793. The merging of the two forces in what was then the
wealthiest nation in the world, and the leadership of a military
genius, made Napoleonic France the arbiter of all continental
Europe for a few years. British naval power kept Europe's Atlantic
and Mediterranean islands out of Napoleon's grasp, but that was all.

If Napoleon had not overreached himself, if he had had the self-
control once exercised by Augustus after successful wars (and more
recently by Prussia's Frederick II), the Continent would have then
found peace and quiet and for a while considerable economic
progress — possibly even a brief literary and artistic golden age — in
an authoritarian system more efficient, and so more effectively
repressive and suppressive, than the ancien régime. Happily for the
future of liberty, Napoleon did overreach himself. In September
1812, only the decision taken by an all-powerful despot stood
between an authoritarian and a relatively free future on the
Continent. In Moscow Napoleon delayed his decision, and lost.
Defeated on the battlefield in 1813—15, Napoleon disappeared from
the continental scene and his radical despotism collapsed.

It is fashionable to admire Napoleon and — derisively — to call the
immediate post-Napoleonic period on the Continent the Restoration.
Once an institutional structure has been destroyed it is nearly
impossible to resurrect it; except formally, there was little or no
restoration. The upheaval caused by French imperialism had sealed
the doom of authoritarian traditionalism in Germanic, Italian, Iberian
and Scandinavian states, as effectively as the short-lived later imperial-

ism of half-a-dozen European nations sealed the doom of authoritarian traditionalism in tribal and civilised societies in Asia, the Middle East, Africa and Australasia.

In many instances there was not even formal restoration. On the post-Napoleonic Continent, there was liberal constitutionalism with free elections (even if suffrage was limited) and considerable freedom of expression and association, in France, the Netherlands, Sweden, Switzerland and several minor Germanic states. Constitutions guaranteed the liberty of all male citizens in Norway, and of large minorities in Hungary and Congress Poland, three dependent states which had considerable autonomy.

In France — in spite of military defeats still by far the premier continental nation — with the help of Russia's autocrat and Austria's all-powerful minister, the liberal minority led by former revolutionaries like Talleyrand and Fouché, and by intellectuals like Constant and Royer-Collard, gave their unwilling fellow-citizens (in about equal numbers devotees of the old despotism and the new) a constitution. Although a restricted one, it made the French of 1814 as different from the French of 1788 as the number one is from zero. The small French electorate expressed a variety of tendencies and voted freely. In the French parliament sat traditionalists, Bonapartists, right-of-centre and left-of-centre liberals and republicans. There was sufficient freedom of the press for the first major spokesman for modern authoritarian socialism, Saint-Simon, to publish his books, and enough freedom of association for his followers to organise themselves.

More important than limited but genuine constitutionalism was the fact that during the twenty-five years of turmoil caused by the upheaval of 1789, there had been a clarification of positions. In 1814 there were more liberals in continental nations than there had been before 1789. Moreover, thanks to a certain amount of freedom in ten or twelve states, and to inefficient despotism in several others, liberals had possibilities for action that had not existed before 1789, or during the Napoleonic period. Rather than a restoration, there was, however unsatisfactory for liberals, a radically different situation on the Continent in 1814 from that which had prevailed a quarter of a century earlier.

POST-NAPOLEONIC COURSE OF CONTINENTAL LIBERALISM

Wherever they could — and this means in all continental states with the exception of Austria and a few smaller ones — liberal revolutionaries began agitating, conspiring and revolting shortly after Napoleon's defeat. They were already active in Spain in 1814, in Italy and

Germany in 1817, and soon after in other countries from Portugal to Poland. Their example was contagious. Outside the Continent, liberals conspired in Russia and organised anti-Ottoman uprisings in the Balkans, and won independence for their countries in the Western hemisphere (see Chapter 6). After several decades of agitation, when there had been limited constitutional liberty, decades of conspiracies, insurrections and wars, when there had been absolutism, the institutional structure was loosened.

In the late 1860s and early 1870s, just a little over half a century after the collapse of Napoleon's radical despotism and the attempt to revive traditional absolutism, continental liberalism was successful, or seemed well on the way to success. With free elections and universal male suffrage, Switzerland and France were half-way towards being liberal democracies. In the North German Confederation (after 1871, the German empire) and the Austro-Hungarian empire elected national assemblies did not have much power, but the assemblies were there, elections were free (on the basis of universal male suffrage in Germany), and if the citizens' representatives were determined enough and acted together, they could exercise considerable influence. In the remaining countries (fifteen in 1914), liberal constitutionalism was triumphant.

The essential articles of the liberal programme were being pursued everywhere: government by discussion in an assembly of freely elected representatives of the citizens; power from below; laws equal for all, impartially enforced; freedom of conscience and of the press; diffusion of lay education and universal literacy; a market economy; and separation of church and state. The final goal of communities of free and equal citizens was still distant, but the institutions for achieving it peacefully were there.

The variety of religious, philosophical and ideological—political positions; the multiplicity of parties, also of non-party private organisations of all kinds, including trade unions and co-operatives; the birth of new movements; the advancement in all scientific fields, in technology, in social disciplines; the expansion in industrial and agricultural production and in transportation, in education, health and other services; the open expression of dissent and opposition; the increase in physical and social mobility; the restlessness not only of dynamic minorities but of growing sectors of the population in what had been stagnant societies: these, and more, indicate that the loosening of institutional structures had led to a liberalisation in ways of life. There was unhappiness, more than before 1789, alongside achievements; but continental liberals were confident that with more achievements the discontent resulting from change would soon give way to satisfaction.

CONTINENTAL LIBERALS AS AN INFLUENTIAL MINORITY

After the establishment, or widening, of liberal constitutionalism, there were enough liberals among the voters to give them, at times, a parliamentary majority in the Swiss, Scandinavian, Dutch and Belgian nations. In France, liberals had been a small minority in 1814, and also at the time of the revolutions of 1830 and 1848. In 1870, including groups from former Orléanistes (moderates) to progressive constitutional republicans and democrats, liberals were still a minority when they established the Third Republic. Their numbers increased somewhat later, but at most they never were more than a bare majority of French citizens. In the North German Confederation and its successor the German Empire, liberals at first had a plurality in the Reichstag but soon lost it. (Even at the time of their greatest electoral success, in May 1848, they had never been more than a large minority.) In Italy, Austria-Hungary, the Iberian states, liberals were small — in the Balkan states minuscule — minorities, and they governed thanks largely to restricted suffrage. Considering their small numbers, the attachment to authoritarian traditionalism of millions of all classes in most large nations and several small ones, and the unrelenting attacks made by authoritarian and anarchic progressives, liberalism's success on the Continent as a way of life, as well as a political structure, is indeed strange.

The passivity of large sections of the population had contributed to liberalism's success (only among the Swiss, the Scandinavians, the Dutch, the French, was inertia not a major feature of national life). Military events in nationalist and imperialist wars had also contributed: the defeats Austria had suffered in 1859 and 1866, and France in 1870; the victories achieved by Italy with foreign help in 1859—60; the wars of 1827—9, 1854—6, as the result of which victorious foreign powers imposed liberal-constitutional regimes on Balkan nations emancipated from Ottoman rule. British intervention in favour of liberal constitutionalists in Greece, Belgium, Portugal, Spain and Italy also contributed. So, for several generations, did the convergence of liberal aspirations with nationalist passions and, for a shorter period, of liberal advocacy of a market economy with capitalist interests developed in it.

THE POLITICAL REALIGNMENT OF THE 1870s

There was a realignment of ideological—political forces on the Continent during the generation that witnessed the partial failure of liberalism in 1848—9, and its partial success two decades or so later. The strength of authoritarian radicalism among continental Europeans made the situation more complex, and for liberals more difficult, than that which prevailed in English-speaking nations; but the realigning did not differ essentially from what had taken place in North America and Great Britain.

Once the major goal of a liberal constitution had been achieved, liberals with a leaning towards moderatism (or who had always been moderates at heart) moved towards the position of constitutional conservatives: defence of constitutional liberties, yes; solution of problems on the basis of equality, no. The passage of Guizot's party of Resistance from liberalism to conservatism in France, in the wake of the revolution of July 1830, was partially made in Italy by members of the parliamentary Destra after 1861; in Austria-Hungary by many who, like Schmerling, had been liberals in 1848–9, after the issue of the October Diploma and the February Patent in 1860–1; in Germany by many former National Liberals after 1867. There was a loss to the right but a gain on the left: a majority of democrats now joined the liberal ranks. The gain was greater than the loss.

For about two generations continental democrats (a smaller minority than the liberals) had shared basic Jacobin convictions and values. They did not doubt that once the privileged groups had been eliminated, the 'people' would form a cohesive and uniform whole, and harmony would reign: universal suffrage, the first article in the democratic creed in the post-Napoleonic period, would endorse 'the sacred unity of the people'. 1848 was a revelation: manhood franchise in France and the Germanies led to the election of assemblies in which the representatives of the people were even more divided than those of privileged classes; it was evident that free universal suffrage caused divisions. Furthermore, the 'people' had put Louis Napoleon in power and had supported the Second French Empire; and the 'people' were behind Bismarck in Prussia, in the North German Confederation, in the Second German Empire. Clearly, both the unity of the people and the identification of the will of the people with liberty were myths. The choice lay between unity which required dictatorial coercion, and the people's will expressed through free universal suffrage, which would bring divisions and (as liberals had warned since 1789) the possibility of arbitrary reactionary rule, unless the people's will was contained through constitutional rules. A minority of democrats chose unity (in practice conformity imposed from above), many joining the fast-growing socialist movement. For the majority of democrats who chose free universal suffrage, the gap between themselves and the liberals had narrowed.

TOWARD LIBERAL DEMOCRACY

Sheltered in Great Britain by British liberalism, which they despised or hated, or both, Ledru-Rollin, Mazzini and Ruge (exiles from

France, Italy and Germany), spokesmen for the 1848—9 democrats, created a democratic international in London, dedicated to Jacobin ideals. Their followers were not many, and in time they dwindled. There could not have been agreement in 1848 between d'Azeglio and Mazzini in Italy, Dahlmann and Ruge in Germany, Barrot and Ledru-Rollin in France; but there could be, and there was, co-operation between Cavour and Manin in 1856, between Richter and Löwe in 1867, between Thiers and Gambetta in 1870.

Liberals who overcame fear of dictatorial tendencies in the masses agreed to pass — if not immediately then at some not too distant a date — from liberal constitutionalism to liberal democracy, through universal suffrage. In the decades immediately preceding the First World War, Clemenceau in France, Preuss in Germany, Giolitti in Italy, Canalejas in Spain, Sverdrup in Norway, Borgesius in the Netherlands, Venizelos in Greece — except for Preuss, at one time or another heads of government — were all liberal democrats. In the ideological—political spectrum, they occupied the same place as Wilson, Seddon and Lloyd George in English-speaking nations. In the years preceding the First World War, liberal democrats in France and the smaller states of north-western Europe, constitutional liberals elsewhere, were the dominant political force in all continental states, except, tragically, the largest, most populous and most powerful — Germany.

THE SIN OF PRIDE

Wherever there is some liberty, 'dominant' does not mean 'exclusive'. All through the post-Napoleonic century, continental liberals had to contend with traditionalist upholders of 'throne and altar' — in liberal terminology, of absolutism and obscurantism. As time passed, the traditionalists' numbers declined in relation to the total population and their influence waned; however, they remained a powerful force in Iberian states, and also in Germany, where militarism, even more widely diffused after unification than before, strengthened dynastic loyalties. Considering the Continent as a whole (and excepting the progressive small nations in the north-west) liberal institutional structures were undermined by four major forces born from the emancipation that liberal successes had brought. They were represented by the dogmatic sectors of the intelligentsia, by capitalist exploiters, by frenzied revolutionaries, by nationalists quickly sliding towards racism and imperialism.

There are no data about the extent of tendencies within the intelligentsia (or other groups of the population) of continental nations during the period of liberal ascendance. *Post facto*, and speculatively, it may be stated that at times in the more advanced nations a majority of the intelligentsia, most of the time in most nations no more than a plurality, was committed to liberalism. Traditionalists held second place. Third place belonged to members of non-traditional illiberal tendencies, dogmatically convinced not only of possessing the truth (many people have that conviction) but sure of the truth's forthcoming victory, and righteously contemptuous of everyone else. They knew, they were right, they were superior. Without usually giving it much thought, they started from the postulate of the omnipotence of reason. Their followers acted on the basis of the corollary that power belonged rightfully to them. Their pride at the intellectual level became authoritarianism at the level of political activity. Dogmatism, extremism (no optimum, always a maximum — see Chapter 1), despotism, were by 1914 the unholy trinity guiding expanding sectors of the continental intelligentsia.

Sooner or later the expanding sectors gave birth to ideological—political movements. Any listing is inaccurate in relation to importance as well as being incomplete. Each sector had its prophet: Rousseau, Hegel, Comte, Mazzini, Marx, Nietzsche, Sorel; some prophets were imported — the Russian Bakunin, the British Spencer; at times a school of kindred spirits acted as prophet — free-market economists whose speculations had little foundation in fact, neo-Thomists working hard to reformulate the catholic position at the theological and the practical levels, and racists. (Freud joined the ranks of the prophets later.) The literature about individual thinker-prophets or groups of thinker-prophets is large, and of great interest, but unimportant from the point of view of continental ideological—political movements: first of all because what followers got from the prophet mattered more than what the prophet said, and the relationship was sometimes vague (for instance the position of 'revolutionary' syndicalists and of social Darwinists mattered more than that of their respective prophets, Sorel and Spencer); second because no one knows whether merit or plain luck made a thinker popular (by the time racists found de Gobineau their racism was already established).

While the continental liberal minority was trying to consolidate the liberal-institutional structure at the intellectual level — important where the intelligentsia exercises paramount influence (see pp. 122ff.) — their position was undermined by those who in the name of 'absolute truths' rejected the right of all to give free rein to spontaneity, and the institutional system aimed at guaranteeing the peaceful coexistence of different tendencies born from spontaneity.

SINS OF GREED AND FURY

Revolting against economic as much as political and intellectual authoritarianism, continental liberals advocated a free market, free enterprise and free labour. They foresaw that economic growth would be the outcome; it was. Differences in growth were due more to the numbers and capacity of entrepreneurs than to natural resources, availability of capital or labour and state protection of business. Belgium was the first country on the Continent to industrialise on a large scale (with the help of British technicians and British capital). France followed, but entrepreneurs were less numerous than they had been, or were, in English-speaking countries; fewer too, than they would be when, after a delay of several decades, the German economy 'took off' quickly and efficiently, providing an early example of an economic miracle. Less numerous and less energetic were entrepreneurs in Austria-Hungary (except for Sudeten Germans and Jews), Italy and Spain. The Swiss, the Dutch and the Scandinavians, chronologically in that order, did as well as, or better than, the Germans.

   Liberals had not foreseen that economic expansion, accompanied by large-scale population transfer from agricultural to industrial areas, and concentration in cities, would lead — under conditions of political liberty — to growing tension between wage-earners and entrepreneurs, bent on maximising profits by keeping wages down (thus stupidly restricting the market for their products). Economists of the classical school had formulated dogmatic principles: law of supply and demand, law of the market, iron law of wages, law of rent, quantitative law of money, law of diminishing returns — none of them 'laws', at the utmost tendencies that can be manipulated. One cannot say whether these were a reason or a rationalisation for Liberal parties and Liberal statesmen in power, to decide not to interfere with the activities of entrepreneurs or to maintain the balance between management and labour, producers and consumers — to ignore in the economy the equality stressed in the legal and ethical fields. The fact is that there was no interference, or not enough. Greed had a green light. For too long liberals were *libéristes* (see Chapter 2). When in power they acted illiberally by allowing an excessive concentration of economic power to be in the hands of entrepreneurs, who more and more found their political home in conservatism, preferably its authoritarian wing. The *libérisme* of British Liberals was checked to some extent by humanitarianism; North American liberals soon adopted *dirigisme* as the guide to their economic policies; as a result, in Great Britain opponents of capitalism did not become influential as a political force until early in the twentieth century, and in North America they remained a largely uninfluential minority. The dogmatic *libérisme* of continental liberals left a vacuum which was filled by socialists.

Born in France early in the nineteenth century, at a time when liberals were few and the loyalty of most French people went to either traditionalist, Bonapartist or Jacobin authoritarianism, continental socialism differed radically from the British version. It also has had by far the greater impact in the world at large; from the Russian Herzen and the German Marx to the Vietnamese Ho Chi Minh and the Syrian Bakdash, many foreigners who played an important role in the socialist movement formulated their ideas in France or patterned them on French ones. As an idea, socialism (or communism) had been formulated by, and appealed to, Frenchmen of the Enlightenment and of the Revolution; as an ideological—political force it appeared in France in the early 1830s, when agitation was made possible by the liberalisation of French institutions and of the French way of life in the wake of the 1830 revolution, and of government by moderate liberals. Agreeing on a collectivist economy (variously interpreted), French socialists divided on the basic question of liberty (which in theory they considered secondary) and ranged all the way from pure anarchists to upholders of strict absolutism. Most called themselves 'democrats', but their democracy was the Jacobin authoritarian one.

It would be out of place to go into details of French and continental varieties of socialism and their evolution. Suffice it to say that in continental socialism there have been 'revolutionary' wings since the 1830s, and that to be a socialist 'revolutionary' came to mean primarily (and still does) rejection of the liberals' basic institution: government by discussion in an assembly of freely elected representatives of the citizens. Rightly, anger moved socialists deeply concerned with the plight of too many workers; rightly, socialists agitated for labour and social legislation which should have been, and was not, part of the liberal programme, and of policies when liberals were in power. But anger turned into irresponsible fury in the case of 'revolutionaries' who, in order to eliminate capitalist greed and to increase the workers' share of what had been produced, turned against everything connected with the liberal position, from freedom of expression and free elections through which spontaneity expresses itself, to tolerance and the spirit of compromise which enable different tendencies to coexist peacefully and to alternate in running public affairs. On the eve of the First World War, the major factions of 'revolutionary' socialism were the anarcho-syndicalists and the minority wing of Marxism: among their spokesmen were the Spaniard Ferrer, the German Liebknecht, the Pole Luxemburg, the Italian Mussolini (who all met violent deaths) and the exiled leader of the Russian Bolsheviks, Lenin.

The variety of socialist positions clearly indicates the priority of inner convictions over outer conditions. Socialists agreed on the problem to be solved — the inferior status of workers — and on the solution — collectivism. Most socialist thinkers and leaders came from the same social group: the intelligentsia. They had similar educational backgrounds. Through the inner process of individual thinking and through individual emotions, socialists differentiated themselves through a spectrum that went all the way from revisionists, who differed from liberals on minor|matters (a larger public sector for the economy, more generous social services), and 'revolutionaries', who rejected liberalism *in toto*.

THE SIN OF ARROGANCE

As a meaningful and passionate idea distinct from patriotism, appealing to many and providing a powerful stimulus to action, nationalism was born among the French emancipated by the events of 1787—9. For a considerable time, to be a liberal (moderate or progressive) meant on the Continent to be a nationalist also. The German liberals who rebelled in 1813—14 were nationalists, and so were those who failed in 1849. For several decades, German moderates called themselves National Liberals. Liberal revolutionaries of 1820—1, 1830—1 and 1848—9 in Spain, Poland and Italy were nationalists, and so were those who governed Italy after unification in 1860, who failed in Poland in 1863, who were in power in Spain in 1874 — so were the many liberal revolutionaries in non-Western civilisations at the end of the nineteenth century and early in the twentieth.

Once the process of establishing basic free institutions nearly everywhere on the Continent had been completed, the parting of the ways between nationalists and liberals became evident. Free institutions having a diverse effect, nationalists (seldom numerous except in France but influential among the intelligentsia and the higher socio-economic groups) instead aimed at a maximum of cohesion in the nation: the liberals' state is weak, the nationalists' strong. After the parting of the ways in the 1880s and 1890s, the incompatibility increased. Continental nationalists enthusiastically embraced racism and imperialism; racism justified one's superiority over other peoples and nations, and imperialism (then mainly as colonialism or expansion in tribal areas and areas of civilisations deemed 'inferior') was the implementation of that superiority.

Aware of their own attachment to the nation-state, many liberals, particularly the moderates, were ambivalent towards both racism and colonialism. The liberals' near-universal acceptance of the theory of evolution, the evidence provided by the rapid progress in all fields of endeavour in what many called Teutonic nations, and nations presumably deeply influenced by ancient Teutonic tribes like the Franks, and what circulated as scientific evidence about mankind's past, justified concepts of racial differentiation and of Indo-European, Indo-German, Aryan, Nordic or Caucasian (words devoid of scientific precision) superiority. The commitment to equality between peoples, never strong among moderates, weakened also among progressive liberals.

The nationalists' aspirations for expansion were favoured by the economic growth which had been the outcome of the emancipation of economic forces; which increased individual ability to act, strengthened states and modified the international balance of power in favour of fast-developing nations. They were favoured also by freedom of movement (passports were then symbols of backwardness), with travellers, adventurers, traders, missionaries, scientists and the idle rich going everywhere, disturbing traditional cultures, causing resentment and at times violence (Egyptian risings in 1881, the Boxer rebellion in China in 1900) which called for, or was a pretext for, revenge in the form of aggression.

The autonomy of tribal areas which early in the nineteenth century occupied over half the land area of the globe, and were mostly thinly populated (a few tens of thousands of people in Australia, the southern-most area of the Western hemisphere, the Siberian and North American north, African deserts, a few hundred thousand in central areas of South America, the American West, vast African bush lands, central Asian steppes), ended during the period of liberal ascendance on the Continent. The two phenomena overlap, and only in a few cases is there a relationship of cause and effect. What English-speaking North Americans did in the United States and Canada, Spanish- and Portuguese-speaking South Americans did in South America, incorporating (nominally for several decades in some cases) interior and southern districts covering millions of square miles. The government of Russia incorporated thinly inhabited central Asia, the nearly uninhabited far east and north, and the more populous Caucasus — areas as vast as those included in the 1920s in the French colonial empire. During the seventeenth and eighteenth centuries the Chinese government had added to the empire nearly twice the area of the eighteen provinces of traditional China. Egypt expanded briefly in Africa nearly to the Equator (in the process enslaving much of the black population) and in western Arabia. Mainly in the 1890s, Ethiopians added to their homeland an area twice as large. Having been compelled to abandon their isolationism, the Japanese expanded at their neighbours' expense.

Of the thirteen states into which, within the boundaries indicated in the first section of this chapter, the Continent was divided in 1914, four participated in the rape of Africa; a fifth, Portugal, saw its claims restricted, and a sixth, Spain, held to coastal strips and islands occupied or claimed since the later Middle Ages. Outside Africa, Spain lost American and Asian dependencies when the country was governed by a Liberal party which was unwilling, more than unable, to engage in military action; Denmark got rid of its possessions in the West Indies; the Dutch completed only in 1910 the establishment of their control over Indonesian islands (in vast areas the inhabitants never saw a Dutch official, tax collector, trader or planter). In three cases continental liberals supported colonialism: when Radicals in power in France resumed in the 1880s the policies which, initiated by the authoritarian regime of Charles X and continued under the Second Empire, had led to the French occupation of Algeria, the Senegal area in West Africa, southern Indo-China, and to interference in Mexico and Madagascar; when the Liberal government in Italy tried to placate nationalists by annexing Libya; when a large faction of German liberals supported the colonialist policies of William II.

With regard to colonialism, for continental liberals there was an ugly debit side. On the credit side, liberal institutions enabled anti-imperialist and anti-colonialist forces at home to organise and to increase the awareness of people in all classes about the evils of aggression; and they provided inhabitants of dependencies (and their advocates — British humanitarians, for instance, in the case of the Congolese) with a bar at which they could be heard and some abuses, at least, could be curbed; checked compulsory assimilation and helped subject peoples to keep their cultural identity; and made it possible for anti-colonialists at home to join hands with leaders of liberation movements in the colonies. All this is deemed irrelevant by many who are deeply involved emotionally in anti-colonialist agitation. However, on all four counts, the colonialism of countries in which liberals had introduced free institutions was radically different from all other imperialism, both ancient and modern. German and Italian colonialism ended as the result of military defeats inflicted by liberal-constitutional and liberal-democratic states. The colonialism of liberal-constitutional and liberal-democratic states ended largely because of anti-colonialism at home.

LIBERAL DECLINE AFTER THE FIRST WORLD WAR

As the result of the First World War and revolutions there was political fragmentation in central Europe. To the territorial expansion of cultural Europe between 1821 and 1913 in the Balkans was added some expansion to the east (in 1917—18) with the emancipation of five nations of Western culture from Russian rule. Without counting mini-states and self-governing territories under the jurisdiction of the League of Nations, there were twenty-five sovereign states between the Atlantic and Russia (after 1922, the Soviet Union). Early in 1919 they were all structured as liberal-constitutional states with universal male suffrage, or as liberal-democratic states with genuine universal suffrage. For Bryce, convinced that democracy had come to stay, and for Wilson dreaming of peace in a democratic world, all continental states were democracies in the sense given to the word in English-speaking nations, i.e. liberal democracies.

Names of parties and movements varied, and so did their relative strength in each nation. However, under conditions of freedom such as existed everywhere, at least for a short while, continental Europeans had a wide choice of ideological—political positions. In the immediate post-1919 elections, Liberal and kindred parties received from larger electorates a smaller percentage of votes than they had received in pre-1914 elections. The decline was linked to the wide-spread conviction that liberalism itself (and not, as was the case, large authoritarian residues in the central empires and Russia) had been a major factor in bringing about the war. Even more widespread was the certainty that post-war problems could not be solved with liberal policies.

In favour of liberal-democratic systems (or liberal-constitutional systems if women were excluded from the suffrage) were, besides liberals, all revisionist socialists (labourites, social democrats and plain democratic socialists), constitutional conservatives, and the still relatively small Christian Democratic wing of political catholicism (the latter a major force in all states except five homogeneously protestant ones in the north and four prevalently or largely orthodox or moslem in the south-east). As previously noted (see p. 7) support did not necessarily mean commitment to free institutions. Opposed to parliamentarianism, and to most or all institutions connected with it, were five major ideological—political forces: nationalists; those who in increasing numbers blended socialism and nationalism; lay and confessional traditionalists; the authoritarian 'revolutionary' socialists organised in 1918—22 in communist parties; anarcho-communists, numerous in Spain as anarchists and anarcho-syndicalists and present elsewhere as 'revolutionary' syndicalists.

SHORT-LIVED FREEDOM IN 'SUCCESSOR' STATES

Including states originating in secessions from the Ottoman empire, those organised in liberated areas of Russia and Germany, and those replacing the Austro-Hungarian empire, thirteen of the twenty-five continental sovereign units were 'successor' states. Liberals were numerous, and could count on the co-operation of other parties for the support of free institutions, among Finns and Czechs (the latter, however, forming only about half the population of Czechoslovakia). Liberals had been influential before 1918 among Hungarians, Poles, Rumanians, Serbs and Greeks, but their numbers were small, and many — too many — were also committed to illiberal nationalism. There were hardly any liberals in other 'successor' states.

In the immediate post-1919 period, all thirteen states had, formally, liberal constitutions based on free manhood or universal suffrage. As already noted, authoritarian regimes do not need much popular support to survive, but free institutions collapse without the active support of at least a plurality of citizens. In eleven of the thirteen states, that support was lacking. Sooner or later, dictatorships (mainly nationalist, some monarchical, one clerical, all with national-socialist or fascist overtones) replaced parliaments and free elections. Twenty years after the end of the First World War, free institutions survived only in Finland and, for just four more months, in a truncated Czechoslovakia.

During all or most of the nearly six years of the Second World War, the whole area was controlled directly or indirectly by Hitlerian Germany, or was within the German sphere of influence. Except for most of Finland and Austria and parts of Greece, Soviet troops, or communist partisans then closely linked to the Soviet Union, overran the entire area in 1944–5. British intervention in 1944–7, American in 1947–9, defeated communists in Greece. Nearly 200,000 square miles with 25,000,000 inhabitants were annexed to the Soviet Union; the rest of the Soviet- and partisan-occupied area was reorganised under communist dictatorships. Liberals who were not executed, or imprisoned, went into exile. The ideas disappearing with those who carried them in their minds, all traces of liberalism vanished, except perhaps in Czechoslovakia. So too vanished democratic socialists, organised in small socialist parties and larger agrarian parties. Constitutional and authoritarian conservatives, both lay and confessional (except to some extent in Poland), were eliminated, squeezed out as exiles and silenced.

There were minor uprisings against the new rulers: in East Germany in 1953 and in Hungary in 1956. There was agitation in Czechoslovakia in 1968 and in Poland in the early 1970s. Some interpreted the uprisings and agitation as harbingers of a less authoritarian future; instead they could also be the last flickering of a past not quite dead, when liberty was meaningful to sectors of the intelligentsia and the socio-economic groups it influenced. Events in Yugoslavia, Albania and later Rumania were not a departure from dictatorial repression but factional squabbles within the communist movement.

WEST OF 'SUCCESSOR' STATES

In this area Italians were the first nation to abandon free institutions and to come under dictatorial rule. At the elections of 1919, held with universal male suffrage, the liberals — divided into three main factions — lost the parliamentary majority they had had since the unification of the country. There were two years of violent anti-war reaction, spear-headed by the socialists (among whom the *massimalista* majority looked with admiration and longing at the Soviet dictatorship). These were followed by two more years of a minor civil war fought between fascists (Italian national-socialists first organised early in 1919, already by the end of 1921 the party with the largest membership) and nationalists on one side, and socialists, both authoritarian and democratic, on the other (most liberals looking with sympathy at the fascists). The Fascist party seized power in 1922. It stayed in power until overthrown as a result of Commonwealth and American victories in the Second World War.

Even when voting for parties supporting the liberal-democratic republic proclaimed in 1946, a large number of Italians were impatient with free institutions, seeing them as inefficient and basically unimportant, or opposed to them, seeing them as obstructive and harmful, or perhaps they were simply indifferent. Liberal democracy was established in Italy and survived, at first, largely thanks to the Allied presence and abundant American aid. It survived later largely thanks to the balance between catholicism and communism, the two major political forces in the nation; unable to eliminate their opponent, catholics and communists compromised on a political structure in which both could operate.

Committed to democratic republicanism were those (about one-tenth of the electorate) who in 1976 voted in Italy for three small parties representing progressive and moderate liberalism; also those who voted for the Socialist party (another tenth) and a plurality, perhaps a majority of the nearly two-fifths of the electorate who voted for the catholic Christian Democratic party. In the mid-1970s, the attention of politically concerned people was focused world wide on the development of Euro-communism in Italy. Since the liberation of half of the country by the Allies in 1943–4, leaders of the Italian Communist party had decided to replace 'revolutionary' tactics of all-out opposition to democracy with Lassallean (see p. 149) tactics: using the electoral process in order to win power. The 1968 occupation of Czechoslovakia by Soviet troops was criticised by, among other communists, the Italian Communist party; then came criticism of other Soviet foreign policies, followed by criticism of some internal policies; then came official statements advocating a mixed planned economy within a framework of liberal-democratic political institutions. If criticism and statements were taken at their face value, Italian communism would have veered close to the revisionism of democratic socialists. The Italian lead was followed by communists of other continental countries.

In less than a year from the fascist seizure of power in Italy, the leaders of the military establishment — supported by millions of lay and confessional traditionalists and by nationalists — took over in Spain. The liberal minority, in power since 1874, had been weakened by its divisions and, even more, by defeats suffered in 1898 and 1921 in wars waged against Spain by Americans and Moroccans. Agitation (made possible by the inefficiency of the military dictatorship) led to the establishment in 1931 of the Second Republic, under liberal leadership (the moderate Zamora was President and the progressive Azaña Prime Minister). However, liberals and other groups willing to support liberal democracy were still a minority. Hated by traditionalists and nationalists, disrupted from the beginning by the bloody violence of anarcho-syndicalists, weakened by the ambiguity of majority socialists unwilling to work within a framework of free institutions, and later by deep resentments caused by communist ruthlessness, the republic collapsed in 1939 after a cruel three-year civil war — the prelude to the Second World War. A coalition of rightist authoritarian forces, held together by the military establishment, governed Spain for over three and a half decades. After the death of the military dictator, his successor, at the instigation of his advisers, decided in 1976 to move cautiously towards the establishment of a limited democratic regime. Political movements began to take shape, several combining into two coalitions, deeply divergent in socio-economic policies but both committed to the establishment of a liberal-democratic political structure. In 1926 Portuguese generals did in Lisbon what Spanish generals had done in Madrid in 1923. Their civilian successors patterned the Portuguese dictatorship on the Italian fascist regime. The dictatorship was overthrown in 1974 by a faction of officers tired of fighting insurgents in African dependencies. Elections which in 1975 were about as free as those of November–December 1917 in Russia (i.e. from which were excluded not only reactionaries but also constitutional conservatives), and in 1976 were considerably freer, showed a majority of Portuguese favourable to a liberal-democratic political framework and to public management of a mixed economy. Divided into three major sections (revisionist socialists, social democrats co-operating with progressive liberals, moderates co-operating with Christian Democrats), the majority was opposed by traditionalists, Stalinists and other Leninists, and anarcho-communists.

After the 1917 victories on eastern and southern fronts, the 1918 defeat on the western front took Germans by surprise. The defeat caused the collapse of the semi-authoritarian monarchical regime and of the military dictatorship established during the war, and opened the road to power to a coalition of socialists, catholics and progressive liberals. Suddenly faced with the problem of political responsibility, the majority of German socialists (four out of five at the elections of January 1919) opted for revisionism, supporting the liberals' democracy as organisation of liberty, for the state's political structure. Many realised that free universal suffrage would make unlikely, might even postpone indefinitely, the establishment of a collectivist economy — the first article in their creed. For socialists who called themselves Marxists, this was a grievous and traumatic renunciation. It goes a long way towards explaining vacillation, ambiguities and tensions within their ranks. Among catholics of the Centre party, many were committed to free institutions, most were not. Divided between the moderate People's party and the progressive Democratic party, less numerous than either socialists or catholics, liberals exercised considerable influence until the elections of 1930. The Weimar constitution of the German state (officially not a republic) was largely the work of liberal progressives headed by Preuss, and the moderate Stresemann was the leading statesman of the Weimar period.

The liberal-democratic German state weathered the storm of the critical years 1919—23. When a second storm hit the Germans in the wake of the 1929 American financial debacle, liberal democracy foundered. In 1932, nearly three-fifths of the electorate — marshalled in the Nationalist, Communist and National Socialist parties — wanted an authoritarian regime. Rejecting the liberal principle of the priority of the citizens' inalienable rights over the will of the majority, and fearful of civil war, socialists decided not to use force against the majority. By then, most Centre party catholics had passed from ambiguous acceptance of liberal democracy to open advocacy of a so-called 'strong government'. In power early in 1933, National Socialists, numerous, enthusiastic, disciplined and efficient, bent on avenging the 1918 defeat and on imperial expansion, in 1939 started the Second World War; they were defeated in 1945. One-quarter of Germany was annexed by Poland and (a small district) by the Soviet Union, and its German population expelled (two million out of over ten million expelled died in the process); one-quarter was organised as a rigid Stalinist dictatorship (and was abandoned by over three million Germans who chose exile). A conservative catholic—protestant Christian Democratic party, close to liberal moderatism, received a majority of votes in the elections that accompanied the 1949 establishment of a liberal-democratic Federal Republic in the western half of pre-1939 Germany, and governed efficiently for more than two decades. Continuing, this time without vacillation and ambiguity, the evolution towards liberal democracy begun in 1918, under Schumacher's leadership West German socialists further clarified their stand on basic principles, and proved to be the most reliable and committed supporters of the Federal Republic. During much of the 1970s they governed in coalition with the Free Democrats, the small party formed by the remaining progressive and moderate liberals.

In France, liberals (left-of-centre Radical Socialists and right-of-centre Independents) were more numerous in the immediate post-1919 period than in Germany, Italy and Spain. Largely because of their divisions, low morale and inefficiency when partners in government coalitions, they lost electoral support in the 1930s. The liberal-democratic Third Republic had difficulty in weathering the political storm which reached its climax in 1934, when nationalists and national socialists (fortunately for the republic divided into several competing groups) agitated and tried to bring about its downfall. (Actually the republic was saved by the unexpected support it received from the small disciplined Communist party, suddenly fearful of a fascist dictatorship.) The collapse took place as the result of a successful German invasion six years later. The authoritarian regime which in June 1940 replaced the republic was patterned on the Spanish one: a coalition of rightist authoritarian groups, held together by leaders of the military establishment. After liberation in 1944, the Fourth Republic, organised as an improved version of the Third, received the support of only a third of the electorate. It was sabotaged by the communists (one-fifth to one-quarter of the nation) and actively opposed by Gaullists, the movement in which most rightist tendencies merged. As the result of nationalist agitation linked primarily to events in the colonial empire, the Fourth Republic was replaced in 1958 by a Gaullist semi-authoritarian presidential republic (the Fifth). Liberals were by then a dwindling minority. The old Socialist party had also practically disintegrated.

The cause of liberal democracy (to be strengthened by progressive socio-economic policies) was taken up in the early 1970s by the renewed Socialist party, organised and led by Mitterand, formerly close to radical socialism. It was favoured for a while by changes in the governing majority coalition, the moderate Independent Republicans, who had been the Gaullists' junior partners, gaining in influence through the election of their leader to the Presidency of the republic in 1974. On the basis of recent general elections, and not counting the socialist left wing wavering between free and unfree institutions, nearly half of the French voters may be said to support liberal democracy.

All through this period liberals remained the dominant political force in Switzerland. In the Scandinavian and Benelux states, conservatism – lay in Scandinavia, mainly confessional in the Benelux area – had in practice already become liberal moderatism. The same happened more recently in Austria, after the disastrous authoritarian experiment of 1933–8 which was followed by seventeen years of foreign occupation. In all these states, socialists (in Austria, after painful soul-searching and a bitter debate between upholders of democracy and advocates of dictatorship in 1918–23) moved deliberately towards acceptance of liberal democracy as the proper organisation of a free progressive society.

Scandinavian social democrats and Dutch labourites prefer, for their countries, the expression 'social democracies'. Power being in the hands of citizens' representatives elected through free universal suffrage, and peaceful transfer of power from one section of the electorate to another being guaranteed, they are correctly described as 'liberal democracies'; mixed welfare economies justify the term 'social'. Institutions and policies, not words, matter, so the label is unimportant. There are differences in degree between those who put the emphasis on the word 'liberal' and those who put it on the word 'social', but in the small democracies of northern and central Europe, liberals and socialists agree on the superiority of liberal democracy with advanced social legislation, and mixed welfare economies, over other systems. All tend to subscribe to the slogan formulated by German socialists after the renunciation of Marxism in 1959: 'as much liberty as possible, as much planning as necessary'.

ON THE ROAD TO LIBERAL SOCIALISM

Only in the United States do democratic socialists allow themselves to be described as 'liberals'. Elsewhere, particularly on the Continent, socialists are still deeply conscious that their movement, although made possible by the liberties introduced by liberals, emerged as opponent of liberalism. However, large sections of continental socialists have veered towards a liberal position during the last two generations. Whatever the phraseology still in use, they have accepted political structures founded on free universal suffrage, freedom of expression and association, and mixed welfare economies with a considerable role for free enterprise. Their differences from liberals are no longer in kind, but in degree. At the mid-1970s, Brandt in

West Germany, Mitterand in France and Saragat in Italy were as liberal as Scheel, Servan-Schreiber and La Malfa. Socialist parties with the labourite and social democratic label, and large sections of organised labour, are the strongest bulwark of free institutions in several continental states.

The liberalisation of an important wing of the continental socialist movement, at the practical level first, then at the ideological level too, was the outcome of clarification made necessary by the rise of totalitarianism. On the eve of the First World War, the overwhelming majority of the ten million or so supporters of continental socialist parties (half of them in Germany) rejected the liberals' pluralistic and free-wheeling democracy — at best a superstition (as the British Marxist Bax stated), a fraud for most, a meaningless paper game for the Austrian Adler and the Italian Mussolini. They were committed to a 'centrist' position. Heeding Marx, they saw themselves as a world apart, rejected the notions of equality between socialists and non-socialists and participation in political activities as a party among other parties. Heeding Lassalle, they were willing to use universal suffrage instead of violence. This they considered a concession to what they contemptuously called 'bourgeois' democracy (it was the only concession). In the opposition, they rejected participation in the parliamentary process for the formation of governments. As government, they would not allow any future non-socialist majority to govern the country, thus rejecting the democratic process. This, in the 1970s, is the position of what is described as the 'left wing' of democratic socialist parties. This was the position of the Chilean Allende, and of many who, describing themselves as 'revolutionary' socialists, are critical of orthodox and heretical communism, but can in no way be called 'democrats' — if democracy is individual spontaneity, pluralism, a process for alternating different (possibly antagonistic) tendencies in power.

Beginning in the late 1890s, a small group of continental socialists, whose major spokesman was the German Bernstein, advocated acceptance of liberal democracy. The 'revisionists', as they were called, wanted a socialist party to be like other parties, bound by parliamentary procedure and by the democratic process. Expelled by the centrist majority from the French, Italian and other socialist parties, revisionists were tolerated in the German party — then by far the most important in the world — but virtually ostracised. A revolutionary small wing of the socialist movement rejected the Lassallean compromise with democracy, and advocated violence as the road to power; it was resented at times by centrists but not expelled. (In the small Russian Social Democratic party the antagonism between centrists and revolutionaries — there were no revisionists — led to the formation of two autonomous factions, the centrist Mensheviks and the revolutionary Bolsheviks.)

At the time of the outbreak of the First World War, many centrists decided to co-operate with non-socialists in the effort to win the war. This was supposed to be just a temporary retreat from the position of complete separation between socialists and non-socialists. At the end of 1917, revolutionary socialists led by Lenin seized power in Russia (see Chapter 6). They established a dictatorship and kept themselves in power by means of mass terror — which horrified most other socialists. A year later, the victory of the Allies on the western front put power in Germany in the hands of the Socialist party, the largest in the Reichstag. The centrist position, tenable in opposition, no longer made sense; the choice, as voiced by the Austrian socialist Otto Bauer, was between dictatorship and democracy — the despised liberals' democracy. The majority of German centrists opted for democracy and became revisionists. This was not done enthusiastically, and German socialist chancellors, from Scheidemann to Müller, did not enjoy being heads of a government limited by parliamentary rules and subject to the changing moods of the electorate (nor did the socialist Blum enjoy it when he was Prime Minister of France in 1936). Enthusiastically or not a major corner had been turned, through the rejection not only of dictatorship but also of the centrists' democracy for socialists exclusively (as illiberal as democracy for whites only, such as existed in the South of the United States, and lingers on in the 1970s in the Republic of South Africa).

By 1920, socialist parties of Scandinavia and Belgium had wholeheartedly adopted revisionism as their position. Fascist revolutions completed on the Continent the large-scale socialist conversion to revisionism, begun as response to dictatorship in Russia. Even some Marxists and near-Marxists of the Frankfurt School, who had been unrelenting in attacking the 'repressive' Weimar republic, had to acknowledge — reluctantly — that the Weimarian rule of law they despised and found intolerable was radically different in its limited repressiveness, its responsiveness to public opinion and its flexibility from nazi arbitrary rule. When the Second World War ended, centrism had become a fringe position everywhere on the Continent west of communist dictatorships, except in Italy. In most continental states, socialism was clearly divided between a revisionist majority and an authoritarian minority. To the extent to which it adopted basic political and intellectual liberal positions, revisionist socialism could be correctly described as 'liberal socialism'. Because of their firmer commitment to equality within a framework of free institutions, many revisionist socialists were more liberal than members of liberal parties.

LAY AND CONFESSIONAL CONSERVATISM VEER TOWARDS LIBERAL MODERATISM

Increasing awareness of the superiority of free over authoritarian institutions on the part of many continental socialists, and their veering to a revisionist position close to that of liberal progressivism since 1919, had their counterpart in the post-1945 period in corresponding awareness and veering towards liberal moderatism by lay and confessional conservatives.

In Germany, both the Conservative (later Nationalist) party and the Centre (catholic) party had been inclined towards authoritarianism. In this century, the Conservative party supported the military dictatorship informally established in July 1917, opposed the Weimar Republic, and in 1933 added their votes to those received by the National Socialist party to give Hitler the majority needed to legalise his rule. The Centre party opposed the military dictatorship largely because it was a manifestation of imperial protestant authoritarianism; however, after years of ambiguity, it helped the National Socialist party to gain power and to consolidate it. Italian lay and confessional (clerical) conservatives were enthusiastic about fascism and formed the bulk of the *fiancheggiatori*, those who supported the 'black shirt' dictatorship without sharing the fascists' principles and values. French conservatives nearly overthrew the liberal Third Republic at the time of the Dreyfus affair, and in 1934 (when agitation by rightist groups reached a climax early in February), and were the mainstay of the 1940—4 dictatorial regime. In Spain the catholic Popular Action party aimed at replacing the liberal Second Republic, in the 1930s, with an authoritarian regime patterned on the Italian and Portuguese ones. In Austria the catholic Christian Socialists established their own dictatorship in 1933. Conservatives supported dictators who seized power in ten Balkan, Danubian and Baltic states between 1919 (in Hungary) and 1938 (in Rumania).

The continental conservative scene is now radically different. No longer clerical or exclusively catholic, the Christian Democratic party of the German Federal Republic is the political home of lay and confessional constitutional conservatives: whatever the innermost thoughts of voters, members and leaders, it has been the main pillar of the liberal-democratic republic (established in 1949) throughout the more than two decades when it was in power. The same can be said of its Austrian counterpart. In France all strains of conservatism rallied behind de Gaulle after 1944, and contributed to the huge majority which in 1958 voted for the Gaullist presidential republic. But after de Gaulle's departure from the political scene in 1969, his party broadened its constitutionalism and later helped the leader of the liberal moderates (Independent Republicans) to become President of the republic. Governing alone or in coalition for over three decades, while perhaps inefficient the Italian Christian Democrats were not authoritarian (though doubts arose when crises threatened political stability in 1953, and even more in 1960); in 1976 they were strengthened by the votes of lay conservatives. Many Spanish catholics, in the uneasy transition from dictatorship to democracy in 1976—7, aligned themselves with democrats; in so doing they abandoned the authoritarianism that had been their political trade-mark. In Greece, the leader of a Gaullist-type conservative movement who had been Prime Minister for several years was a major figure in the opposition to the 1967—74 military dictatorship. After 1974 his party gained first place in elections and upheld democratic republicanism. Everywhere, authoritarian traditional conservatism weakened to the point of near extinction, and constitutional conservatives became nearly indistinguishable from moderate liberals.

ELEMENTS OF WEAKNESS

In Great Britain, expanded liberalism with a small 'l' survived the waning of Liberalism with a capital 'L' (see Chapter 4). This happened also in several smaller nations on the Continent. There was the same development on a minor scale (i.e. affecting a smaller percentage of the population) in the four major continental nations and the rest of the small ones. Both the original enemy, conservatism, and the later one, socialism, have largely been assimilated. Institutionally and as a way of life, there was more liberalism in the mid-1970s in the truncated Continent (three-quarters of the area of 1789) than there had been two generations earlier on the eve of the First World War. This was the credit side, which is encouraging, but perhaps not good enough in the event of crises of any magnitude. There were also several elements on the debit side.

About a fifth of the population of the truncated Continent lived in the small democracies of north-western and central Europe. There, three decades after the end of the Second World War, free institutions — centred on the first and second of Roosevelt's four freedoms, and on political liberty — appeared to be solid. Among the other four-fifths, the survival (in Spain, the re-establishment) of free institutions depended primarily on what revisionist socialists close to liberal progressivism, and confessional conservatives close to liberal moderatism, would do.

Concerning these four-fifths, many of the conservatives who had veered towards moderatism, and many revisionist socialists, were still vacillating between allegiance to, and rejection of, free institutions.

Second, even among those who could be relied on not to switch to authoritarianism, commitment to liberal democracy was generally weak — as it had been among Italian and Spanish liberals in 1922 and 1923, French liberals in 1940 and 1958, and German revisionist socialists in 1933. Third, commitment, more important than numbers, was particularly weak among the intelligentsia, fascinated by authoritarian and anarchic variations of communalism and its economic corollary, collectivism.

Besides the considerable power of organised illiberal forces (neo-fascist national-socialists, unreconstructed Stalinists and other national-communists, anarcho-communists), there were other elements of weakness in the major nations and several smaller ones. In France, many supporters of the Gaullist Republican Democratic Rally were committed to the 1958—74 semi-authoritarian system in which considerable liberty for private activities was allowed by a strong government over which citizens had little direct control. In West Germany, evidence of the recent and not so recent past justified doubts about the strength of the attachment to free institutions of Germans who voted liberal, socialist, and conservative. In Italy, the ever-changing balance between catholicism and communism still mattered more for the survival of free institutions than party state-ments and programmes. In Spain, polarisation at the extremes of the ideological—political rainbow was a present possibility as it had been a fact in the past. In Portugal, the parties led by Soares and Sa Carneiro had been supported by voters who would have preferred undemocratic candidates had they been allowed to run for office. In the island state of Malta, nationalism prevailed over revisionism among dominant socialists, who felt the attraction of Arab national-socialism. In Greece, 'revolutionary' socialists participated in the democratic process but were as unreliable with regard to free institutions as 'revolutionary' socialists have been always and everywhere. In many countries native and imported terrorism, partly criminal but largely linked to the major illiberal forces, weakened free institutions.

6

LIBERALISM IN LATIN AMERICA, EASTERN CIVILISATIONS AND THE ARABIAN/AFRICAN REGION

LATIN AMERICA: INDEPENDENCE WITH LITTLE LIBERTY

During the first quarter of the nineteenth century, continental Europeans who had once conquered (or simply occupied without fighting anyone) most of the Western hemisphere — the Spaniards, the Portuguese, the French — were ruled despotically in an efficient way by Napoleon, his relatives and his marshals, or in a less efficient way by princes committed to traditional absolutism and conformity. Millions applauded the despotism of new and old masters. The militants among liberal, democratic and nationalist minorities, conspired and organised revolts, and generally (until the 1830s) failed. Non-militants sat it out, waiting for a new situation to arise, many thinking longingly of Great Britain and the distant United States. During that twenty-five years, European wars, insurgencies and counter-insurgencies favoured political emancipation in the Western hemisphere.

Heavily engaged in Europe, the French government in 1803 sold vast and nearly uninhabited (fewer than a quarter of a million people) Louisiana to the United States, and in 1804 abandoned the more populous Haiti to black insurgents who had wiped out the white settlers. France was out, though — many Frenchmen not wanting out — she held on to islands and a small mainland area, landing troops in Veracruz, Mexico, in December 1861, encouraging Quebecquois a hundred years later to secede from Canada and to re-establish close ties between France and Nouvelle France.

More importantly, French invasions of Portugal and Spain in 1807–8 weakened Spanish and Portuguese control over their five sparsely inhabited (fewer than twenty million people all told) vice-royalties on the mainland of the Western hemisphere, extending nearly 6000 miles from north to south. The liberal revolutions of 1820–1 made it impossible for the two Iberian states to send the

armed forces necessary to maintain their rule, or to re-establish it
where it had been overthrown by insurgents. The British helped the
insurgents: at the government level subsidising and arming patriots
and harassing authorities in Madrid and Lisbon; at the private level
organising and leading patriots.

Between 1806, when de Liniers replaced the Spanish viceroy in
La Plata's capital Buenos Aires and Miranda briefly liberated Coro in
Nueva Granada, and 1824 when Sucre won the battle of Ayacucho
in Peru, eight independent states replaced the viceroyalties. Through
secessions, the eight states soon became sixteen, and later twenty,
through further secessions and emancipation from colonial rule.
Among the leaders of the few tens of thousands of patriots who won
independence for their countries on the battlefields, many were
(rather vaguely, most of them) liberals: Belgrano, Miranda, Artigas,
Allende, Morelos, Pedro de Bragança, San Martin, Sucre (Bolivar's
right-hand man), O'Higgins. Six of the eight newly established states
were republics with liberal constitutions, often patterned on that of
the United States. The constitution of the ephemeral Mexican empire
of 1822–3 was semi-liberal; so was that of the more lasting Brazilian
empire (1822–89). There were Liberal parties in Nueva Granada
(Colombia) and in Central America, and liberally inclined movements
existed elsewhere.

Latin American wars of independence (possibly excepting the
Haitian one) would seem to deserve the label 'liberal' just as much
as the war of independence of the thirteen North American colonies:
independent states should have free institutions. However, within a
short while liberalism ceased to be an effective political force in Latin
America, and liberal constitutions were dead letters. A mean version
of authoritarian conservatism was in control, and remained so for a
long time (rather less in Chile and Uruguay, where liberals survived as
an organised force and made a come-back, reasserting their leadership
in 1861 and 1872 respectively). In most of the area — two-thirds of
the twenty republics — it still is in control.

OLIGARCHIA

Again, terms can be misleading. Post-independence Latin American
conservatism was not the law-abiding paternalism of European
continental conservatives, and was totally unlike the moderatism of
former right-wing liberals who had joined hands with constitutional
conservatives, as in English-speaking nations (see Chapter 4). The
geographical distance between southern Europe and Latin America is
greater than between North America and Great Britain or Scandinavia, but the cultural distance is considerably smaller. Ideologically

and temperamentally, Latin American conservatives were of the same breed as authoritarian traditionalists of Latin European nations. They were blood brothers of Iberian Carlistas and Miguelistas, of Italian clericals and *codini*, of French *vendéens* and *ultras*. They were firmly committed to rigid, irresponsible power from above, and to close connection between state and Roman church, in order to maintain hierarchically structured societies and a conformist elite monopolising wealth and arbitrarily ruling docile and ignorant masses. They belonged to the *ancien régime*.

Latin America was the child of the stagnant branch of Western civilisation (see page 70) in the Western hemisphere. It was archaic as well as stagnant, in that it had never felt the innovating, vivifying spirit of the Reformation; also in that ideas and values of the intellectual revolution, the Enlightenment and the scientific advancement, of changing economic processes, of the political revolutions in Great Britain, North America and France, had had a minimal impact there. Except for members of a minuscule intelligentsia, few in Latin America had cared for the liberal content of the three political revolutions: liberty as the independence of a community made sense to large sections of the politically active minority; liberty as the autonomy of the individual entitled to his or her identity, as civil rights, above all as citizens' self-government, was rejected. In contrast to those who had been raised in eastern civilisations, educated Latin Americans understood the concept of liberty as autonomy of the individual, which was implicit in Western cultures; their rejection was not the instinctive response of people who cannot grasp an unfamiliar concept, it was a deliberate decision.

Once the French, Portuguese and Spanish garrisons and expeditionary forces had been withdrawn, native authoritarian traditionalists had a freer hand in Latin America than they had had under colonial rule. In most cases they proved more tyrannical than European viceroys and their officials had been. Whether power was in the hands of creoles (native-born whites), as it was almost everywhere immediately after independence, or of blacks, as in Haiti, or, later, of mestizos in republics from Paraguay to Mexico, and of mulattoes in states of the West Indies, independence brought no emancipation.

Liberals, moderate or progressive, were few. They had organised the original conspiracies and insurrections. They fought and helped to win the wars of independence. They drafted liberal constitutions. That was all. There were not enough of them to fight successfully against the more numerous traditionalists and, a century later from about 1930 on, the authoritarian radicals.

The rural masses, demoralised by three centuries of harsh colonial rule, kept ignorant by the bigoted clergy (which had the monopoly on education), vegetating more than living at a bare subsistence level, were apathetic. If roused, they sided with dictators steeped in traditionalism, even inhuman ones like the Paraguayans Francia and Lopez, and the Haitians Soulouque and Duvalier. In the twentieth century, the masses sided with radical dictators, Vargas, Perón, Castro. In the course of time millions of Europeans migrated to Latin America, mostly from authoritarian states or from societies in which authoritarian ways of life prevailed. After the First World War, they and their descendants applauded Latin American fascist and near-fascist dictators, while their cousins in the Old Countries were applauding Mussolini, De Rivera, Salazar and Hitler.

SLOW BEGINNING OF EMANCIPATION

Thanks to divisions within the *oligarchia* caused by ambition and greed, to mainly inefficient dictatorial rule, to wars won and lost, to the impact of outside factors (for instance the all-pervading French cultural influence among educated Latin Americans, British economic and cultural influence in the Argentine, and American in Mexico), liberals had other chances.

In Colombia, the small liberal minority had the upper hand in 1849–53, long enough to abolish slavery. Out of power, it was often cohesive and influential enough to prevent the consolidation of the rule of the *oligarchia*, and to overthrow a dictator in 1909. In Mexico, Juarez — one of the major nineteenth-century figures in Latin America, actively aided after 1865 by the United States in his struggle against a Habsburg intruder and his French supporters — led the Liberal party to victory in 1867, in the ten-year civil war waged against traditionalists. The victory was followed by nine years of liberal-constitutional rule by Juarez and Lerdo. The aged general who in 1876 had revolted against Lerdo and had governed Mexico dictatorially was overthrown in 1911. The successful revolutionaries elevated to the Presidency their leader, the liberal Madero. Madero was assassinated in 1913, but liberal forces were not definitively crushed until a military triumvirate seized power in 1920. In Uruguay, a long period of strife ended in 1872, with the victory of the Colorado (liberal) party. A generation later the Colorados, under the leadership of Battle, engaged in a policy of radical reforms: genuine government by the assembly of freely elected representatives of the citizens, a generous system of social security, universal instruction, disestablishment of the Roman church. In Chile, liberals, led by able statesmen such as Errazuriz (father and son), completed the unification of the country in 1884, consolidated parliamentary institutions, introduced administrative and socio-economic reforms and made progress towards the democratisation of the political structure. In the Argentine, under the energetic leadership of Lisandro de la Torre, the progressive Union Civica (founded in 1891) began agitation aimed at weakening the hold of the *oligarchia*. In Brazil the Progressive party, established in 1882, was instrumental in replacing monarchical rule with a constitutional republic; it was too weak, however, to check the power of the *oligarchia*, which ran the affairs of the republic as it had run those of the empire. The anti-Spanish revolt in Cuba in 1895–8, and agitation against conservatives subservient to the U.S. government, reached a climax in 1906 in the revolt of the Liberal party, whose leader, José Gomez, remained President of the republic until 1913.

ONWARD

There were some liberal successes in Latin America after the First World War. In Uruguay, Battle's successors continued policies that for nearly two generations made the small republic a showcase of liberal democracy. In the Argentine, the Radical party (successor of the Union Civica), in power in 1916, governed the country under the leadership of Irigoyen and Alvear. Liberal policies facilitated the assimilation of immigrants to the Argentinian nation and stimulated economic development. Argentinians then enjoyed the reputation of being the most dynamic and advanced Latin American nation. In Chile, *oligarchia* and the military combined in their opposition to liberal institutions and policies, and established a dictatorship in 1925. After a liberal-led revolution overthrew the dictator in 1931 the moderate A. Alessandri was President of the republic until 1938, to be succeeded by the progressive liberal Cerda. In Peru and neighbouring republics influence was exercised for decades by the Apristas, members and sympathisers of the People's Revolutionary Alliance (APRA), founded in 1933 and led by Haya de la Torre, a social democrat close to liberal progressive positions. Not strong enough to become the government, the Apristas were nevertheless strong enough to prevent the consolidation of traditionalist and military dictatorships; as late as 1975, the social-nationalist dictator general Velasco accused de la Torre of being the main cause of the instability of the regime, and the Apristas of having organised the revolt that nearly overthrew the dictatorship. Colombia was governed constitutionally by the Liberal party for nearly two decades after 1930; the assassination of the Liberal leader Gaitán was followed by a civil war which enabled national-socialist generals to seize power briefly. The liberals Gallegos and Betancourt led agitation in the 1930s against the dictatorial military establishment of Venezuela.

Established in 1919, liberal democracy has survived in Costa Rica
ever since — a case unique in the history of Latin America.

Around 1960 the outlook for liberal constitutionalism, even for
liberal democracy, seemed fairly favourable in many Latin American
republics. Both in Brazil and Cuba, internal and external pressures
had compelled one dictator to resign in 1945, the other in 1944, and
a brief interlude of liberty ensued. Both dictators were back a few
years later, but one committed suicide in 1954, and the other was
defeated early in 1959 by *guerrilleros* of a movement then pledged
to reforms within a liberal-democratic structure. Dictators close to
fascist radicalism had been overthrown in the Argentine in 1955, in
Colombia in 1957, in Venezuela in 1958. It seemed reasonable to
hope that Chile, Costa Rica and Uruguay would no longer be small
oases of liberty in a vast authoritarian desert.

BACKWARD

It seemed reasonable, but it did not come about. At the mid-1970s,
the Latin American outlook for free institutions was bleak. Imitation
was, as usual, taking its toll. Latin America was part of a new entity,
the Third World, which was forming in the minds of many. Latin
Americans should act no differently from Africans, Middle
Easterners, Asians — most of them quick to discard any trace of free
institutions, to replace citizens' government with dictatorial rule, to
make ideas and the economy state monopolies.

The outlook was bleak, not so much because of political events
which did not differ from previous ones (conspiracies, *golpes* or
military *coups d'état*, insurgencies, revolts), but because of what the
citizens expressed when they were free to do so. In Brazil and the
Argentine (with Mexico, by far the most important countries of
Latin America) *integralismo* and *justicialismo*, organised in the
1930s and 1940s and led by Vargas and Perón respectively, were
Latin American manifestations of the world-wide national-socialist
movement (both closer to Italian fascism than to German nazism).
When the tide of war turned against the Axis powers, Vargas resigned.
As a result there were free elections in 1945 and in 1950. Vargas's
candidate in 1945, and Vargas himself in 1950, were elected with
about 50 per cent of the votes. After Vargas's death, throughout ten
years of liberal constitutionalism and free elections, most votes went
to the two parties derived from the dictatorial *integralista* party. The
liberals, organised in the Democratic National Union, and led by
Lacerda, remained a small even if at times influential minority. In
the Argentine a military *golpe* overthrew Perón in 1955, but during
eleven years of liberal constitutionalism and free elections

justicialismo remained the major political force, strong enough to paralyse governments headed by Frondizi and other leaders of the liberal Radical party. The military dictatorship established in the Argentine in 1966 held free elections in 1973; two-thirds of the votes went to the Presidential candidate designated by Perón, then an exile. Shortly after, Perón returned to a triumphant reception. He, and after his death his widow, ran the country amid growing government inefficiency. In 1976 the military again took over; the personnel changed, but not the institutional structure.

In Uruguay, the aspirations of liberal *battleismo* proved to exceed the endurance of the nation. Specifically, the economy collapsed, unable to support an all-embracing generous social-security system. In Chile, liberal democracy opened the road to power first to the catholic Christian Democratic party, which respected the democratic process, then to a coalition centred on the Socialist party, whose position was of the Marxist—Lassalleian centrist variety (p. 149): elections, not violence, to attain power; once in power, 'irreversibility' (as Allende stated in 1970), i.e. disregard of the democratic process. There was government paralysis in both Uruguay and Chile; it provided the military with opportunity to establish their dictatorial rule in 1972 and 1973 respectively. In Cuba, Castro — leader of victorious anti-fascist insurgents in 1959 — faced the choice that other revolutionary leaders, Lenin in 1918 and Mussolini in 1924, had faced after seizure of power: whether to respect the democratic process and accept the fact that the opposition had majority support, or crush the opposition by establishing dictatorial rule. Castro took longer to make his choice than Lenin, a little less long than Mussolini. Finally he opted for the easy dictatorial road, justifying his choice by proclaiming his conversion to communism. In Peru, the minority government of the moderate Belaunde was swept away by social-nationalist officers in 1968. A military *golpe* also ended, in 1963, the brief tenure of the progressive Bosch as President of the Dominican republic (as a result he switched from liberal progressivism to socialist authoritarianism). In Mexico, the one-party authoritarian regime established in the 1920s remained solidly entrenched; a small measure of political liberty, the organisation of impotent opposition groups, and the failure of attempts at rural and urban guerrilla warfare, were evidence of the support the regime enjoyed among the population.

At the mid-1970s there were only three exceptions to dominant authoritarianism in Latin America. Oscillating between moderatism and progressivism, liberal democracy survived in Costa Rica, where the Unification party tended to moderatism, while the Liberation party moved to a social-democratic position. In Venezuela the brief constitutional experiment of 1945—8, under the leadership of Betancourt, had been revived after the overthrow of a military dictatorship in 1958. It survived the internal and external attacks of authoritarian radicals and anarcho-communists, who — with the help of the Cuban dictatorship — made Venezuela their main target in the 1960s. The liberal progressive Democratic Action party, back in power in 1974 after a Christian democratic interlude, pursued social policies that enabled the Venezuelan nation to become, instead of one of the most backward, one of the most advanced in Latin America. In Colombia, after the defeat in the civil war that followed the assassination of its progressive leader Gaitán in 1948, the Liberal party was instrumental in re-establishing a constitutional regime in 1957. Although less progressive than its Venezuelan counterpart, it did guarantee the basic liberties essential to the nation's further advancement. The Liberal Lopez Michelsen who had followed in the footsteps of Gaitán, was elected President of Colombia in 1974.

Regardless of ethnic and class distinctions, the majority of politically conscious citizens among the three hundred million or so inhabitants of Latin American states (and of some Caribbean former colonial dependencies which have recently become independent) prefer dictatorship to democratic self-government. Since independence, conflicts have been primarily between antagonistic authoritarian forces. During the last fifty years, on one side there have been the traditionalists who still monopolise power in a majority of republics, from gigantic Brazil to tiny El Salvador; on the other side have been those whose position is centred on authoritarian, or even totalitarian, nationalism, and on command economies controlled by the nationalists. The convergence of national-socialist and national-communist movements (see p. 129) since the late 1950s is one of the chief features of the contemporary Latin American scene. Argentinian Peronistas, Brazilian *integralistas* and Castroites were all together on the authoritarian side of the political fence, together with the Peruvian and Panamanian military dictatorships and the less extremist one-party regime in Mexico. Varying in the opposition to traditional authoritarianism, they were equally committed to opposing free institutions.

There are some liberals in most republics and in the commonwealth of Puerto Rico. In general, they represent a weak political force. All they can do (together with revisionist socialists, of whom there are still fewer) is to use every possible opportunity to try to establish free institutions. When attempts fail, and dictatorships of one kind or another are re-established, there is nothing left to do but to try again.

'ORIENTAL DESPOTISM' IN EASTERN CIVILISATIONS

Through a common heritage shared until the beginning of the modern era, and through contacts at times difficult and rare but never completely interrupted, links have existed between Western progressive nations and Latin American peoples among whom archaic forms of Western civilisation prevailed. Thanks to these links, liberalism and everything pertaining to it could, even if at times with difficulty, be understood (and then accepted or rejected). But there were no links with peoples inhabiting eastern empires five to ten generations ago, before the empires were subjected to pressure from Western states, and peoples felt the disrupting and upsetting influence of Western dynamism.

Each major empire (Russian, Chinese, Ottoman, Persian, Mogul, Japanese) was the home of a different form of civilisation. Gods and rituals differed, as did class relationships, family structures, educational curricula (but not educational methods), art forms, literary activities, manners, modes of dressing and eating. All, however, had in common five identical features as foundation of a strongly entrenched static social order: autocratic absolutism, rigid conformism, strict communalism, subjection of the masses supplying labour and food, and inefficient agricultural techniques. The arbitrariness, repressiveness and recurrent waves of cruelty when stability was threatened, implicit in the time-honoured expression 'oriental despotism', applied to all.

Taking liberty as a criterion, however great the differences (as great for instance as those between Bolivian and Cambodian dictatorships today) eastern civilisations were variations of the same authoritarian species. Absent were concepts and values related to individual autonomy and responsibility, to spontaneity, originality, right to dissent; absent also were concepts and values related to self-government, and to peaceful coexistence on a footing of equality of groups differing not only in functions and in goals, but also in ways of thinking and living. After the first contact with Western carriers of new ideas and values, the curiosity of a few was squelched by the revulsion of the many. Later, when contacts increased, most people at all levels of education and responsibility found free-wheeling Western ways of life repellent. Resented generally were the greater wealth and power of Western progressive nations, their economic and cultural penetration, their political superiority — resented specifically was everything pertaining to liberal ideas, values and institutions. In some cases (Russian rulers intermittently since the early eighteenth century, Ottoman rulers also intermittently between 1839 and 1913, Japanese rulers since the 1860s, Chinese rulers feebly in the 1890s, decidedly after 1949, and Iranian rulers in the post-1945 period) efforts were made to use Western technology while keeping out the concepts, values and institutions from which the technology had resulted. In much of the area covered by these empires (post-1919 Turkey, post-1945 Japan and India the main exceptions) revulsion and resentment are now even stronger and more widespread than they were early in the century.

At times as a result of decisions taken by rulers, but more often of pressure exerted by outside forces, and in two instances of the initiative taken by small progressive revolutionary groups, stagnation began to be disturbed on a scale large enough to lead to change: in the Russian empire around 1700, in what had been the Mogul empire in the 1760s, in the Ottoman empire in the 1830s, in China in the 1840s, in Japan in the 1860s, in Persia around 1900. However (as in most of Latin America) the breakdown of traditional authoritarianism did not imply a popular surge in favour of freer institutions and a freer way of life. It simply opened the door to a new, more efficient (and thus more coercive) authoritarianism which satisfied the general desire for quiet and stability.

RUSSIA'S CLOSED SOCIETY

Since the last years of the seventeenth century, fair numbers of Westerners went to Russia as envoys, teachers, merchants, artisans, craftsmen, or simply as visitors. A small minority among educated Russians learned about Western, particularly German and French, ideas and ways. Peoples of Western civilisation, first the Balts, then most Poles, the Finns, some Swedes, were incorporated in the Russian empire between 1721 and 1815. From Peter the Great on, czars and their ministers at times followed policies patterned on Western ones. They did not want Western values to corrupt Russian subjects and to weaken the hold of autocratic absolutism and orthodox conformism, but they did want Western efficiency and, above all, technology.

After the middle of the eighteenth century there were masonic lodges in Russia which acted as centres for the diffusion of ideas of the Enlightenment, and later of the French revolutionary slogan *liberté, égalité, fraternité*. Between 1799 and 1814 Russian troops fought in central Europe, even occupying Paris, and many officers were impressed by what they saw. Imitating what was done in post-Napoleonic Europe, officers in garrisons abroad, officers and civilian friends with liberal leanings at home, organised secret societies (none numbering more than a few hundred members). Liberal conspirators even tried a *coup d'état* against autocratic rule in 1825. Still, Western influence, through diffusion of basic concepts and values and imitation of Western ways, was limited. The Russian way of life remained distinct and unique. When the efficient autocrat Nicholas I died in 1855, there were individuals inclined towards liberalism in Russia but there was no liberal movement.

THE RUSSIAN 'THAW' OF THE 1860s

A new situation came about in the 1860s, initiated by the czar himself. Alexander II, not a liberal but somewhat tolerant, compassionate and open to new ideas, adopted a partial imitation of progressive Western ways as a solution to the problem of strengthening the Russian state, defeated in the Crimean war.

Representative institutions, constitutional guarantees and the free market had made Great Britain the premier state in the world: just a touch of the institutions and the guarantees, and the partial freeing of the market, might help Russia without endangering the autocracy. Starting with the relaxation of censorship and police repression in the late 1850s, continuing with the reform of legal institutions, the emancipation of serfs in 1861, the increase in the number of schools, the creation of provincial (1864) and municipal (1870) boards and councils entrusted with some functions (the *zemstvos*), there was a liberalisation from above which made for a new climate.

To use an expression current in the 1950s in relation to the Soviet scene, there was a 'thaw' in the Russia of the 1860s — i.e. less coercion. Those Russians who took advantage of the thaw went in various directions. There were articulate and sophisticated champions of traditional autocracy, and nationalists fired by the conviction that God or history or something else had entrusted the Russian people with an all-important mission. There were radicals (ideologically close to what will be the New Left in liberal democracies of the 1960s and 1970s), combining communalism (with or without collectivism) and anarchism in varying measure, some totally pacifist, others advocating violence and practicing terrorism. Liberal ideas appealed to members of the military and civilian bureaucracy, of the nobility (the novelist Turgenev was the best known and the most influential), of professional classes. Spokesmen for ethnic and religious minorities made their voices heard. Compared with the dynamism and variety in English-speaking and continental nations, it was not much — but starting from total inactivity even a little movement is a great deal. Liberals belonging to the establishment could use channels opened by the reforms of Alexander II: the *zemstvos* became hotbeds of liberalism.

1917: THE TRAGIC FAILURE OF LIBERALISM

The thaw of the 1860s ended when authorities decided that repression was needed to curb radicalism. Radicals went underground, while liberals continued to operate prudently wherever they could. Taking advantage of a minor thaw, in 1903 liberal-minded members of the *zemstvos* and their friends formed their own organisation, the Union of Liberation. When defeats inflicted by Japan in the war of 1904–5 led to a deeper crisis than the Crimean war had caused half a century earlier, the Union was instrumental in inducing the well-meaning but weak Nicholas II to replace autocracy with semi-constitutional rule. Given the background, elections which were partially free, political parties, a nearly independent and highly respected judiciary, some independence of the press and some freedom of movement, were more of a radical innovation in Russia than they had been in France four generations earlier. In 1905 the institutional structure of Russia loosened through a genuine progressive revolution.

The liberals divided. The moderate Octobrists, followers of Guchkov and Rodzianko, satisfied with the limited constitutionalism of the October 1905 Manifesto, went their own way. For the Constitutional Democrats or Kadets whose main spokesmen were, among others, Maklakov, Miliukov, Petrunkevich, Struve, Tyrkova, limited constitutionalism was only a meagre beginning. The division between Octobrists and Kadets was a disaster, because liberals were few, most Russians of all classes were loyal to the autocracy, and authoritarian and anarchic radicals opposing autocracy were numerous and deeply committed.

In the elections of 1906, 1907 and 1912, first the Kadets and then the Octobrists elected a plurality of deputies. During the First World War these two groups and smaller ones formed a parliamentary Progressive Bloc. The general consent of experts in Russia and abroad was that liberals would soon take over the government in Russia, and that the world's largest and potentially most powerful and wealthiest state would join the then growing number of nations organised along liberal-constitutional and liberal-democratic lines.

The events of March 1917 seemed to bear out the experts' predictions. Unplanned agitation in Petrograd, and soon in other major Russian cities, became a revolution when soldiers and sailors joined the demonstrators. Leaders of the Progressive Bloc organised a provisional government, headed by Lvov and formed at first by progressive and moderate liberals and a revisionist socialist. Moderates soon dropped out, and the provisional government underwent several reorganisations as a coalition of progressive liberals, anti-authoritarian (but not necessarily revisionist) socialists and non-party experts.

The liberals' success proved ephemeral. Two major developments occurred. Acting on the basis of their convictions and of a tradition to which they felt ideologically close (French events of 1793, 1830, 1848 and 1871, and the short-lived Russian soviets of 1905), the Petrograd leaders of the two largest socialist movements, Mensheviks and Socialist Revolutionaries (S.R.s), organised a council or soviet supposedly representative of working people, and acting as a counter-parliament. What little authority could be exercised in a period of revolutionary upheaval was divided. The second development was the widespread insurgency of industrial wage-earners in the cities, accompanied by mutinies in the armed forces, and soon followed by revolts of the peasantry in the countryside. Insurgencies, mutinies and revolts caused the Russian state to disintegrate.

The obtuseness of members of the provisional government and anti-authoritarian soviet leaders, and the political ability of Bolsheviks, are commonplaces. In fact, Miliukov, Kerensky, Chkheidze, Chernov on one side, Lenin and his right-hand man Trotsky on the other, were all intelligent people. As is usual in times of crisis, each simply acted on the basis of his own convictions, Miliukov giving priority to political reforms and to the war against imperialist Germany, Kerensky deferring to a constituent assembly to be elected as soon as feasible, Chkheidze and Chernov trying to make the soviets the sole repository of authority, Lenin and Trotsky exploiting every opportunity to set up the Bolsheviks' autocratic rule. These were the things about which they had been thinking and writing, for which they had waited for years.

Liberals, divided between progressives and moderates and influenced by nationalism, and anti-authoritarian socialists divided into antagonistic factions, lacked the cohesion of disciplined organisation indispensable for political success — especially during a crisis. Instead, the small but highly disciplined party of committed Bolsheviks found in the growing chaos the opportunity to seize power and to restructure Russia as a totalitarian one-party state. For Lenin and all Bolsheviks (from 1918 on, communists), heeding 1860s nihilists and Marxism's co-founder Engels, liberalism was the main enemy. Censorship, abolished by the provisional government, was re-established a few days after the November coup d'état, and a powerful secret police, the cheka, was organised in the middle of December, primarily to deal with the liberal opposition labelled as 'czarist reaction'. The terror of 1918—22 began in January 1918 with the murder of Shingariov and Kokoshkin, two prominent liberals and former members of the provisional government. Force had to be fought with force; the liberals Vasilenko, Krym, Pepeliaev (later assasinated) were prime ministers in provisional governments in the Ukraine, Crimea and

Siberia; Astrov and Struve were in the southern Special Council whose armed forces held until the end of 1920; Dolgorukov was not the only one who returned clandestinely from exile to organise a democratic underground, and was executed.

In the course of the terror, the civil war and the accompanying famine, five to six million people died. As many as were able (possibly three million) fled abroad. Among these millions were almost all the Russian liberals. An idea dies when those who carry it in their minds die; in Russia, liberalism ended. Sakharov and the small band of liberal and near-liberal dissidents of the 1970s are voices crying in the wilderness.

Leninists maintained that capitalism was their enemy. Aside from the advantages and disadvantages of rigid state capitalism in a command economy (called 'collectivism') versus ever-changing private capitalism in a market economy, Leninist communists once, and all national-communists and national-socialists today, reject even more than a market or mixed economy the freedom of conscience with which liberalism began (see Chapter 3), the freedom of expression, which is liberalism's first liberty, self-government, which is liberalism's basic institution. Lenin's totalitarian one-party state was a return to the norm of authoritarian societies. What happened in Russia two generations ago affects the world today as much as what happened fifteen centuries ago in the Greco-Roman empire affected Mediterranean peoples.

TURKISH PROGRESSIVISM

On the eve of the period of liberal ascendance, autocratic Russia had been Europe's only neighbour in the north-east, and the vast, slightly more populous, autocratic Ottoman empire — stretching at the time of its greatest expansion from the Sudan to Poland and from Morocco to Persia — the only neighbour in the south-east. It had been ruled by Turks and Turk-assimilated people, but present-day Turkey is just one of over a score of successor states into which the empire splintered. In the mid-1970s two of the successor states had liberal-democratic regimes and three were governed by authoritarian traditionalists. Fifteen were radical dictatorships ruled despotically with varying degrees of efficiency (or, rather, inefficiency) by national-communists of Soviet or other persuasion in Europe, by social-nationalists and national-socialists in Asia and Africa. Turkey is a case apart: the first example of a nation in which officers seized power and used that power for emancipation of the people from traditional or other authoritarianism, without coercing them to accept a new authoritarianism. As a case apart, Turkey is often included culturally in the

Western area, instead of in the Middle East, to which the state belongs historically and geographically.

Military defeats, financial difficulties and the expansionist aims of powerful foreign states induced some Ottoman leaders, from Reshid in the late 1830s to Midhat forty years later, to introduce Western-type innovations. These were primarily in the civilian and military organisation but also in the economy and in education. The aim was to strengthen the empire. The climax of these efforts, deeply resented by the traditionalist majority of the ruling classes and by the masses, was the short-lived liberal constitution of 1876. Midhat paid with his life for his efforts at reform.

With little or no attention given to what was going on in the small circle surrounding the autocrat, contacts with the outside world had multiplied. Because of the government's concern with the efficiency of the armed forces (wars against neighbours and insurgents were frequent), officers, trained abroad or at home by foreign instructors, acquired the status of a highly educated elite. During the first decade of the twentieth century, progressive officers formed clandestine societies, and opted ideologically for a version of national liberalism attuned to Turkish culture. Their position was close to that of distinguished civilians such as Kiamil and Talaat.

Niazi, the most dynamic of the progressive officers, organised the military coup which in 1908 overthrew the autocracy. A major bastion of 'oriental despotism' had fallen. Kiamil was Prime Minister, and liberal expectations were great. But before long the small band of reformers divided; liberals were swept aside by nationalists pursuing imperialist goals by dictatorial means.

The defeats suffered by Ottoman troops in 1917—18, the flight of national imperialists who had governed the country during the war, the collapse of the empire and ensuing political chaos, the end of the caliphate and weakening of cohesion among traditionalists and the post-1919 rivalries among the victorious Allies enabled a faction of nationalist but not imperialist officers who had participated in the revolution of 1908 to establish the Turkish republic in 1919—22.

Organised in a People's party led by Kemal, Ismet and Bayar, the republicans tried — despite the opposition of the traditionalist majority of the population — to provide the Turks with a parliament, with elections which at times were free, civil rights, a responsible judiciary, a bureaucracy of efficient and honest officials, and secular education. In order to end the subjection of women, polygamy was abolished, public education made available to girls, equal voting rights were given. A mercantilist economy with a planned public sector and a state-controlled private sector was criticised — and somewhat loosened — by those who organised the Liberal Republican party led by Fethi in 1930, the Democratic party led by Bayar in 1946, the Justice party led by Demirel in 1961. Most post-1946 elections were won by the Democratic and Justice parties.

For more than half a century periods of relative liberty (and considerable tension) have alternated with periods of military rule (most recently in 1960–1 and again in 1971). After the Second World War authoritarian radicals added their opposition to that of the traditionalists. Guidance, however progressive, is not compatible with liberal spontaneity. Nevertheless, Turkish guided democracy has been different in kind from the guided democracy of Brazil in 1930–45 and of Indonesia in 1949–65. There, guided democracy was another term for Leninist 'democratic centralism' — for dictatorship as the permanent organisation of society. In Turkey the goal was originally, and has remained ever since, responsible government of free citizens. At the mid-1970s the goal was not as distant as it had been in 1922.

Smallest of the autocratic empires in the Eurasian land mass, Persia (Iran since 1935) — the France of the Middle East — had had a far longer and more splendid past than the Ottoman and Russian empires. Dynasties had come and gone, but at the middle of the nineteenth century Persians did not doubt the legitimacy of their autocratic king of kings any more than it had been doubted when, in the eyes of ancient Greeks, Darius and Xerxes were the personification of 'oriental despotism'. The present, however, was squalid. A small group of progressive Persians, some educated in Europe, all admirers of Western ways and institutions, carried out a successful revolt in 1906. There ensued a constitution, a parliament, elections, some freedom of the press, some reforms of the administration, some economic improvement; but there was no movement strong enough to support the reformers, who were hated by traditionalists and undermined by factions siding with this or that foreign power. Prominent figures like Nasir ul-Mulk and Sayyid Zia were at best national liberals, their authoritarian nationalism prevailing over liberal convictions. In 1921 a soldier of fortune, Reza Khan Pahlavi, seized power and quickly put an end to the constitutional experiment.

THE 'CLOSED' CONTINENT CLOSES AGAIN

In China two minor wars, waged by European powers righteously pursuing the wrong goal of international free trade, compelled the Chinese authorities (apparently ignorant of what was happening outside their borders) to open the boundaries of the vast state occupying the 'closed' continent, controlling vast, thinly populated (except in the south-east) dependencies and separated from the rest of the world by mountains, oceans and deserts. It was a traumatic experience for a nation believing itself superior to all others, and for a government which for 400 years had deliberately cut its subjects off from contact with foreigners.

Many Europeans and Americans went to China to trade, and many also to teach and preach. A few Chinese from the educated and well-to-do elite were sent abroad to learn about foreign ways, while the uneducated migrated in their hundreds of thousands near and far, not to settle in foreign lands but to return wealthy to their homes. In 1896, the middle-aged scholar Yen Fu began to publish Chinese translations of the works of Huxley, then those of Mill and Spencer; others followed suit with more translations. Foremost among them was Liang Ch'i-ch'ao (known also as Jen-kung), who wrote copiously, popularised British and French ideas, considered himself liberal, and became the central figure in a group of young people committed to the transformation of the Chinese state and society along liberal lines: freedom of expression, self-government, market economy. The fact that there was no word in the Chinese vocabulary to render the concept of liberty as individual autonomy and capacity for choice is indicative of the difficulties reformers had in formulating their positions.

A regent, more aware of events in the outside world than other members of the ruling clique, showed a leaning towards changes patterned on those taking place in Japan, but he was dismissed in a palace *coup* in 1881. In the 1890s a few high officials (among them Yuan Shih-k'ai and K'ang Yu-wei, whom Liang considered his mentor) suggested reforms along liberal-constitutional lines. There was even a 'hundred days of reforms' in 1898. It ended in another palace *coup*, when courtiers, firmly committed to traditional despotism and conformism, seized the emperor and banned the reformers. Soon after the dawn of the 20th century, in exile or in new industrial cities and distant districts not easily controlled by the central government, the small band of reformers among the educated elite organised societies advocating constitutionalism. With or without permission of the authorities, several thousand young people went abroad to study, particularly to Japan, the United States, and Germany.

K'ang, Liang and Chang Chih-tung, whose main field of interest was the reform of the educational system, may be described as moderate liberals. (It is reported that their writings were avidly read by young Mao Tse-tung and his friends.) Among progressive liberals then was Sun Yat-sen, who in 1905 organised the Combined League Society advocating the establishment of a liberal-democratic republic. The republic came into existence — formally at least — in 1911, as the result of insurgencies in which Yuan played a major role. For liberals everywhere, unaware that insurgencies were mainly xenophobic explosions of anti-Manchu hatred, the downfall of the most perfect form of 'oriental despotism' was an astounding event and a great success.

After 1911 and until 1924, dynamism compensated for smallness of numbers among advocates of reforms. Liang returned from exile and established the Chin-pu Tang or Constitutional party. Back from exile likewise, Sun founded the Kuo Min Tang or Nationalist party. In newly established literary societies, and in schools and universities set up and financed mainly by Americans, political ideas and policies were being discussed: nationalism, liberal constitutionalism, democracy, socialism, anarchism, and their conceptual frameworks from positivism to idealism, from dialectical materialism to voluntarism. The young writer Lin Yutang distinguished himself as an upholder of liberal ideas.

While intellectuals discussed, and all sorts of groups came into existence, merged, disintegrated, faded away, the state was collapsing. Officials left over from the previous regime had little authority, new officials were incompetent. Local leaders became *de facto* independent rulers. Under the guidance of Soviet agents, Sun's Nationalist party was reorganised in 1924. A clique of officers trained by German and Russian instructors took over the leadership of the Nationalist party after Sun died in 1925. Their first aim was to re-establish the unity of the country. All pretences at constitutional reforms and democratic process were swept away. The attempt to emancipate the Chinese from absolutism and dogmatism had lasted about as long as in Persia, and with the same negligible results. There were, however, economic achievements of foreign and Chinese entrepreneurs: factories, roads and railways, a growing number of skilled industrial workers, of competent technicians, of able executives.

The major event in Chinese life after 1925 was the division within the authoritarian Nationalist party between two main factions, and the civil war they waged against each other from 1927 to 1949 — a civil war complicated by the occupation of large sections of the country by the Japanese between 1931 and 1945, and by involvement in the Second World War. In terms of the times, one faction of the Nationalist party was close to the national-socialist or fascist position. It remained dominant until 1947. The other faction leaned towards the Communist party organised in 1921, and was finally absorbed by it. In 1947 the communists (or, more accurately, the national-communists, who combined Trotsky's confused concept of permanent revolution with Stalin's clear-headed ruthlessness) suffered their last defeat. Two years later they achieved total victory. By means of recurrent waves of terrorism in the late 1950s, all traces of liberal ideas and aspiration were eliminated from the Chinese nation as effectively as it had been done in Russia thirty years earlier. Totally authoritarian and totally conformist, ethically and intellectually at a higher level than ever before, Chinese society was again a closed society. After nearly four decades of bloody turmoil, the overwhelming majority of the Chinese felt immensely relieved.

JAPAN: A QUESTION MARK FOR LIBERALS

Of the Eurasian autocratic empires, feudal Japan had seemed the least promising for intellectual innovation and political emancipation when, soon after the middle of the nineteenth century, and under coercion, rulers gave in to the pressure exerted by Western powers and abandoned the policy of complete isolation deliberately pursued for over two centuries. However, just one generation later, by the late 1880s, Japan had become a promising candidate for joining the expanding number of liberal-constitutional states.

For Westerners who — as is normally, and wrongly, done — evaluated others on the basis of their own experiences, feudalism meant the Dark Ages, a lower cultural level than that attained in Europe during the age of centralised absolutism. It was not realised that feudalism as decentralised despotism, in which to the hierarchy of those who cultivated, managed and owned agricultural land, corresponded the hierarchy of peasants, vassals and great nobles, and in which sovereignty was divided among hundreds of nobles and (as was the case in Japan and had been in Europe) twin central authorities, provided possibilities for innovation which did not exist in highly centralised bureaucratic autocracies. Also it was not known that the system of ideas and values within which operated the minds of educated Japanese, closely related to the loose beliefs of the national religion, lacked the precision and therefore the rigidity of traditional systems of thought in other autocracies.

Whatever may have been the role of a decentralised institutional system and an unsystematic way of thinking, the fact is that in the wake of the 1853 American show of force, members of the political and intellectual elite deliberately decided that imitation was the road to survival. They were numerous enough to form a faction bent on modernising (within limits) Japan so that it might withstand the impact of Western dynamism. By 1868 that faction had defeated the traditionalists and was in control of the state. Thirteen years later, advocates of liberal constitutionalism organised a right-of-centre moderate party and a left-of-centre progressive one (symbolically, and approximately, corresponding to the two-party systems in the major English-speaking nations).

The first elections in Japanese history took place in 1890, the year following the granting of a constitution. The franchise was as restricted as it had been in Great Britain before 1832, but the fact of having elections and an assembly whose members discussed freely was a tremendous step towards emancipation. For about forty years the voters, more and more of them as the franchise was extended, had some voice in running public affairs. During that period the executive was not controlled by elected representatives or officials as in Great Britain, France, and the United States, but some participation in the government process there was.

No one knows to what extent office-holders (from Okuma and Itagaki in the 1890s to Wakatsuki and Inukai in the early 1930s, just before the establishment of a military dictatorship with fascist overtones), and millions of Japanese who joined parties and voted, were committed to liberalism, constitutional or democratic. Discipline continued to be a major feature of the homogeneous Japanese nation: the liberalisation of political institutions, the alteration in the status of various classes, the transformation of the economy, the establishment of a modern educational system, all had been wanted by the reformist wing of the oligarchy. People responded to decisions taken by a small ruling group; they had not asked for a transfer of power from the few to the many. There had been Japanese sincerely committed to the ideas and values of a society of free and equal citizens; for instance, at the end of the nineteenth century Nakamura, Fukuzawa, and later Tatsukichi Minobe. From 1889 to 1932 there had been a liberal-constitutional structure, dominated by an efficient, dynamic and forward-looking oligarchy. Beyond that, the rest is speculation.

Three decades after the end of the Second World War, any assessment of the solidity of free institutions in Japan is also speculation. The liberal-democratic structure is there — it functions. The executive is responsible to the majority of a parliament of freely elected representatives of the citizens. There is freedom of expression and of association. There is a mixed market economy leaning towards welfarism, and, in practice more than in law, a fair degree of security of tenure for employees. There is self-government at all levels. There are universal public education, good secondary schools, plenty of institutions of higher learning, excellent research centres.

The structure was not the work of the Japanese. It had been wanted by the Americans who occupied the island empire in 1945, and ruled it autocratically and efficiently for several years. Within that structure there was a radical transformation in the way of life — from family relationships to religious beliefs. The economic expansion which turned a small country without natural resources and, at the start, with little capital, into the third-ranking industrial power in the world is a manifestation of the transformation. In the late 1970s, Japanese are as different from all other Asians east of the Dead Sea as Israelis are from all other inhabitants of the Middle East.

At the instigation of the American occupiers, the two major pre-1932 political parties were revived. The Seiyukai became the Liberal party, decidedly moderate, and the Minseito became the Democratic party, dubiously progressive. In 1955 they merged as the Liberal Democratic party, and during the following twenty years received a majority of votes. The presence of genuine opposition parties, and the activity of extra-parliamentary groups, from passionate nation-alists to anarcho-communists, show that political emancipation has been real. Politically and economically, Japan had joined the liberal-democratic world. The way in which the Japanese will respond to major internal and external crises will show whether they belong to that world intellectually and emotionally.

INDIANS TRY LIBERAL DEMOCRACY

Emancipation from moslem rule (which in some sections of the Indian subcontinent had lasted more than 800 years) in the second half of the eighteenth century meant expanding freedom of expres-sion for the hindu majority in India, and some freedom of action. Between 1764 and 1818 British rule replaced moslem rule in most of the predominantly hindu areas; elsewhere hindu and moslem monarchs were no longer able to tyrannise over their subjects and wage war. British coercion was restricted by parliamentary supervision at home, by the control increasingly exercised through the press by public opinion in Great Britain and in India, and by militant co-operation between Britons (including high officials of the Indian civil service) and Indian opponents of British rule. Relatively secure, and able to formulate their own ideas and to express them (particularly when studying in Great Britain, as many did), the Indians' awareness of their distinctive identity deepened.

For progressive Indians, liberalism was less of a foreign import than it was for subjects of Eurasian autocratic empires. Authoritarian features in the Indian way of life did not lack, from castes and hereditary monarchical rule to the subjection of women and a rigid family structure. There were also non-authoritarian elements. Self-government was practiced, however limitedly, at the local community level in many areas of the subcontinent, through *panchayats* elected by most, and at times by all, adults. In the absence of the long and difficult process which in the West has led to the concept of the dignity of the individual, there were widespread respect and compassion for the individual. Whatever the legalities, the Indian tried to achieve economic independence through his own efforts, and he was entitled to enjoy the fruits of his own labour. Whatever theologians said to the contrary, in practice hinduism was polytheism and, notwithstanding occasional flare-ups of religious fanaticism, worshippers of different gods in the hindu pantheon tended, if not to respect one another (which they usually did) at least to leave one another alone.

Among the hindu majority there was a good deal of tolerance in a varied, complex and pluralistic society. In the eyes of the majority, arbitrariness, conformism, intolerance and cruelty characterised the way of life of the moslem overlords, not theirs. After elimination of the last important residue of moslem control in 1857, British liberals never doubted that India would one day be independent, and that Indians would govern themselves through free institutions. This was the gist of statements made during the parliamentary debate on the 1858 India Bill, and of arguments causing British governments led by the Liberals Asquith and Lloyd George to put forth, and parliamentary majorities to approve, the Indian Council Act of 1909 and the Government of India Act of 1919. The latter created an Indian Parliament and provincial legislative councils, two-thirds of which was to be composed of freely elected representatives.

Banerjee, Gokhale, and others who founded the Indian Association in 1876 and the National Congress in 1885 were in a position not unlike that of North American patriots one hundred years earlier, and of most Latin American patriots two generations earlier. They wanted greater autonomy first, then outright independence. They were also committed to giving independent India citizens' self-government and an improved version of other free institutions which, even if first evolved in Great Britain, in India were Indian and not British.

Tilak, Motilal Nehru, Mohandas Gandhi of the next generation, were primarily nationalists, but they agreed that independent India would be a liberal democracy pursuing progressive goals by means of social reforms and a mixed economy. Authoritarian traditionalists were numerous in all classes of the population. After the First World War there were active and at times influential advocates of national-communist and (until 1945, with the support of Axis and Japanese dictatorships) national-socialist radicalism; but when independence came in 1947, and even more in 1949 with the enactment of a republican constitution, India was structured as a federal liberal democracy.

The Indian majority party, the National Congress, was a coalition in which for several decades national liberals, both moderate and progressive, collaborated with revisionist socialists, and also with confessional conservatives and other groups which were neither

liberal nor socialist. In 1958, liberals — mostly moderates, with a
small progressive wing — who had co-operated for decades with
Mohandas Gandhi and Jawaharlal Nehru, but inclined less than the
majority of the National Congress towards passionate nationalism,
sometimes veering (for instance in relation to Kashmir) towards
imperialism, and thought further expansion of the public sector of
the economy unwise, formed the small but influential Swatantra
party. Its leader was Rajagopalachari, heir to Gokhale's position. In
early 1977, led by Mody, the Swatantra party (merged in the Janata
or People's Party) was dedicated to democracy as the organisation of
individual liberties, to respect for the many ethnic–cultural groups into
which the population was divided, to local self-government, to education as the development of the autonomous personality, and also to a
market economy and diffusion of property through peasant ownership of land, increase in the number of shareholders in private and
semi-private corporations, and increase in the number of independent
artisans. Led by Patel and Desai, 1969 secessionists from the National
Congress organised in 1977 the anti-authoritarian People's party.
Specifically concerned with the fate of peoples with distinct
cultural identity, leaders of minorities (for instance the Tamil
Karunanidhi) were committed supporters of federal democratic
republicanism. There were several groups of socialists: authoritarian
Leninists, Marxist-Leninists, and Maoists prevailed numerically, but
higher in prestige and political influence from 1947 to 1977 were
liberal socialists, deeply committed to humanism as respect for the
individual's dignity, and to humanitarianism as action to help the
needy (in India perhaps a larger section of the population than in any
other major nation).

In 1975, the Prime Minister and leader of the National Congress,
Indira Gandhi (daughter of J. Nehru and no relation to Mohandas
Gandhi) found herself in the position described earlier in relation to
the Cuban Castro (see p. 160). Opposition was growing, and the
moment came when a choice had to be made between acting democratically and resigning, or acting dictatorially and ending the
democratic process. To the surprise of those acquainted with the
position held publicly and privately by Ms Gandhi during her father's
lifetime, with her repeated statements concerning India's debt to
liberal thought and the liberal tradition, with liberal socialists policies
pursued during her premiership, Ms Gandhi chose dictatorial rule.
Opposition leaders were arrested by the thousands; freedom of
communications media was first curbed and then suppressed; the
military establishment was strengthened and the judiciary deprived of
its independence; steps were taken to replace a partially efficient
market economy (through which considerable progress had been

made) with a largely inefficient command economy; close ties were established with the dictatorial Second World and with some of the more obnoxious dictatorships of the Third World. According to Ms Gandhi's supporters, dictatorial authority was needed to solve pressing socio-economic problems. There was a brief political lull, then opposition forces regrouped and gained ground. Like de Gaulle in 1968 and unlike Lenin in 1918, Ms Gandhi and her advisers decided to appeal to the people. Instead of harsher policies being adopted, emergency measures were rescinded and free elections held in March 1977. Having lost to the opposition Ms Gandhi resigned. The twenty-month authoritarian interlude may have been just that — an interlude. Liberal democracy had a new lease on life.

THE OTHER INDIES IN THE EAST

Outside the British-ruled empire of India, on the eve of the Second World War one could meet liberals and liberally inclined people in the one independent state (Thailand) and the many protectorates, semi-protectorates and colonies into which were divided the rest of the subcontinent and the vast continental and insular area to the east once known to Westerners as trans-Gangetic India — French-ruled Indo-China, Dutch-ruled East Indies, British-ruled Malaya, and so on. Today, liberals are few in the fifteen continental and island sovereign states (and the one minuscule protectorate) which occupy the same area, and are inhabited by nearly one-eighth of the world's population.

Peoples and cultures vary in the fifteen states — so, for the time being, do political structures. In the past there had been resistance to authoritarianism both native and foreign. There is little today. A Liberal party was active in Filipino politics when the archipelago was a self-governing commonwealth linked to the United States. It went underground during the 1942–4 Japanese occupation, and surfaced in the post-1945 period under the able leadership of Roxas as one of the two strongest parties in the nation. For two and a half decades after independence in 1946, it alternated in power with the Nationalist party. Fearful of losing the Presidential elections, in 1972 the Nationalist leader declared martial law, suspended the constitution and jailed Liberal leaders, among them the Presidential candidate senator Aquino. Impotent politically, the Liberal party nevertheless continued to be part of Filipino life.

In Thailand, the traditional authoritarian regime was replaced in 1932 with a liberal-constitutional one, as the result of the agitation of civilian and military members of the elite organised in a People's party. Constitutionalism found little support, the reformers divided, and a succession of *coups* and counter-*coups* ensued. The agitation

which in 1973 overthrew a dictatorial military faction had a wider
base and clearer purposes than that of 1932. The liberal Sanya
Dharmasakti headed a provisional government until free elections were
held early in 1975. After the elections, the country was at first
governed by a left-of-centre coalition led by progressive liberals, then
by a right-of-centre moderate coalition. Although wider, the popular
base was still insufficient; after a bare three years, generals and
admirals ended self-government.

When abandoning (under pressure, or sometimes of their own free
will) protectorates, semi-protectorates and colonies, efforts were
made by Western powers to effect a legitimate transition from colonial
administration to responsible constitutional government. It had been
done successfully in the Philippines, where constitutionalism lasted
twenty-seven years. In the mid-1970s, constitutional or semi-constitutional self-government continued in Malaysian states, and in Sri
Lanka (despite severe restrictions on freedom of the press); this was
partly the result of the presence of a fair number of citizens
committed to self-government, but more, perhaps, of the balance
between antagonistic racial or religious sections of the population.
Everywhere else intolerance, fanaticism and dogmatism prevailed,
and self-government was quickly replaced by dictatorial rule. In the
post-1945 period, events in that part of the world have been so
horrible that the word 'tragic' is inadequate to describe them: the
slaughter of half a million people and the desperate flight of as many
as fifteen million in and near the Punjab in 1947; the twenty-nine-year
war in Vietnam and the crimes committed by all parties involved; the
massacre of political opponents and members of ethnic minorities
(for a total, it was reported, of 300,000 people) in Indonesia in 1965;
massacres for which no estimates could be made in Bangladesh in
1971 and in Cambodia in 1975. Natural disasters compounded the
suffering. Whatever the events, and not counting India, there was no
liberty anywhere except, at the end of 1976, in two small nations;
the rest of the Indies had rejoined mankind's authoritarian main-
stream.

FROM THE EUPHRATES TO THE ORANGE RIVER: INDEPENDENCE AND DICTATORSHIP

With over a fifth of the planet's land area, an eighth of the population
and nearly half of the U.N. membership in 1977, at that date the
Arabian/African region was a desert where anything approaching
liberalism intellectually, ethically and politically was concerned.
Besides being an illiberal desert, the region had another major feature:
until recently it had been subjected to foreign powers. With the
exception of Moroccans and small communities of south-east Arabia,

Arabs had been Ottoman subjects from the early sixteenth century until emancipated (a few, in the western and central Arabian peninsula) by European powers victorious against the Turks, or brought under European administration between 1830 and 1920. Africans south of the Sahara, for periods varying from a few years, in the case of Ethiopians, to over a hundred in the case of southern African and Senegalese peoples (and, for longer periods, communities of small coastal enclaves), had at first been in part (in the Sudan and eastern Africa) subjects of Arab overlords, then, all of them, of European states. U.S.-sponsored Liberia was a case apart, but not as different as it appeared to be formally.

In four of the twenty states in which Arabic-speaking people form 70 to 100 per cent of the population, European powers, successors of Ottoman rule, made attempts to replace absolutism with constitutionalism — the first step, it was once taken for granted, towards developing a comprehensive system of free institutions, emancipating minds, loosening socio-economic structures. The response was mainly negative. The British, exercising over-all political control but usually respectful of cultural identity (except for what was then deemed ethically unacceptable, like slavery and torture), set up constitutional regimes in Egypt in 1883 and Iraq in 1924. As mandatory power, the French did likewise in Syria and Lebanon in 1930. Liberals were not numerous enough in these four countries to form a group of political consequence; also, they were not particularly strongly committed to holding their own against prevailing traditional authoritarianism and (from the 1930s on) expanding radical authoritarianism, actively helped before and during the Second World War by European national-socialists and after 1945 by national-communists as well. Prominent figures like the Egyptian Ali Maher, the Iraqi Nuri as-Said, the Lebanese Chamoun, sometimes described as 'liberals', were at best 'national liberals' with the emphasis on 'national'. There were ups and downs, periods of some liberty alternating with periods of none. Constitutionalism was finally obliterated in Syria in 1949, in Egypt in 1952, in Iraq in 1958, in Lebanon in 1975. The most distinguished Lebanese liberal, Charles Malik, statesman and educator, remained as nearly isolated in the Arab Middle East as Sakharov was in the Soviet Union. In Algeria, a small group of national liberals genuinely committed to free institutions, organised in the 1930s, gained influence when two of its members, Ferhat Abbas and Ben Khedda, headed a revolutionary government in exile in the 1950s. In the 1960s the group lost to Algerian social-nationalists.

In some of the twenty states there probably are individuals harbouring liberal ideas and aspirations, but they are few, and when old age and sickness take their toll are not replaced. In recurrent bitter conflicts among Arabs one authoritarian tendency fights another; there is no conflict between advocates and opponents of free institutions. There is one small enclave: Israel, which, with its unique culture, belongs politically to the progressive branch of Western civilisation. Labourism, deeply committed politically to liberal democracy, is the major ideological–political force; national liberal moderatism characterises a right-of-centre coalition which in the mid-seventies had the second-largest number of deputies. Against Israel, anti-semitism makes a united front of Second and Third World dictatorships and large minorities of the First World nations. For dictators near and far Israeli free institutions are a greater cause for resentment than is the Jewishness of the Israeli state.

To the south of Arab areas, German, Italian, Portuguese and Spanish colonial authorities ruled African dependencies autocratically. British, French and Belgian authorities followed policies founded basically on three principles derived from what was taken for granted at home: to administer with as little expenditure as possible; to leave to private initiative the function of developing the economy and social services; to interfere as little as possible with the ways of life of the many peoples and tribes (except, again, for what then seemed ethically unacceptable). During the two decades of devolution, British, French and Belgian authorities provided self-appointed leaders of the population of the various territories with blue-prints for setting up constitutional regimes, to which power was transferred when colonies, mandates and protectorates became independent states. Some constitutional regimes lasted several years, some only a few months.

During the early phase of devolution, African experts prophesied that within ten years from independence all African states would have regimes characterised by personal or one-party dictatorships, a high level of nationalist emotionalism with heavy racist overtones at times, state monopoly of communications media, strict supervision of educational and religious activities, command economies. The prophecy proved universally correct. Variations within the pattern have of course been considerable: there have been benevolent and malevolent dictators; in several states racism led to genocide while in others dictators protected minorities from overzealous majorities, or majorities from powerful minorities; there was a wide range in the efficiency of censorship, of supervision, and of command economies.

From the perspective of liberalism, the situation in areas ruled by Afrikaners was no different from that in the rest of the Arabian/ African region: the Afrikaners' democratically organised closed oligarchy belonged to the authoritarian camp, differing in degree but not in kind from one-party, collective or personal dictatorial regimes. Located primarily since the 1830s north of the Orange River in districts recently depopulated by wars between Bantu tribes, Afrikaner communities were given independence within the Union of South Africa in 1910. Since 1948 (see Chapter 4) they dominated the English-speaking minority and ruled all non-whites autocratically. They institutionalised the policy of *apartheid* or separate development, and strengthened their position with the proclamation of a republican form of government in 1961. As is usually the case, repressiveness within a structure allowing for some freedom of expression caused greater tensions and deeper hatreds than the suppression carried out in efficient and monolithic authoritarian states. In conjunction with the mounting wave of self-awareness among black people everywhere, and stimulated by the collapse of Portuguese rule in 1974–5 in two large territories adjoining the republic, both external pressures and internal tensions and hatreds increased. Leaders of South African Bantu peoples rejected independence in small undeveloped and 'undevelopable' districts, and claimed equality of rights within the republic. Equality was asked for also by non-Bantu racial minorities. After 1975 an atmosphere of crisis prevailed and violence increased. Also there began to be heard the voices of a few liberal-minded Afrikaners who joined liberals among the English-speaking minority and other groups in demanding the dismantling of the institutions of *apartheid*. Likely alternatives to liberal success are either the stiffening of the coercive policies followed since 1948 or the triumph of authoritarian opponents of the Afrikaner nationalists' oppressive oligarchy.

A major effect of colonial administration in the Arabian/African region was the loosening up of traditional social structures. New ideas circulated and (limitedly, but not so much so compared with other modern imperialisms) fields of autonomous action opened. Nationalism, involving deeply felt emotions focused on an overriding idea and a simple goal, made sense to the educated minority of dependencies which became (or soon will be) independent states. Variously interpreted, authoritarian socialism was easily grafted on traditional communalism. The combination of nationalism and socialism produced the social-nationalism and national-socialism prevailing among the ruling Arabian/African intelligentsia, while the masses either carried on with traditional authoritarian ways, concepts and values or abandoned them without finding a replacement. South of the Sahara, variations of national-communism have gained considerable ground since the early 1970s. Autonomy and responsibility of the individual, the right to be oneself and to dissent, free inquiry, freedom of expression, equality within a differentiated society, citizens' self-government and the rest of the liberal position were absent in pre-colonial times and were still absent in post-colonial times. The parallel lives of pre-colonial and post-colonial Libyans such as Karamanlis, against whom the United States waged war early in the nineteenth century, and dictator Qadhafi, of West Africans Samory, ruler of an empire until 1898, and Sekou Touré, dictator of Guinea, of East Africans Mwanga, Kabaka of Bagandas, and Amin, dictator of Uganda — just to mention three instances — show that the colonial interlude had little effect on the principles and values which are the foundation of a way of life. Projections into the future are speculation; with this in mind, on the basis of vigorous dynamism, ability to master modern techniques, enthusiasm for discovering new horizons, one may hazard the guess that black communities, less set in the 'cake of custom' than Asian nations, will in the not distant future exercise considerable influence on the international scene. It will be an authoritarian influence.

7

SUCCESS BRINGS FAILURE

THE IMPACT OF LIBERALISM

A cursory glance at world events during the last 300 years shows that the liberals' influence has been disproportionate to their numbers. This was because they aimed at emancipation — from intellectual subservience, political oppression, economic scarcity — not just for themselves but for all members of the community. Therefore, to what liberals did (good or bad) one must add what was done (good or bad) in liberal-constitutional and liberal-democratic states by those (usually the majority) who had not participated in the liberal movement — opposing it, or indifferent to it — but who were also emancipated from subservience, oppression and scarcity.

Factory workers in Great Britain several generations ago, Jews in the Austrian section of the Dual Monarchy at the end of the nine-teenth century, blacks in the United States in recent decades, had, as the result of successful liberal agitation, opportunities for action they had hitherto lacked and that they lacked in authoritarian states. British factory workers pioneered the labour movement, Austrian Jews the Zionist movement, American blacks the Black Power movement. The deep-seated crises which in the 1960s and 1970s disrupted Marxist ranks intellectually and catholic ranks both intellectually and institutionally (the two largest and until recently among the most cohesive movements in the world) originated in liberal-democratic societies where coercion could not be used to punish deviationists and heretics.

A comparison between what life was and what it is now shows how radically societies have been transformed by the liberal heresy. Liberalism gave birth to the existing democracies of which a score are in western Europe and North America, and a dozen or so elsewhere. It disrupted authoritarian traditional cultures in eastern Europe, the Middle East and Latin America. It shook dormant civilisations in Asia and caused some of them to collapse. It speeded the painful passage from tribal organisation to the complex structure of the state in African and Pacific areas.

Everything non-traditional of importance today was born in nations endowed by liberal revolutionaries with free institutions. Democracy as the liberal organisation of individual autonomy, or as the authoritarian organisation of the general will, thought founded on reason and the revolt against reason, capitalism, collectivism, trade unionism, corporatism and co-operativism, socialism in its many versions, nationalism and internationalism, scientific advancement, the progress of technology, secularism, humanitarianism, urbanisation, industrialisation, have all been the children of liberty.

Liberal successes, however limited and brief, through their general emancipating effect have been a major revolutionary force, with a cumulative effect surpassing the liberals' goals and expectations. Have the consequences been good or bad? The answer depends on one's values. One thing is certain: there has been radical change. For better or for worse, the liberal minority, directly through its actions, indirectly through the energies it freed, has provided the stimulus that today makes mankind dynamic, restless, and above all unhappy.

THE LIBERALS' DEMOCRACY

Self-government is the tedious process of nominating candidates, campaigning, engaging in apparently endless discussions, making compromises, aiming high and far, and most of the time making ridiculously short steps, if any at all.

This tedious process is the foundation of the liberal political structure. It enables people to take initiatives, to agitate, to work together towards common goals. It transforms subjects into citizens. For liberals, self-government is valuable because it has fostered the emancipation of submerged sectors of national communities: wage-earners, peasants and other proletarians; minorities of all kinds; women. It is valuable because it is the key to the peaceful coexistence of opposites — progressives and conservatives, collectivists and free enterprisers, internationalists and nationalists, unbelievers and believers — who all contribute to the richness of a way of life; and because it makes for improvement. Horrors are present in all societies and errors are made by all, but horrors can be eliminated and errors corrected, to the extent that they are exposed, that citizens agitate, and that there are channels of action.

Denials of personal liberty have been essential features of organised societies for thousands of years until recently. The right of government to mould citizens, to impose a way of thinking, to decide arbitrarily what people should do, is taken for granted in more than one hundred authoritarian states. Forced labour, regimentation in communes, in *agrorods* or other collectivities, the impossibility of finding an occupation and making a living if one is 'unreliable', are the external manifestations of severe restrictions on personal liberty in societies ruled by surviving traditional despots and the more numerous radical ones.

Denials of personal liberty have been eliminated in so far as free institutions have replaced authoritarian ones, and in the measure in which liberal-democratic values have exercised pressure over authoritarian ones. In liberal democracies governments do not mould citizens; the citizens, if they make the effort, can control the government. Limitations to personal liberty due to economic pressure are being eased, in welfare and other mixed economies, in the measure in which self-government makes progress. These have been no mean achievements.

LIBERALS SUPPRESS SLAVERY

Of all denials of personal liberty, slavery is one of the cruellest, even if making slaves of prisoners instead of killing them had originally been a step towards a less barbarous way of life. Slavery was part of social organisation in early and later civilised societies, and, like many in Africa in recent centuries, in those passing from tribal to the more complex organisation of the state. There has never been an abolitionist movement in nations of Far Eastern and Middle Eastern civilisations — only, at most, a recommendation that slaves be given decent treatment. The 1861 Emancipation Edict in Russia was the outcome of imitation — not of a spontaneous movement among Russians. Western Christians opposed slavery in their communities but, unable to conceive the equality of all races of the human species, continued to condone the enslavement of blacks, considered to be not quite human.

It was left to liberals to make abolitionism a movement and to lead it to success. It took over a hundred years of agitation and action to stamp out slavery, from the founding of anti-slavery societies in London and Paris in the 1780s to the rounding up, in the 1890s, of the last slave raiders and traders by the British in the Great Lakes area of Africa, and by soldiers of the French Third Republic in the Sudan. (Slavery lingered for a few more decades in countries on or near the Red Sea, and variations of it continue to this day with forced labour in *gulags* of totalitarian dictatorships.)

The British navy put an end to the slave trade on the Atlantic Ocean, then on the Indian Ocean. This meant interference with public and private property rights, and intervention against the sovereignty of independent slave states, on the east and west coasts of Africa and in the Americas. Freetown, Liberia and Libreville — as the names indicate — were shelters for freed slaves built by British, American and French abolitionists respectively. For liberals everywhere, and for tens of thousands of young people who died, the civil war of 1861—5 in the United States was a war to end slavery. Late in the nineteenth century, the British fought slavers from Malawi to the middle Congo and upper Nile valleys, and the French from present-day Guinea to Chad. The outcome of liberal action, ending slavery and, in much of the world, outlawing kindred institutions from serfdom and forced labour to peonage and the subjection of the untouchables, were among the greatest achievements of the period when liberals were influential.

ESCAPE FROM DESPOTISM

Whatever the anti-liberal tendencies of most of those who write, speak, organise and agitate, more people flee from authoritarian states than from those in which liberals still have some influence. Despite the fact that movement is usually restricted and often made impossible by rigid controls, in so far as people have moved, the main flow has been from states where there is much repression to states where there is less — in the twentieth century, from dictatorships to liberal democracies.

Surviving Armenians abandoned Turkey after the atrocious massacres perpetrated by Ottoman troops before and during the First World War. Three million refugees and exiles fled Russia after the dictatorial *coup d'état* of November 1917 — most of them finding shelter in liberal-democratic countries. In the 1920s, as new dictatorial regimes replaced liberal constitutionalism (chronologically, in Hungary, Mexico, Italy, Spain, Persia, China, Poland, Portugal, and so on), or inefficient traditional authoritarianism, tens of thousands chose exile in lands where there was some liberty. Hundreds of thousands abandoned Germany during 1933—9, after Hitlerian national-socialists seized power, and many times that number (no one can estimate how many, figures run into the millions) later took to the mountains, the hills, the forests, hid in cellars and attics from the Pyrenees to the Volga, to escape from nazi governors, their puppets and the omnipresent S.S. Five to six million Germans, Koreans and Vietnamese fled East Germany, North Korea and North Vietnam in the immediate post-1945 period, while only a trickle left West Germany, also South Korea and South Vietnam, where dictatorial repression was then less severe or less efficient than in the north. Even after the building of the Berlin Wall in 1961, in a fifteen-year period many thousands managed to escape from East into West

Germany. A quarter of a million Spaniards, Catalans and Basques crossed the border into France when the Republicans were defeated in the civil war of 1936—9, and over half a million Cubans fled to the United States after the Castroite takeover. Intelligent people of goodwill write that conditions are terrible in liberal-democratic Italy because of capitalism, and thanks to collectivism wonderful in dictatorial Yugoslavia; but several times more people abandon Yugoslavia than Italy, or try to. Numerous visitors to national-communist China return impressed by dictatorial achievements (just as visitors to national-socialist Germany in the 1930s were), admiring the spirit of solidarity, the discipline, the devotion to the common good; but there are several million refugees from China in Hong Kong, Taiwan, south-east Asia and Western nations. Nearly a tenth of all Tibetans fled to India after 1959, and of all Laotians to Thailand after 1975, and tens of thousands every year swim through shark-infested waters for fourteen hours to find a shelter in 'colonial' Hong Kong. There was an exodus from Chile after the *golpe* of 1973, but none since the overthrow of a dictator in 1958 from Venezuela, the butt of terrorism and armed raids by authoritarian radicals and anarcho-communists during the Presidencies of the liberals Bétancourt and Leoni.

THE BREACHING OF THE INTELLECTUAL DYKE

Throughout history and pre-history, conformity enforced through censorship and monopoly of education has been the dyke holding back intellectual development, reducing the expansion of knowledge to a trickle, smothering the search for truth. It was breached in modern times through the efforts of seventeenth- and eighteenth-century forerunners of liberalism. Those for whom Milton and Voltaire spoke were not many. Their courage and dynamism compensated for smallness of numbers. Few are aware today of growing censorship and monopoly of education the world over — or pay little attention to it. Still fewer stop to think that, as said before, once freedom of expression and free inquiry are lost, they may never reappear — and humanity will stagnate.

'The one object in life is the development of the mind, and the first condition for the development of the mind is that it should have liberty,' wrote the French philosopher Renan. The first and second freedoms of Roosevelt's famous statement of 6 January 1941 are, in reality, one, worship being the way of speaking with God.

Elimination of censorship and liberation from dogmas have been paramount in the preoccupations of liberals. The struggle for liberty of the mind, as free inquiry and free expression, has been an uphill

one. While the old enemy, conformist traditionalism, was being
defeated, a more dynamic and more aggressive new enemy appeared,
conformist radicalism. The ups and downs of the struggle for political
liberty have been ups and downs for free inquiry, for freedom of
communications media and education, for freedom to teach and to
worship.

Ignoring the distinction between optimum and maximum (see
Chapter 1) and between liberty and licence, enemies of liberalism
gleefully point to instances of restrictions on activities of the mind in
several liberal democracies. There is plenty of evidence of the reverse:
multiplicity of ideas and values, expansion of knowledge in all fields,
variety and innovation in literary and artistic styles. The impressive
creativity among English- and French-speaking European people in
the eighteenth and nineteenth centuries, and the more recent
creativity among North Americans, are connected with conditions
of freedom. What Germans, Russians and others produced when
censorship relaxed and dogmatism weakened, what Chinese and
others contributed in free foreign environments, has been astounding.
Intellectual vigour, the desire to experiment in the most varied fields
(and the possibility of doing so), the restless search into the
philosophical, religious, scientific, literary and artistic unknown,
today are found in liberal democracies, not in disciplined conformist
societies dominated by old or new authoritarian forces.

Free inquiry has played the most important role in expanding
scientific knowledge, in developing technology and in enabling
people to achieve higher standards of living through the control and
exploitation of the forces of nature: the life-giving powers of soil,
water and air, electricity, the energy contained in solid and liquid
minerals and the enormous amount of it condensed in the atom. Free
inquiry is needed now more than ever, to redress the baneful consequences of recent industrial expansion, to save nature from the
despotism of the human species, in the end to save the human species
from itself. Dogmatism strengthens people, but cannot cope with
problems whose solution requires analysis and reflection, application
of the canons of the scientific method, open-mindedness, and the
patient (often dull and always wearisome) process of trial and error.

Believing in the value of education, liberals aimed at schooling for
all — schooling as the forming of responsible citizens, respect for
spontaneity, and the development of individual capabilities, not as
mere socialisation through indoctrination. The schools applying the
principles of Basedow, of Pestalozzi and his disciple Froebel, the
people's school movement in Scandinavia in the nineteenth century,
the workers' university movement later, did as much as political
agitation to liberalise and transform the way of life in the Germanies,

Switzerland and Scandinavian nations — a more difficult feat than
the liberalising of institutions. When in 1809 von Humboldt created
a new university in Berlin dedicated to the principle of academic
freedom, he took a revolutionary step and made that university a
revolutionary centre. Missionary schools in which teachers treated
pupils as independent individuals endowed with dignity and
responsibility, and trained them to think with their own minds, did
more to shake the foundations of conformist traditionalism in
stagnant civilised and tribal societies of Asia and Africa — from
China to Benin — than the cannons of imperialist powers.

THE BREACHING OF ECONOMIC DYKES

Eighteenth-century progressives in North Atlantic nations had rightly
seen a major obstacle to economic progress in the coercive structure
of mercantilism. They clamoured, successfully in several countries,
for the abolition of restrictive policies and repressive practices, and
for the establishment of a free market with free enterprise, free
labour, free movement of goods and people. The economic dyke was
breached, and there was a flood in the form of sudden expansion of
economic activities. It was greeted enthusiastically by progressives, as
yet unaware that the breach was releasing socio-economic forces
alien, even bitterly hostile, to liberal principles and values.

    The central idea guiding eighteenth-century physiocrats and
admirers of Adam Smith, who advocated breaching the economic
dyke, was simple: let nature take its course. Later came awareness of
the suffering caused by market economies. There was, however,
another side to the coin: when free enterprise operating in a free
market represented a major share of the economic process, for the
first time economic stagnation was overcome on a large scale; it
seemed that instead of permanent scarcity for most there could be
abundance for all.

    Statistics are not the best yardstick for what goes on in a society,
but they do give an idea of what happens. Between independence and
1850, the American national income multiplied about eight times,
and again sixfold between 1850 and 1913. The British national
wealth was estimated, in constant monetary units, at £2 billion in
1812 and at over £12 billion in 1912. Nations with little or no
capital in the form of minerals, fertile soil and other resources, like
the Swiss, became prosperous, or, like the Japanese, advanced
towards prosperity rapidly. In the nineteenth century Danish liberals
evolved a six-point programme which led their nation from poverty
in a backward economy during the first half of the century to
moderate and evenly distributed affluence at the end of it:

constitutionalism, agrarian reform, diffusion of education, co-operativism, encouragement of foreign investment, and stimulation of foreign trade. The Swedish socio-economic model developed since 1932, which is — rightly — the pride of social democrats everywhere, was made possible by the expansion of production during the previous two generations, after Liberals restructured the state in 1864. There was a pre-1914 economic miracle in Germany, when in a few decades a largely agricultural country, whose national product had been half the British one, outstripped Great Britain to become by 1900 the second industrial power in the world (after the United States).

India, as poor as all of Asia when the British East India Company took over the administration of Bengal from its moslem rulers in 1764, was more advanced economically than any Asian independent state (except for Japan) in 1947. In Kenya, in the sixty-odd years between the colonial administrative structuring in the 1890s and independence, wealth in Colin Clark's international units increased from a few million (represented by domestic animals, parcels of cultivated land, rudimentary home-made products, and what was owned by Arabs living in a few small coastal cities) to several billion.

In the twentieth century economic expansion has become general. The achievements of some command economies (bureaucratic collectivism in the Soviet Union, corporatism in Germany during the nazi period) have been remarkable. Liberals, who condemn command economies because their functioning requires dictatorial coercion and because of the stultifying effect on citizens transformed into docile subjects, point out that the economies most efficiently fulfilling the basic function of supplying goods and services are today those in which the market plays a dominant role (the Australian, Canadian, Japanese, Swiss) or a considerable one (French, Israeli, Swedish).

With hindsight, many are convinced that the emancipation of economic activities in a few North Atlantic nations in the eighteenth century was harmful. Whatever the evaluation, there has in fact been economic expansion as the result of that emancipation, and more people have led a better life than they would have done without the revolutionary developments of 200 years ago. The liberals' contribution to the expansion was the original breaching of the economic dyke in Great Britain, the United States, and France, and the formulation of ideas which served as guidelines in choosing policies.

The infatuation with *laissez-faire* lasted too long (see Chapter 2), but even so it was not absolute. When in power liberals were responsible for the development of the economic infrastructure, without which production lags and distribution is hampered.

Although labour legislation came late, it achieved the goal of raising the status of labour to that of management and proprietorship in the market and mixed economies of liberal-democratic states, and provided one more section in the bridge being built between progressive liberals and anti-authoritarian socialists during the last two generations. Scandinavian revisionist socialists and Commonwealth liberals were the architects of the welfare economy, which provides a temporary solution to the social problem; Keynesian liberals were for several decades in the forefront of the effort to find a better and more lasting solution; in the forefront in the mid-1970s were statesmen, administrators and intellectuals of the calibre of Dahrendorf, La Malfa, Servan-Schreiber and Samuelson.

TOWARDS EQUALITY

As equality is a fact not of nature but of culture (see Chapter 1), the road leading to it is, if anything, more difficult and longer than the road leading to liberty. Not only is each human being different from all others, and therefore, in the eyes of most, unequal, but organisation, indispensable for survival and even more for advancement, produces inequalities. It is easy to talk about equality, but it takes effort to find out what institutions make it possible to pass from the theoretical to the practical, and to establish them. All that mankind has achieved in the past — and is achieving today in states ruled by authoritarian radicals — is uniformity of ideas and values through the use of extreme coercion, which demands the ultimate inequality between those who coerce and those who are coerced.

Requiring as it does the suppression of liberty, uniformity is totally illiberal. It is liberal, instead, to put differing individuals and groups on the same level. This liberals have tried to do by emphasising the moral equality of all and embodying it in society's institutional structure.

It is fashionable to deride the notion of moral equality as a convenient screen to hide *de facto* inequality, and to counter it with that of socio-economic equality. In reality there is no contraposition and so no screen. Morality (in elementary terms, what by general consent is considered right and good) is the foundation of laws and thus of politics, the process through which laws are made and enforced: laws regulate relationships among citizens and between citizens and state, inclusive of course of socio-economic relationships. Socio-economic equality, like legal and political equality, is a part of the whole: moral equality.

Moral equality means that all citizens have the same status, none superior and none inferior; it means laws equal for all and equal opportunities to participate in public life. Ethically, it means the abolition of the double standard, of the discrimination between 'us' (those who are like me) and 'them', who are not entitled to do what I may do. Rejecting dogmatic absolutes (see the section 'The *optimum* is not the *maximum*' in Chapter 1), at the practical level of socio-economic relationships, having balanced what is right against the requirements of the economic process, moral equality means keeping differences in standards of living within a range compatible with the proper functioning of self-government as government for all. What that range should be depends on a number of conditions; the one to five income range once mentioned by an American President is a good starting-point. As is often the case, enunciation of the principle is easier than its application.

In view of what had generally been taken for granted everywhere for thousands of years, and in most of the world still is, to have conceived moral equality was no small achievement. Whatever the praises of love and brotherhood sung by believers in the major religious faiths, those same believers never considered infidels and heretics as their equals. Today likewise, nationalist, authoritarian socialist, and anarcho-communist believers in secular religions do not conceive of equality between those who share their creed and those whose convictions, goals and interests differ. In the over a hundred authoritarian states, laws for subjects are not the same as the laws for rulers and the servile oligarchies enforcing their will. In liberal democracies, however imperfectly, laws are equal for all; enforcement is not easy but the dismissal, resignation, and imprisonment of American and Japanese highest officials in the mid-1970s show that it can be done.

Today, where an aspiration for equality is widespread, and organised enough to become a political force, it concerns primarily not rights and duties but incomes and status. Opponents of free institutions point to economic inequality in liberal democracies, to extremes (particularly noticeable in the United States) of wealth and poverty. Evidence shows that not enough was done by liberals to lessen inequality when they had political influence (see Chapter 2), and that not enough is being done now by labourites, social democrats and other revisionist socialists, who in many nations are spokesmen for the liberal position and carry out liberal policies. Nevertheless it is a fact that many liberal democracies, mainly through raising wages, have gone further along the road of diminishing economic inequality than most dictatorial societies (see also p. 105). There is, moreover, a greater awareness of economic inequality in liberal democracies than there is in any authoritarian state, and from that awareness comes stimulus to action.

In the mixed economies of liberal democracies (in which the role of welfare policies becomes more and more important), division of labour and the complex organisation required to produce and distribute goods and services lead to differences in functions, in training of skills, and in levels of responsibility. The differences justify higher incomes for those who fulfil functions of which not everyone is capable, whose training is more costly in terms not so much of money but of time and energy, whose responsibilities are greater. Awareness of inequality, resentment leading to agitation, pressure of organised groups, strikes, free voting – possible in liberal democracies and not in dictatorships – have an equalising effect.

For several generations the European nations that were the most egalitarian economically, Switzerland and Norway, were also the freest; New Zealand came closer to being an egalitarian society than any other. Today there is less inequality of economic conditions among the thirteen million inhabitants of the Netherlands than among the thirteen millions of the Kazakh Soviet republic, and less inequality among twenty-three million Canadians than among twenty-three million subjects of the Iraqi and Algerian dictatorships.

In all economies, the average real income (the sum of disposable personal income and social-services benefits) of five basic classes – farmers, blue-collar workers, white-collar workers, professional people, executives – differs, but the range is narrower even in the United States, where inequalities are great, than in the Soviet Union (in the late 1950s about one to six as against one to twelve). Besides the productive socio-economic classes there are the parasitic ones: members of ruling oligarchies in dictatorial states, *rentiers* and speculators in liberal democracies. Liberals who are also economists. for example Servan-Schreiber in France, and Keyserling in the United States, and members of the liberal minority who agree with them, recognise the need for state action in order to eliminate parasitism in market economies. Parasitic oligarchies in dictatorial states cannot be eliminated because they monopolise political power.

In the 1950s, Yugoslavia was often mentioned as the country where economic inequality had been abolished. China was the country most mentioned in the 1970s in this respect. It became evident in the mid-1970s that what was once said about Yugoslavia was not correct, and that a major source of economic inequality was the dictatorial political inequality between the ruling clique (leaders of the Communist League) and the subjects. Little is known about China that is verifiable, but reports from areas where foreign visitors are barred indicate that the range in living standards between, for instance, peasants in western mountain provinces and members of the dictatorial elite in eastern cities, is greater than that in the United

States between Appalachian farmers and miners and Washington
officials of the federal bureaucracy.

Social mobility helps to shorten the road to the goal of socio-
economic equality. To open all careers to talent was once a powerful
liberal slogan in nations of continental Europe, and equality of
opportunity has been a powerful liberal slogan in North America.
The slogans inspired action aimed at breaking the rigid mould
created in all communities by desire for security of income and
status (thus for tenure) on the one hand, and on the other by the
ambition of most parents to use their achievements as a spring-board
for their children.

Liberals are convinced that market economies in which the private
sector (not necessarily dominant) has considerable autonomy provide
wider avenues for social mobility than command economies, and
that physical mobility — the free movement of all — an essential
article in the liberal programme, contributes to social mobility. Of
those who take advantage of the opportunities provided by market
economies to try to improve their standard of living and social status
many fail — but many succeed. Success is often easier for the
outsider, not inhibited by mores and by ties with others, than for
those who stay in their native community. Mass migrations,
facilitated by the abolition of restrictions on movement during the
period of liberal influence, helped tens of millions to improve
economic conditions and social status.

EMANCIPATION OF HALF THE POPULATION

More fundamental, and even more difficult to solve than the
narrowing of income range, is the problem of equality between men
and women. The inferior status of women is one of the most
repulsive features in nearly all societies, whatever the level of development. Inferior is an understatement: women have often been no more
than chattels, with no rights in a man's world, no life and property of
their own. Their children were the father's children. The man's
adultery and other so-called 'lapses' were condoned, the woman's
savagely punished. The double standard was taken for granted, and
still is by nine-tenths and more of mankind. The *machismo* in
Spanish-speaking nations; the contempt for women in islamic
societies; the prevalence of women in menial occupations in
national-communist dictatorships; the diffusion of material titillating
male sexuality and extolling virility, through various media, in liberal
democracies — all are manifestations of the same revolting
phenomenon: men asserting their superiority.

The emancipation of women did not begin in the modern world

until traditional authoritarian structures had been, at least partially, replaced by liberal-constitutional ones. Equality of rights was not achieved until the establishment of liberal democracies. The most prominent early champions of women's equality, besides Holbach and Holberg in their liberal moments, were two outstanding liberals, Condorcet and J. S. Mill. Olympe de Gouges's *Declaration of the Rights of Women*, Mary Wollstonecraft's *Vindication*, M. S. Fuller's *Woman in the 19th Century* would never have appeared if there had not been freedom of the press in France, Great Britain and the United States respectively. Mary Lyon could not have started a women's college in 1836, and Mary Bethune a college for black women in 1904, if there had not been freedom of teaching in Massachusetts and Florida. Mary Baker Eddy and Annie Besant could not have been founders of religions if there had not been freedom of worship in English-speaking nations. The first women's rights convention would not have met in 1848 if there had not been freedom of association and agitation in the United States. Liberalisation in ways of life created the climate that enabled de Staël, Austen, Sand, Stowe, Lagerlöf and Deledda to be the first widely read women authors in their respective countries. The impact of liberalism gave legal equality to women, led to women's suffrage in three major nations immediately after the end of the First World War, ended harems, suttee, bound feet, infanticide of baby girls, tore the veil from the faces of moslem women.

Equal rights are an important step in emancipation. Harder to accomplish is the next step: equal treatment, or emancipation in the field of mores. Women's liberation movements are indispensable to create the pressure that can upset and destroy the tyranny of custom — at times a worse and more enduring tyranny than that of despots. Articulate spokeswomen of liberation movements are often against liberal democracy, but it is only in liberal democracies that such movements can be organised, and be successful. Without free institutions there would be no more agitation for the end of discrimination of all sorts in North America, continental Europe, and Japan than there is in Eurasian and Third World dictatorships.

HUMANITARIANISM

The crusade for the world-wide abolition of slavery generations ago, and the organisation of welfare economies in recent decades, testify to liberal humanitarianism. Plagues, famines in the wake of crop failures and civil wars, suffering caused by natural disasters, have always led to responses from liberals in the form of humanitarian action. Whatever their personal convictions, the British Florence

Nightingale, through her dedication to nursing during the Crimean war, the Swiss Henry Dunant through the creation of the Red Cross shortly after the Franco—Austrian war of 1859, the American Herbert Hoover through the organisation of relief in famine-stricken areas of Russia in the early 1920s, joined in the liberal era's humanitarian crusade. Revulsion for human sacrifices widely practised in many communities in the eighteenth and nineteenth centuries, for refined cruelties sanctioned by tradition in otherwise highly civilised Asian nations, for massacres in the Balkans in the 1870s and in Armenia later, for pogroms, affected the policies of governments in countries where liberals were influential.

Liberals also carried out a vigorous campaign for penal reform, for the abolition of torture and the death penalty, for reducing terms of imprisonment, for the improvement of conditions in jails and penitentiaries. They championed Roman legal principles conveniently overlooked in authoritarian regimes: that punishment can be inflicted only on those who have actually committed a crime or offense — not on those who, whatever their intentions, have not begun to perpetrate a criminal act; that there is no such thing as the crime of a collectivity — of capitalists or communists, of kulaks or East African Asians, of Masons or Jesuits, of Jews or Germans; that one is presumed innocent until proved guilty; that laws must not be made retroactive.

No liberal disparaged the efforts of Friends to help those everywhere in need of it; the initiatives, often doomed to failure from the start, for understanding between conflicting groups and for cooperation; the efforts of societies for the prevention of cruelty, to children, to all human beings, to animals; the Y.M.C.A. and the Y.W.C.A; Booth's Salvation Army, Baden-Powell's Scouts and Guides, Schweitzer's Lambarene, Ceresole's *hilfdienst* (service to help, the 1920s' Swiss forerunner of the Peace Corps and all such initiatives of the 1960s and 1970s), the recent Amnesty International.

Unlike Quakers, liberals are not integral pacifists. Most of them are agreed that, since tyranny is founded on force, force may have to be used to destroy it, and that force is at times necessary to contain waves of fanaticism. Liberals also agree with what Lincoln said on the question of slavery: that it is one thing to live with evil in order to maintain peace, but quite another to appease evil and help it to expand. From the Geneva convention of 1864 to the protection of the rights of conscientious objectors, liberals have tried to limit the savagery of war. It was, and is, liberal to adopt a forgive and forget policy after a conflict, as Lincoln wanted to do in 1865, as British and American liberals wanted to do in 1919, as American Fair Dealers did in relation to Germany and Japan after 1945. It was liberal to send relief supplies to South and North Vietnam, to help

Bengalis oppressed by Pakistanis and Biharis oppressed by Bengalis. For a liberal there is no end to the scope of humanitarian work, and much remains to be done on a private individual basis after bureaucracies have been organised to deal with human suffering.

For liberals, humanitarianism has meant help to others, for no other reason than that they need help. It has meant to treat giver and receiver of aid as equals, and to enhance the dignity of the receiver by making him self-sufficient, thus strengthening individual autonomy. Liberal humanitarianism is compassion for the individual in need, whoever he or she may be, neighbour or stranger, friend or foe. It is not the elitist superiority lurking behind the charity asked of religious believers; it is not the pseudo-humanism of Leninists, who divide mankind into those to be saved, who may be helped, and those who are damned and therefore should be destroyed — whose humanism is belied by their approval of cruelty practised in the dictatorial systems they admire, and by their absence of compassion.

THE INDEPENDENCE OF NATIONS

Since the end of the nineteenth century, nationalists everywhere (with partial exceptions in India and smaller areas once administered by the British) have been firmly opposed to liberal constitutionalism and liberal democracy, and today are opposed to revisionist socialists taking liberal positions. As a minority of nationalists now side with authoritarian traditional forces and the majority with Leninist, 'African', 'Arab' and other versions of authoritarian socialism, nationalism and dictatorship are practically synonymous. However, evidence shows that the emancipation of nations — one of the major developments of the last 200 years — has been successful to the extent that liberalism has been influential. Liberals have been advocates of the formation of nation-states and have contributed to the disruption of colonial empires.

A score of nation-states came into existence in Europe between 1822 (when Greeks declared their independence) and 1921 (when independence was granted to Irish catholics) during the period of considerable liberal influence. When national-socialist Germany reached the peak of its power, there remained on continental Europe only six other independent nation-states. Between 1920 (when Ukrainians were defeated by Russians) and 1948 (when Soviet paramount rule was consolidated in Czechoslovakia) twenty nations west of the Urals lost their independence to the Soviet Union.

Advocates of independence for subject nations have opportunities in liberal-constitutional and liberal-democratic states which are lacking in authoritarian ones; from Virginia in 1765 to St Lucia in

1976, in the self-governing British territories of the Western
hemisphere, citizens could agitate for independence. They also
received the support of large and influential sectors of the public in
the ruling country, a public which could make its voice heard.
Hindus, Cypriots, Sudanese had under British administration
opportunities for achieving independence they would not have had
had they remained subjects of Moguls and Ottoman Turks, of
Egyptians.

As can be seen in countless legislative acts introducing self-
government, and leading, step by step, to independence in overseas
territories, British Liberalism, and its ideological and political
successor, liberal-socialist Labourism, were the main forces in the
gradual transformation of the British empire into a commonwealth
of independent nations, and in recognising the right of nations to
opt out of the Commonwealth if a majority of citizens desire to do
so. In the United States, liberalism was the major force checking, and
ultimately putting an end to, American imperialist thrusts. There is
no internal force in Arab states that can do for Nilotes, Kurds and
Berbers, and in the Soviet Union for Balts, Georgians and Uzbeks,
what American liberals did for Caribbeans, Central Americans and
Filipinos who had come under U.S. rule.

As revolutionaries in dependencies and mother countries, and as
groups exercising pressure on governments of influential foreign
countries (the United Kingdom, the United States), liberals contributed to the independence of Latin American nations. Liberals first
weakened the Habsburg multinational empire, then prevented its
survival after the military defeats of 1918. From the independence
of Greeks in the immediate post-Napoleonic period, to that of
Saudi Arabs and Yemenis at the end of the First World War,
independence came to nations included in the autocratic multinational Ottoman empire, when defeated by powers in which liberals
were influential. If liberals and democratic socialists of the 1917
provisional government had not been defeated in Russia by authoritarian socialists, nations conquered by the czars would have kept the
independence briefly regained or achieved, for the first time, in
1917–18. In Eurasian dictatorial states there are, from Berbers in the
Atlas mountains to Miaos near the South China Sea, over one hundred
million people belonging to over thirty subject nations — and no
independence movements.

The recent colonial version of the age-old phenomenon of imperialism has been a tragic feature of modern civilisation. That colonial
empires created during the last few generations by five nations
belonging to the progressive branch of Western civilisation collapsed
was largely due to the pressure of anti-colonial forces which developed

thanks to liberal-democratic institutions. No Gandhi and Nehru would have arisen in India, no Sukarno and Aidit in Indonesia, no Kasavubu and Mobutu in Zaïre, no Senghor and Houphouet-Boigny in West Africa, no Quezon and Osmeña in the Philippines, had there not been in Great Britain, France, the Netherlands, Belgium and the United States a liberal movement strong enough to curb imperialism and colonialism, and to help independence movements in British, French, Dutch, Belgian and American overseas territories. If these countries had been dictatorships, and their governments had done what the Japanese did in Korea and Taiwan, the Russians in Central Asia and the Caucasus, the Arabs in Iraq and the Maghreb, the Chinese in territories where live forty million non-Chinese, then the efforts of N'krumah in Ghana, Ben Yussef in Morocco, Hatta in Java, Lumumba in Zaïre and Muñoz in Puerto Rico would have remained sterile.

There is, rightly, a strong reaction against colonialism, and liberals see colonies being replaced by independent states with satisfaction; but it is a mistake to assume that there is a general anti-colonial revolt. Although there has been a successful revolt in areas under the aegis of liberal democracies, there is none where efficient dictatorships are in control.

INTERNATIONALISM

Many admire the *pax romana* which once reigned in the Mediterranean world, and the *pax sinica* which for longer periods reigned in the 'closed' continent at the other end of the Eastern hemisphere. *Pax romana* and *pax sinica* resulted from conquest and the establishment of an authoritarian central power strong enough to repress all movements aimed at independence, and to assimilate, through coercion, all peoples in the dominant nation. In modern times there has been a brief *pax britannica*, when one nation was so strong it could enforce peace everywhere. The liberals' *pax humana* has been the peaceful coexistence of independent nations within an international structure built on liberal principles.

The first peace associations were organised at about the same time, the middle of the nineteenth century, by liberals on both sides of the North Atlantic. Liberals spurred heads of state to take initiatives that led to the first and second peace conferences of The Hague, and to the creation of the International Court of Arbitration, providing channels for the peaceful solution of international disputes. It was not much, and the Court did not do much, but it was a beginning.

The American President who brought the League of Nations into existence was a liberal. What he created mattered more for the advancement of humanity than the deeds of his better-remembered contemporary, Lenin. Together with the abolition of slavery, the League of Nations is the greatest achievement of the era when liberals were influential.

Thanks to the patience, vision and energy of another liberal American President — a greater man than his better-remembered contemporaries such as Stalin and Hitler who ruled vast empires — the United Nations was established. The League of Nations had functioned as long as liberal democracies were able to keep the dictatorial states in check; it collapsed in 1939–40 when frenzied national-socialists, in power in more and more states, joined hands with national-communists in power in the Soviet Union and influential in many countries. The United Nations has been able to function in so far as its liberal-democratic members have been strong. With each dictatorial state that joined the organisation there has been a loss of strength. The weakening of the democratic commitment among Americans, the collapse of the parliamentary republic in France, the decline of Great Britain, the overthrow of free institutions in most states that achieved independence after the Second World War — in brief, the decline of liberalism — is the major element in the impotence of the United Nations. There is no *pax humana* yet. A beginning was made, and there is no certainty that it will ever be more than that; the League and the United Nations may prove to have been the swan song of liberalism — a brave song.

PLUSES

Anyone acquainted with what goes on today can recite a litany of liberal shortcomings and sins, as fashionable among advocates of authoritarian 'new orders' as it was among advocates of old ones. Taking three letters at random, among others under 'a' are acquisitiveness, aimlessness, alienation, anarchy and atomisation: under 'c' callousness, chaos, competitiveness, compromise (excess of), contradictoriness; under 'i' impotence (to solve problems), inconsistency, indifference (to 'real' problems), inefficiency, irrationality; and so on under each letter, passing through pet commonplaces such as divisiveness, individual and class egoism, formalism, greed, hypocrisy, crass materialism, selfishness, etc. For hordes of militant and articulate opponents, the impact of the litany is heightened by passions which blind them to the liberals' actual achievements and also to what — with or without the liberals' participation — the achievements made possible and contributed to advancement.

As mentioned in the first paragraph of the Introduction, pluses and minuses of liberalism will be dealt with in a sequel to this book. However, to have a clear idea of what will be lost if authoritarian tides engulf all mankind, it is proper, even though tediously didactic, to summarise briefly points made in this and previous chapters, bearing in mind that all achievements have been partial, and that often no more than a beginning has been made.

The emancipation of minds from dogmatism and of consciences from fanaticism through free inquiry and freedom of expression, and tolerance of dissenting views — the number-one article in the liberals' ideological position — has been a major achievement even if the number of people affected has been small. A less limited achievement, for a while, has been self-government — the number-one article of the liberals' political programme — implying political emancipation and the reversal of the relationship between citizens and state. Emancipation from stagnant traditional economies has also been a step forward, even if for several generations it was accompanied by too much suffering. The liberal institutional structure (see Chapter 2) is the only one which makes provisions for the peaceful coexistence of different groups and different tendencies on an equal footing, which provides means for peaceful changes in a society and its governing, which provides channels for uncovering defects, errors and horrors, and for correcting those that cannot be eliminated. Among specific goals achieved have been the world-wide abolition of slavery and serfdom, education as concern for the person and not as indoctrination, and the advancement of science for the benefit of all; also, a start has been made in creating an international order founded on law. Liberties wanted by liberal revolutionaries made possible the emancipation of peasants, proletarians, and the rest of the working classes; of women, of nations, of believers in creeds considered heretical, and of those whose secular ways of thinking depart from the norm. The same liberties made possible the agitation aimed at diminishing inequality and injustice, and brought about an astounding expansion of knowledge and a no less astounding expansion of the economy.

Partisans and admirers of Second and Third World dictatorial regimes take for granted that by abolishing the liberals' two key liberties (freedom of expression and political liberty) and replacing them with guidance through dictatorial coercion and censorship, emancipation and advancement in all fields of spiritual and material endeavour will be speeded up. On the basis of historical evidence, it would be better not to take this for granted.

ADVERSE EFFECTS OF THE RELEASE OF ENERGIES

Pluses having been listed, mention must be made of usually ignored elements which have contributed to the minuses feeding the resent-

ment, contempt and hatred against liberalism of the majority of the
world intelligentsia, focused on the shortcomings and defects of
'capitalist bourgeois democracy' (which actually involve all non-
economic features of the liberal experience — features more important than the economic ones). Of these elements, three are implicit
in liberalism: release of energies, responsibility, and freedom of
expression. Another one is the inability of most to conceive moral
equality.

The breaching of intellectual and economic dykes brought about
by liberal agitation and by the liberals' partial successes has already
been mentioned. Breaching may have no effect, especially if the
reservoir behind the dyke is at a low level. On the other hand it may
lead to floods. In English-speaking communities first, then in others,
it produced floods in the form of a vast release of human energy — an
increase in the dynamism of millions of individuals. The flood
eventually affected all mankind; by then, most found it intolerable.

The initiative of a few liberal revolutionaries was sometimes
sufficient to establish free institutions; but free institutions cannot
survive without the support of a large sector of the community — not
necessarily a majority, but at least a plurality with a wide margin.
Already early in this century, in many nations (for instance the large
continental ones), there was more liberty of expression, of conscience,
of association, of movement, than majorities could cope with.

Released energy meant new ideas. The breaching of intellectual
dykes in small communities of the ancient Mediterranean world had
affected only tiny minorities. In the seventeenth century there was
already sufficient intellectual and political awareness, and sufficient
literacy, among the English, Dutch, Scots and French to expose
hundreds of thousands to new ideas. By 1800 those so exposed had
become millions, on both sides of the North Atlantic. There were
various interpretations of Western Christianity; then came rejection of
Christianity, and the formulation of numerous non-Christian ways of
thinking. Differences in basic principles and values, in methods of
thought, were not subjects of debate for philosophers only; they were
of concern to millions who had never heard the name of a philosopher,
who had to find their own way, drawn as they were into the maelstrom created by the clashes of incompatible ways of thinking.

Released energy meant political pluralism. Self-government
necessitated participation in public affairs; it brought into existence
political parties each advocating a set of different, mutually irrecon-
cilable policies. In the area of practical activities there was another
maelstrom, created by the clashes of political forces.

Released energy meant a 'free for all' for entrepreneurs in the
newly established market economies. It meant conflict among owners

of capital, impotence for those who did not own property, efforts by capitalists and entrepreneurs to take over control of the state. Data concerning economic expansion and rising standards of living have already been mentioned. In liberal-constitutional states there was a greater economic distance between 1900 and 1750 than there had been between 1750 and the year 1. However, closer to the concerns of most people than expansion and rising standards were the instability of the economies and the insecurity in which lived tens of millions of the unemployed, employees and self-employed. For most, the economic maelstrom was frightening. Understandably, stability at a level just above starvation was preferable to insecurity at a relatively high standard of living.

Finally, release of energies meant what citizens of liberal-constitutional states, and liberal-democratic ones later, did outside the borders of their own countries. From earliest near eastern states thousands of years ago, to dictatorships today, the normal rule of the politically organised community has been rigid state control over the movements and activities of subjects going abroad. Liberals objected strenuously to control, advocating freedom of movement. In the measure in which liberal-constitutional states replaced authoritarian regimes, citizens became free to come and go, and to do abroad — without supervision and interference by authorities at home — whatever they were able to do on the basis of their own decisions.

FLOODING THE EARTH

Freedom of movement made possible the mass migration of tens of millions of Europeans, primarily to North America, and also to the southernmost Latin American republics and Australasia. Even more important for future relationships, particularly for today's antagonisms and conflicts, was the presence of more and more citizens coming from nations with free, or fairly free, institutions, into hitherto closed civilised societies and tribal communities jealous of protecting their cultural distinctiveness against all outsiders (see also 'The sin of arrogance', p. 139).

Western Europeans and North Americans went everywhere, most of them in search of economic opportunities; many just to settle in a different environment, to explore, to preach, to help; a few also to conquer, for the benefit of a private firm as the British Rhodes did, for their own benefit like the Belgian Leopold of Coburg, for the benefit of a foreign state or of their own country, like the Germans Emin (in Egypt's service) and Peters. Consequently, there was political, economic and cultural expansion of nations affected in varying measure by liberal ideas and values. At times there was government initiative, but the expansion of the area in which six nations endowed with free institutions, and one with semi-free institutions, exercised paramount influence for a while, was mainly the outcome of what their citizens did on their own. More often than not, the flag followed traders, settlers, missionaries, mercenaries, rather than preceding them.

Expansion is a euphemism. The right word is 'imperialism'. In the case of the British in all continents, the Dutch in south-east Asia, Americans moving into Texas and California and taking over Hawaii, Italians, Belgians and Germans in tropical Africa (less so in the case of the French, whose government usually kept the initiative), imperialism was a different phenomenon from the traditional one. Ancient Persian, Macedonian and Roman empires, the Chinese empire, the sixteenth-century Turkish and Spanish empires, today's Soviet empire, have been the result of government initiative and action. What citizens of North Atlantic nations did on their own initiative was disturbing for the home country; it was extremely disturbing for the other peoples who certainly did not want to be taken over and strongly resented the flood of foreigners, even when they came peacefully and with the best of intentions. Liberals released energies, part of that released energy created the colonial imperialism of a few generations ago.

RESPONSIBILITY: A BURDEN FOR MANY

Government by the citizens is ridiculed by sophisticated intellectuals. It is firmly rejected by all those convinced that they hold the key to salvation. It gives the measure of one's smallness: 'what am I? One vote among millions!' It is a major source of frustration. People of goodwill find it hard to understand why the majority of voters are not with them, and attribute their failure to sordid interests and to conspiracies of evil forces. It has already been mentioned (p. 149) how, over half a century ago, people as different as Adler and Mussolini (both spokesmen for tens of millions) described the government process in liberal democracies as a meaningless paper game. For the nazi Hitler, it was 'a preposterous creature of filth'.

Whatever the reasons and rationalisations of articulate opponents, for most people self-government is a burden. The proper functioning of free institutions requires on the part of many, not just a few, the qualities implicit in the word 'character': self-discipline, endurance and patience. It took republican Romans of the fifth and fourth centuries B.C. over a hundred years to find a solution compatible with their relatively free institutions to the problem created by the arrival of new residents in their country. It took seventy years of agitation in Great Britain to pass the Reform Bill of 1832.

A common attitude in existing liberal democracies seems a logical one: 'why wait? Aren't we right? Down with democratic procedure! A little violence and everything will be put straight.' 'Democracy? We are in a hurry!' is a frequent comment of Third World intellectuals and their friends everywhere. Liberals, in contrast, are certain that the short cut of dictatorial arbitrariness and violence is not a short cut at all, but a road ending in the dead swamp of despotism and conformity; that to avoid this so-called 'short-cut' it is necessary to reject dogmatism, utopianism and perfectionism, to control emotions and imagination, to assert intellectually the priority of reason, and ethically the priority of duty, and to accept the heavy burden of responsibility.

THE MOTE AND THE BEAM

It is common to make a sharp distinction between oneself and others, to adopt in matters relating to ethics (laws, at the level of political structures) a double standard. 'We' and 'they' may engage in the same type of action, but if 'they' do it, it is something other than if 'we' do it. Someone else's tyranny, exploitation, cruelty is evil — not one's own. Liberals reject this distinction: laws define the citizens' rights and duties; the struggle for laws equal for all requires total rejection of the moral double standard which has always prevailed in mankind, and in matters of political action is accepted more widely today than it was in a recent past.

Many are revolted by oppression, discrimination, and the suffering thereby caused — as long as those who oppress and discriminate are others. They themselves, when oppressing, discriminating, and inflicting suffering, are unaware of what they are doing or indifferent to it, or shield themselves with an armour of fine justifications. Two generations ago, authoritarian revolutionary socialists, rightly horrified by 2000 victims of czarist repression when Stolypin was in control, felt no concern for the nearly 2,000,000 victims of post-1917 Bolshevik repression; later, they felt no concern for the more than 20,000,000 victims of Stalinist repression. National-communists everywhere are revolted by the cruelty of capitalist exploitation, but find the cruelty accompanying collectivist exploitation legitimate. In the 1930s and early 1940s Hitlerians and Stalinists — tens of millions in each group — accused each other of abominable cruelties: each was as cruel as the other. Middle Eastern national-socialists who champion the cause of Arab refugees from Israel have no thought for the equal number of Jews who fled Arab oppression, and their descendants, now making half the population of Israel. Many who had been outspoken in exposing the brutality of the Cuban Castro and North Vietnamese Ho, kept quiet in the early 1970s about the brutality of the Chilean military junta and the South Vietnamese Thieu.

For most liberals, morality underlies all aspects of individual and collective life. They are convinced that unless there is equality in the moral field, there cannot be equality in social and political fields for any length of time, that moral equality requires the abolition of the double standard, that its abolition is an absolute prerequisite to moral betterment. For liberals, Reformed Christians who once felt guilt about the execution of heretics were on a higher ethical plane than Counter-Reformation Christians who self-righteously approved of it. Americans who felt guilt about atrocities committed by U.S. troops in the Vietnam war were on a higher ethical plane than the many everywhere who justified massacres carried out by national-communist Vietnamese and Cambodians.

Rejecting the double standard means to be aware of one's short-comings and errors. Through this awareness, liberals have bared them-selves to attacks from those whose shortcomings and errors are greater, but who are shielded by their refusal to admit them. For several generations, since English-speaking people have expressed themselves without undue fear of punishment, liberals have criticised every aspect in the societies in which they were influential; they have provided information about the defects and limitations of liberalism. Today they provide information about what is wrong in thirty-odd liberal democracies. To discover what is wrong in traditional and radical authoritarian states, one has to rely on information provided by emotional members of clandestine organisations, by embittered exiles and by unreliable agents of secret services.

Rejecting the double standard means to view reality as it is. Usually what one sees is not pleasant. Between most Christians and reality there has been a screen inscribed with 'love', 'charity' and 'salvation'; between disciples of Lenin of all persuasions and reality, there is a screen on which tyranny is called 'cult of personality', dictatorship is 'democratic centralism', forced labour camps become 're-education centres', recanting under duress is 'self-criticism', class genocide is 'humanitarian concern for toiling masses', aggression is 'war of liberation', indoctrination is 'enlightenment'. Screens enable people to go through life blithely unaware of their evil deeds. Liberals try to remove screens, and come under attack because of what they expose.

LIBERALISM'S ACHILLES' HEEL

The liberals' first freedom, liberty of expression, is the single major source of the twentieth-century revolt against liberalism. The uncovering of errors and horrors, and the providing of means — discussion, association, agitation and free suffrage — for action aimed

at correcting errors and eliminating horrors, is the distinctive mark of
societies organised through free institutions.

The evidence of recent generations shows that the very uncovering
leads many (specifically, a majority of the intelligentsia) to the
belief that free institutions are responsible for errors and horrors.
Through intellectual sleight of hand the uncovering becomes the
source of what is uncovered. Moreover, discussion and agitation
heighten emotions to a pitch that many find unbearable. Freedom of
action provides increased opportunities to overstep the bounds of
what is feasible without disrupting the social order; repression,
through police action and trials covered by the media, becomes
evident.

It is fashionable to concentrate on the many defects of market and
mixed economies (from now extinct *laissez-faire* to welfarism) and
to pass from opposition to economic policies advocated now or in
the past by liberals, to rejection of liberal principles and institutions.
However, evidence shows that mankind's dynamic sector is affected
not by what goes on in the economic field, but by *knowledge* of what
goes on. In market economies each defect is reported and freely
discussed. In dictatorial command economies there is as much controlled reporting and discussion as the dictatorship allows. The result
is disturbing awareness in market economies, ignorance and acquie-
scence in command economies.

A few examples will suffice to show this. Between the First and the
Second World War living standards in Italy declined as the result of
the corporate command economy established by the fascist dictatorship. The decline was not publicised or discussed. Consequently,
dissatisfaction with economic conditions was less than it was in the
post-1945 liberal-democratic republic, when standards rose (albeit
unevenly) thanks to the dynamism of a mixed economy. From the
uprooting of millions of farm workers and forced labour in the Soviet
Union in the late 1920s, to the disruption of economic activities in
1967–9 and forced migration from urban to rural areas in China,
greater harshness has characterised collectivist economies than market
economies, in spite of the latter's depressions and recessions. Collectivist harshness was neither reported nor discussed; depressions and
recessions were widely reported and discussed. Consequently, a
majority of the world intelligentsia looks with admiration at collectivism and other command economies, which provide fewer goods and
services and less economic satisfaction than market and mixed
economies.

Slavery, serfdom and kindred institutions were important features
in authoritarian societies of the Eastern hemisphere. Spokesmen for
descendants of slaves, and leaders of communities once victims of the

slave trade, have turned violently against everything connected with
the movement that opposed slavery and struggled for its abolition.
At the same time they praise those of their own ancestors who had
been slave raiders, and ally themselves with states which practised
slavery and in which the voice of an abolitionist was never heard.

If Germany had not been defeated in the Second World War,
Germans would never have believed the unreported massacre of
millions of human beings perpetrated by the nazis; they would have
denied that anything of the sort had ever happened; there would
never have been a sense of guilt. If atrocities which occurred in
countries where there is no freedom of expression are mentioned,
admirers of those countries shrug their shoulders: 'How can you
prove it?'

In recent years abuses committed by the American chief executive
and his intimates, and by American intelligence agencies, have been
publicised by the media and have disturbed the public profoundly.
Abuses committed by dictators and their secret agencies, about which
no more than vague rumours are known, do not disturb the public
of authoritarian states.

Since passions heighten in the measure in which there is knowledge
and discussion of errors and horrors, freedom of expression creates a
climate charged with emotion. Free communications media mean
that all can share in the sufferings of others. In 1964—72, for the
first time in history (and the last, if freedom of expression is replaced
everywhere by censorship) a whole nation experienced at home the
tragedies and cruelties of warfare, of war as it is. Americans, and
through American free media people the world over, saw My Lai and
the hundred dead. Television viewers in states ruled by national-
communists, their allies, friends and admirers never saw, never heard
of, the three thousand dead, victims of the North Vietnamese in Hué.
The death of four students reported by press, radio and television in
1970 led to a deep wave of revulsion and protest in the United States.
No revulsion or protest followed the death of many times that
number of students in Poland and Egypt in the spring and autumn of
1968, in Uganda in 1976.

Knowledge contributes to action. In the early 1960s, Buddhist
monks set themselves on fire to protest against the tyranny of a
dictator in the American-protected section of Vietnam. Because of
the American presence, the dictator was forced to allow foreign
reporters and photographers to roam at will, or nearly at will.
Reporters and television cameras rushed to the scene. News agencies
of countries in which there was freedom of communications media
made photographs available throughout the world (for small sums).
There was revulsion; the dictator was isolated at home and abroad.

When, thanks to the climate created by revulsion and isolation, the dictator was assassinated, the consent of opinion was: 'well done!' In the summer of 1976 a protestant minister in East Germany and several Buddhist monks in Vietnam set themselves on fire to protest against the suppression of religious freedom. Reporters were not called in. Television cameras were not set up. News of the events reached foreign countries by word of mouth; time had passed, there was no photographic evidence, sources might have been biased. There was no excitement, no response. Censorship had done its job: what one does not know, does not hurt.

In dictatorships, repression is not publicised, and it also precludes possible action. When controls are efficiently applied, action, even at the conspiratorial level, cannot be initiated. In past generations, Indians were deprived of their lands by white Americans, and Tatars were deprived by White Russians of an equal amount of land. In the 1970s, Sioux and other American Indians, helped by white Americans, took widely publicised steps which strengthened the Indians' sense of their own identity, and increased white Americans' awareness that there was a problem and that it should be solved in favour of the Indians. Descendents of Tatars who once lived independently in the khanates of Khazan, Sibir and others, or as nomadic tribes, claimed self-determination in 1918—19. They were shot down. There were no articles in the Soviet press, no television cameras, when survivors or Crimean Tatars, deported during the Second World War, were dispersed by the police before beginning to demonstrate for permission to return home. While Tatars are being denationalised, the public of the Soviet Union is unaware that there is a Tatar problem. Soon there will be no problem. Censorship and repression are doing their job.

8

CONCLUSION

PURGATORY

Liberalism was born in the minds of those convinced that liberty is
not only 'mine', belonging to me and those who agree with me, but
also 'theirs', belonging to those who do not agree with me. Those
holding such convictions were few. They became many. Now they
are not so many. Liberalism acquired significance when dissent —
heresy, deviation and opposition — became legitimate, when 'I' and
'they' were on the same level, when the major political problem was
no longer how to achieve any specific goal, but rather how to
establish an institutional structure enabling people equal but
different, and pursuing different goals, to coexist peacefully.

Liberalism had its political beginning when, at a time of deep
religious emotion, institutions were advocated that recognised first
the equal rights of different groups of believers, later the equal rights
of believers and non-believers as well. It was born in the religious
turmoil that followed the Reformation. What became applied to
different religious groups applied later to different political
tendencies. Liberals maintained that citizens are equally entitled to
look forward and be progressives, or to look backward and be
conservatives, or to look nowhere; entitled to advocate or oppose
church—state connection, to be for or against free enterprise and
mercantilism, later for or against welfarism, co-operativism and other
economic systems, for or against involvement in foreign conflicts.
When nationalism became a paramount emotion, liberals (most of
whom were inclined towards nationalism) respected the rights of
non-nationalists, such as pre-1914 socialists and pacifists, to express
themselves and to agitate for their cause. Later, problems arose
concerning differences derived from the division of labour, the
multiplicity of economic activities, the uneven distribution of
property, the individual's position in the economic structure; it was
implicit in the liberals' institutional system that manual workers
would rise to the level of non-manual ones, that status should be the
same whatever the income, that possession of property is not a
privilege.

Equal rights for all and legitimacy of dissent were among the major disruptive revolutionary innovations which liberalism introduced. They appealed to some, and now frighten most. The deep animosity that advocates of authoritarian regimes and admirers of six-score or so dictatorships have for liberalism gives some idea of the antagonism it meets with everywhere, even in the nations of its birth. Contrary to all other ideological—political creeds, liberalism does not promise salvation, not even the solution to all problems. In the liberal theology there are neither Hell nor Heaven but only Purgatory — a steep mountain one may climb to obtain a wider view and to breathe cleaner air, but without ever reaching the summit.

GUIDANCE VERSUS SPONTANEITY

It is easy to be misled by the multiplicity of movements with different names agitating mankind, and by the protestations of concern for liberal principles and aspirations from advocates of political monopoly and thought control. In the course of a debate in 1946, this writer's opponent said 'we are all liberals'. The fact of the matter is that we are not all liberals, just as we are not all democrats (even if most opponents of democracy would echo the Italian dictator who stated in 1932 that what he stood for was 'the purest form of democracy'), or, indeed, all anything else. As we are not all liberals, as there are areas shared intellectually and institutionally by liberals and non-liberals, and ideas are manipulated to deceive oneself as much as to deceive others, to be aware of the dividing line is important.

To dot the 'i's, those for liberal democracy are: progressive and moderate liberals and small groups of national liberals, also revisionist socialists and lay and confessional consti-tutional conservatives — many words to indicate a shrinking minority of mankind. The illiberal forces fall into two categories: those opposed to change and those favouring it. Their goals and supporting arguments vary, but not the institutional structures based on central-ised irresponsible power, an arbitrary secret police, censorship and command economies.

Traditionalists, nationalists and authoritarian lay and confessional conservatives consider liberty a privilege and reject equality. They are elitists. The corollary of elitism is oligarchy, politically; in the area of activities of the mind, monopoly of communications media and education; economically, command economies favouring property owners, at times tempered by a measure of paternalism towards wage-earners and the working class generally. Oligarchy, monopoly and command economies mean guidance of the many by the few.

Authoritarian radicals favour change. They attack liberals and kindred groups as incapable of fulfilling their promises or unwilling to do so, thereby falling short of the goal of a society of free and equal citizens. Whatever their protestations about liberty and equality, authoritarian radicals have shown themselves to be committed not to the open society in which spontaneity plays a leading role, but to a closed society characterised, in all fields, by guidance of the many by a few who in turn are bound by their own dogmatism. From Jacobins in 1793 to Ethiopian revolutionary officers in 1974, authoritarian radicals — in the name of the good of the people — have restricted political options, censored communications media, monopolised education and established command economies.

In today's ideological—political spectrum, rightist authoritarians favour guidance because of their elitism, and leftist authoritarians are elitists because of their commitment to guidance. All are opposed to the spontaneity which is the foundation of the liberal-democratic heresy, centred institutionally on free elections and on what makes them meaningful and operative. The re-establishment of censorship in November 1917, the creation of the cheka in December of that year and the disbanding of the constituent assembly in January 1918, proved that all traces of liberalism had been eliminated from the March revolution in Russia, that counter-revolutionaries were in power. Similar steps taken today have exactly the same meaning.

Originally, the debate between opponents and partisans of authoritarianism was rightly focused on political structures. During the last three generations or so it has been focused primarily on economic systems and policies, and for many the debate has lost in clarity. In fact the debate always concerns political structures and the entire field of non-material activities, economic arguments usually being only a pretext to persuade people to accept dictatorial systems.

LIBERALS' AND SOCIALISTS' MUTUAL AMBIVALENCE

Today the question of the correct relationship between liberalism and socialism is all-important for liberals, at the theoretical as well as the practical level. Many liberals joined hands with socialists in the past, and many do so now. When clear-headed French progressive liberals called their party (the pivot of the Third Republic) Radical Socialist, they indicated where they stood. As repeatedly stated, labour parties of all continents are largely coalitions of progressive liberals and revisionist socialists. Free trade unionism is as much liberal as socialist (sometimes more), in North America of course, and also in

other nations. Examples of recent cases of collaboration between
liberal and socialist parties have been given. Without going outside
their immediate circles, members of the intelligentsia (the dynamic
minority acting as guide to mankind, one must always remember)
meet people who call themselves 'socialists' and are more committed
to 'liberty, equality, fraternity' and to the institutions of a society of
free and equal citizens, and are thus more liberal, than many who call
themselves 'liberals'. Why not be a socialist?

Aware of economic problems and their social impact, many liberals
(in Great Britain since the immediate post-Napoleonic period) were
moved to action by the moral imperatives that no rationalisation
about market economies justifies the subordination of wage-earners
in a free enterprise or any other system, and indifference to the
suffering of those left behind in the quickening economic race; that
human rights having absolute priority over property rights, the
enhancement of the living conditions of working people comes first
in any social and economic programme; that whatever the need for
differentiation of functions, the goal to aim at is the equal status of
people fulfilling different functions. It was a crime to wait for
generations for agrarian reforms in agricultural societies and for new
deals in industrial ones, and for experimenting with mixed welfare
economies. Once basic liberties enabling citizens to think and act
freely had been conquered, and spontaneity was replacing con-
straints, too many liberals were slow to realise that equality had
first place in political goals.

The ending of workers' subordination and of indifference to
suffering, legislation to improve the quality of life, to raise economic
and educational levels and to achieve equal status, elimination of
parasitism, radical agrarian reforms and new deals, welfarism, the
goal of equality, made many liberals in the past ambivalent towards
socialism, and make them so today. The urge to think, speak and act
freely, attachment to democracy as citizens' self-government,
revulsion against all despotism, made many socialists in the past, and
make them now, ambivalent towards liberalism.

Many, but not most. In the socialist movement now embracing
hundreds of millions, several million are many, but a small fraction of
the whole. Rejecting freedom of thought and expression, and
citizens' self-government through free elections, most socialists are of
communist authoritarian persuasion and entirely illiberal. Denying
non-socialists the liberties and democratic rights accepted for
socialists, centrists like Dubcek's and Allende's followers, like
factions in most parties affiliated with the Socialist International and
their youth organisations, like post-1945 ideologues whose spokesmen are, among others, the Swiss Ziegler and the American Chomsky,

are far from liberal positions. Their vaunted 'democratic socialism' is
akin to Jacobin political monopoly (see Chapter 5), i.e. not democracy
at all. There remain the revisionists, today a majority in parties
affiliated to the Socialist International, for which vote tens of
millions in the thirty-odd countries where elections are free.

When liberals do not have their own political organisation, or for
some reason mistrust it, moderates join constitutional conservatives
in fulfilling the negative function of acting as a brake against change,
and progressives tend to merge with revisionist socialists. These last,
however, are not a homogeneous force. American, German and other
Social Democrats, many New Zealand and other Labourites, humanitarian socialists such as Narayan's followers in India, have committed
themselves (with varying degrees of awareness) to democracy as the
liberals' organisation of spontaneity, as the unchanging method to
achieve ever-changing goals; they are liberal socialists. More numerous
and more influential are other revisionists whose commitment to
civil liberties and democracy does not extend to the acceptance of
spontaneity as a permanent feature of society, whose goal is an
institutional structure in which change can take place in only one
direction, and in which therefore intellectual, political and socio-
economic options are limited. Deep convictions, seldom mentioned
because taken for granted, but underlying action and so easily
verifiable, explain difficulties which in the mid-1970s arose between
Left Radicals and the Socialist party in France, explain the pre-
cariousness of the collaboration between Liberal and New Democratic parties in Canada, the failure of efforts made in Great Britain
since 1924 to achieve a stable alliance between Labour and Liberals,
the reluctance of most revisionists to have anything to do with
liberal organisations.

Major differences between liberals, however progressive, and
socialists, however revisionist, may be summarised as follows:

(i) Liberalism being what is implict in the word (individual
autonomy and responsibility), and socialism also being what is
implicit in the word (priority of the collectivity, and society's
responsibility), primary concerns for liberals are to expand the area
of spontaneity, and for socialists to guide individuals into their
appointed slots.

(ii) Spontaneity stimulates diversity, which to liberals is richness
of life and source of progress, and is a positive feature of society to
be obstructed as little as possible; the liberals' equality concerns
status. Socialists are not concerned with spontaneity and mistrust
diversity; their equality is uniformity.

(iii) The liberals' institutional structure takes people as they are,
and as they evolve under a minimum of government and other

pressures; cohesion is achieved through laws equal for all, enacted in an assembly of freely elected representatives of the citizens. The socialist institutional structure aims at moulding citizens.

(iv) With the important exception of moderates turned conservative because of support for property owners, liberals are people-conscious (historically, people meaning a nation, ideally mankind) while socialists are class-conscious. The whole — nation or mankind — being differentiated, liberals take heterogeneity and the presence in society of 'us' and 'them' (see p. 24) for granted, their formula for coexistence being the equal liberty of all. Revisionist socialists reject the authoritarian slogan 'one class, one party, one idea', but tend towards homogeneity.

(v) Empirical evidence tells liberals that multiple factors are always at work. Reasonableness tells them to choose the *optimum* and not the *maximum* in ideas and policies (see p. 30). Experience teaches them to live with differences (fashionably, 'contradictions'). Revisionist socialists, however undogmatic, make of one factor affecting a situation the only factor, bring ideas and policies to their ultimate 'logical' conclusion, and are horrified by 'contradictions'.

(vi) In the economic field differences are not substantial. Liberals accept *dirigisme*, which can become planning, also limitations to property rights, and mixed economies in which the public sector plays a large role, while revisionist socialists subordinate planning to the freely expressed will of the citizens, recognise limited property rights (but not limited to the point of being insignificant) and accept mixed economies in which the private sector plays a large role. Mixed welfare economies — an improvement over capitalism and over collectivism — are common ground for progressive liberals and revisionist socialists. But they too are unsatisfactory. Where does one go from there? In search of new economic formulas, liberals take the open road of trial and error, of never-ending experimentation which does not endanger institutions that make further experimentation possible. Socialists, still under the influence of the *non sequitur* that since capitalism is bad, collectivism must be good, continue to be committed to the dead-end of the collectivist system.

(vii) To the liberals' spontaneity, diversity, lessening of pressures over individuals, concern for society as a whole, pluralism, limited policies, adaptation to 'contradictions', unending economic trans-formation, socialists oppose guidance, uniformity, moulding of individuals, class, monism, unlimited policies, abolition of 'contradictions', collectivist dead-ends. Differences there are. From the viewpoint of society and of progress, they are an asset. There is, also, the common ground mentioned above; because of it, collabora-

tion between liberals and revisionist socialists is possible. Because of
the authoritarian tide, collaboration is necessary, especially in
nations where free institutions are weak.

LIBERTY ERODES CONSERVATISM

What has been said about the possibility (necessity where authoritarian forces are strong) of collaboration between liberals and
revisionist socialists, is valid also for the relationship between liberals
and constitutional conservatives. The word 'conservatism' implies
opposition to change, and thus incompatibility with liberalism.
However, there is as much of a radical difference between authoritarian and constitutional conservatives as there is between
authoritarian and revisionist socialists.

Bearing in mind that generalisations embrace a wide range of
variations and that there are exceptions in the measure in which
constitutional conservatism is affected by liberal moderatism, it can
be said that constitutional conservatives are class-conscious, are for
guidance and monopolistic property rights, use education to mould
individuals and not to stimulate spontaneity, tend to take ideas and
policies to their 'logical' or extreme conclusion; they accept diversity,
pluralism and differences within a hierarchical structure. On these
counts their distinctive position is alien to that of liberals. At the
same time, being constitutional, they are committed to free political
institutions and what makes them operative.

Empirical evidence shows that where there is liberty, individuals
and society do not stand still. The widely accepted commonplace
about the conservatism of liberty (and, today, specifically of liberal
democracy), formulated by advocates of radical authoritarianism, is
as ridiculous as it is fashionable. In any society, in the measure in
which free institutions replace authoritarian ones, conservatism as a
stand-still position is eroded. Conservatives who opt for constitutionalism — as many did in the past, and quite a few did in the mid-1970s,
from factions of India's Congress party to French Gaullists — become
committed to an institutional system in which change is possible, and
what conservatives hold to be important is jeopardised.

In relation to the three nations that were liberalism's launching
pad, constitutionalism meant that eighteenth-century British Tories
and American Southern planters, and early nineteenth-century French
legitimists, accepted opposition to their privileges, which were first
eroded, finally obliterated. In relation to nations touched later by
the liberal heresy, the constitutional faction of Japanese conservatives
which fought against authoritarian factions weakened the oligarchy
of which they were part, just as the constitutionalism of South

African conservatives is now weakening their oligarchy. Continental
European and Latin American confessional conservatives who moved
from authoritarian clericalism to constitutional Christian democracy,
opened the door to nonconformism, agnosticism, atheism, to the
upheavals transforming the Roman church. Lay conservatives like
landed proprietors and other property owners who stand — as many
did and do, on the basis of deep and sincere inner convictions — for
constitutionalism, accept a system in which property changes hands
easily and forces opposed to private ownership gather strength.

The survival of privilege, of oligarchic rule, of ecclesiastical control
of minds, of private monopolistic property, requires rejection of
freedom of expression, however restricted, and of political liberty,
however limited. This was made clear by ideologues of traditional
absolutisms (just as ideologues of new absolutisms justify censorship
and dictatorship in the name of the defence of this or that
'revolutionary' goal). Constitutional conservatives adopt positions
that make conservatism subject to change; instead of head-on
collision with liberalism, there is movement at different speeds along
parallel lanes. In France, the lanes were close enough in the late
1960s to make collaboration possible between moderate Independent
Republicans and conservative Gaullists, and to check a sudden
anarcho-communist rush. In Portugal, free institutions can last as
long as they are supported with equal commitment by the People's
Democratic party of liberals and liberal socialists, the revisionist
Socialist party, and the Social Democratic party of lay and confessional constitutional conservatives. In Spain, in 1977, the fate of
democracy hung largely on the commitment of Camuñas's liberals,
Gonzalez's socialists and Gil Robles's conservatives.

'MAKING OVERMUCH OF LIBERTY'

Referring not to the *ancien régime* about which he was writing, but
to the dismal present when a large majority of French people waxed
enthusiastic about their dictator, de Tocqueville wrote the above
words, adding 'nowadays . . . no one in France sets any store in it'.
In France, in the 1850s, it was fashionable — and evidence of
advanced thinking — to be contemptuous of those who stood for
liberty (as defined in Chapter 2) and for the simple institutional
structure through which liberty becomes a major feature in a nation's
way of life. It is also fashionable today in many parts of the world.

At the end of the book, this writer reiterates the unfashionable
thesis that liberty (Locke's capacity for choice and Kant's
spontaneity) matters more than anything else, that survival and
progress were made possible in the past by liberty, through inventive-

ness and experimentation, and that on liberty depend progress now, and possibly survival itself sooner or later. Since liberty makes for change, instability, uncertainty, most people reject it: in the historical scheme there is no difference between the appeal of the combination of nationalism and dogmatic authoritarian socialism, the most important force in world society today, and the veneration that once surrounded ancient Pharaohs, Kings of Kings, Sons of Heaven, who were the embodiment of order, stability and continuity. Conditions of liberty have existed in the past not because they were wanted, but because of inefficiency, disruption brought about by conflicts, or antagonism between authoritarian regimes. Liberalism, the movement which produced the revolutions of 1688, 1776 and 1789, and everything that came out of those revolutions, has been the attempt to institutionalise liberty, to make it not an unwelcome accident but the foundation of ways of life. Liberal democracy is still the heresy it was generations ago; dictatorship is still the orthodoxy it always has been with monarchs, theocracies and oligarchies. Once again, what man has created, man can lose; if democracy as the organisation of liberty, now surviving in fewer than one-fifth of the world's sovereign states, is lost, it may be lost forever.

Thanks to greater efficiency and larger populations, the new absolutism is more frightful and frightening than the old. It kills by tens of millions and not by tens of thousands. Excuses for the killing get more and more perfunctory: 'exaggeration!'; 'a passing phase'; eventually to the point of callousness — 'so what?' — and mausoleums in which dictators who were chief executioners are entombed become shrines. Adding political subjection and monopoly of media and education to economic subservience, control over citizens becomes total. Scientific advances perfect control over consciences and minds: 'the strength of civilisation without its mercy [is] the most frightful of all spectacles' wrote the young Macaulay, commenting on brutality in eighteenth-century India. That brutality was only a fraction of that which exists today. Perhaps this writer makes overmuch of liberty; perhaps no one has ever made overmuch of it.

49 B.C., A.D. 1434, . . . ?

Arnold Toynbee, deeply concerned about liberty, in a lecture delivered at mid-century in Troy, New York, reminded the audience that attempts had been made three times to escape from authoritarian moulds, and to replace servile institutions, which are the norm of social organisation, with free institutions; that the third attempt was the one made in modern times, and that the two previous attempts had each failed after 300 years or so.

Limitedly and imperfectly, there was government by citizens in the Roman state after the rebuilding of Rome around 390 B.C. In 49 B.C. Caesar, basking in military glory, launched a brief civil war in which he was supported by a majority of citizens. When the fighting was over, the republic was over too. There was some opposition. There were ups and downs. The last traces of citizens' sovereignty disappeared in the first century A.D. Ever since, Caesar has been widely acclaimed and his opponents (led by Cicero, Cato, Brutus) denigrated.

There had been republican self-government in the Italian city-state of Florence since the first half of the twelfth century. In 1434, Cosimo de' Medici, supported by a majority of citizens including those who today would be styled 'progressives', began his dictatorial rule. There was some opposition. Here too there were ups and downs. In 1530 the curtain came down on the Florentines' experiment in liberty. The Medicis are admired. Their opponents (led by Capponi, Soderini, Ferrucci) have been forgotten.

The end of the third century of the last, rather feeble, attempt to make liberty the foundation of the social order is approaching. The wave of dictatorial despotism begun during the First World War and arrested temporarily in 1945 has caused liberal democracies to be islands in an authoritarian ocean. This is where mankind stands, on the threshold of the 1980s.

BIBLIOGRAPHICAL NOTE

Reasons of space limit the selection of publications concerning liberalism, originally written in English or available in translation. Works listed in this bibliographical note — articles and pamphlets, books in one or more volumes, documents such as constitutions — have been selected primarily on the basis of the importance they have for liberals, the clarity with which they define liberal positions and the accuracy with which they describe aspects of the liberal movement. They represent a small fraction of the abundant and highly diversified literature on liberalism as ideas and values, as institutions, as a central element for several generations of modern civilisation, as the thought and action of individual liberals.

Informative introductions for interested readers are the articles on 'Liberalism' by Harry K. Girvetz in *The New Encyclopaedia Britannica* (London: Benton, 1974), vol. 10, '*Macropaedia*', pp. 846–51; by David G. Smith in the *International Encyclopedia of the Social Sciences* (New York: Macmillan, 1968) vol. 9, pp. 276–82; by Kenneth R. Minogue in *Encyclopedia Americana* (New York: Americana, 1975) vol. 17, pp. 294–6; by Volker Sellin in *Marxism, Communism and the Western Society* (New York: Herder & Herder, 1973) vol. V, sections A and B, pp. 199–207. The pamphlet by Irene Collins, *Liberalism in Nineteenth Century Europe* (London: Routledge & Kegan Paul, 1957) is a useful and perceptive appraisal. D. J. Manning, *Liberalism* (New York: St. Martin's Press, 1976) is an essay on liberalism as an ideological position.

The early formulation of principles later included in the liberal position and incorporated in the institutional structure advocated by liberals, is contained in ten important works. The earliest are two masterful tracts published in 1644. In *Areopagitica: a Speech for the Liberty of Unlicensed Printing*, John Milton championed freedom of expression, the essential liberty and the key to all other liberties. *The Bloudy Tenent of Persecution for Cause of Conscience* by Roger Williams is a statement for the greatest heresy of all, tolerance, without which there cannot be dissent and equality of diverse tendencies. On tolerance, in 1689, appeared the reasoned arguments

of the widely read *Letter Concerning Toleration* by John Locke
(followed by three more *Letters*, the last one unfinished because of
the author's death in 1704). Voltaire's *Treatise on Tolerance*,
published in 1763, was a call to arms in the struggle against
fanaticism on the Continent. Valuable for the philosophical foundation of liberalism are Locke's *Essay Concerning Human Understanding* (which was written when the author was an exile, published in
1690, and should have included 'Some Thoughts on the Conduct of
the Understanding in the Search of Truth', published posthumously),
and Immanuel Kant's *Foundations of the Metaphysics of Ethics*
(1785). The rationale for the system of institutions through which
the citizens' equal liberty in time becomes part of the way of life was
provided by Locke's *Two Treatises of Government* (1690), Charles
de Montesquieu's *The Spirit of Laws* (published in French in 1748
and in English in 1750), and the series of articles published in
1787–8 by Alexander Hamilton, James Madison and John Jay, soon
collected in book form in *The Federalist* (among the many editions,
one of the best is edited by Benjamin F. Wright and published by the
Harvard University Press, 1961). In *An Inquiry into the Nature and
Causes of the Wealth of Nations* (1776), Adam Smith advocated the
emancipation of economic activities from which came an astounding
expansion in output of goods and services.

[The French thirty-three-volume *Encyclopédie, ou Dictionnaire
raisonné des sciences, des arts et des métiers* (1751–72), synthesis of
eighteenth-century progressivism, needs mention on account of its
wide-ranging influence, and because it made of its readers the
collective force which overthrew the *ancien régime* on the Continent
and its dependencies. Articles by Diderot, Voltaire, Turgot and
others, and D'Alembert's 'Preliminary Discourse' were a source of
inspiration for liberal-minded people. One of the publications that
was patterned on the *Encyclopédie* was the *Encyclopaedia Britannica*,
first issued in 1768–71 and widely expanded in each following
edition (two of them appearing before the end of the eighteenth
century), an important vehicle for liberal ideas for several
generations.]

Philosopher, political scientist, educator, deeply concerned with
economic problems (among other important works are *Some
Thoughts concerning Education* of 1693, and *Some Considerations
of the Consequences of the Lowering of Interest, and Raising the
Value of Money* of 1692, followed by *Further Considerations* of
1695), Locke had provided the first synthesis of the liberal position.
In the next place as synthesiser belongs Jeremy Bentham, already a
liberal democrat more than a constitutional liberal; particularly
important were his *A Fragment on Government* (1776) and *An*

Introduction to the Principles of Morals and Legislation (1789); ably translated into French by the Genevese Etienne Dumont, Bentham's works became widely known on the Continent and in Latin America. *Common Sense* (1776), *Rights of Man* (1791–2) and *Age of Reason* (1794) made Thomas Paine popular among progressive liberals on both sides of the Atlantic. What Locke had been for early constitutional liberalism, John Stuart Mill was for the democratic liberalism which incoporated a wide range of social reforms. Among his many works are the *System of Logic* (1843), *Principles of Political Economy, with Some of their Applications to Social Philosophy* (1848), *On Liberty* (1859), *Utilitarianism* (1861) and *Considerations on Representative Government* (1862). In the essay *On the Subjection of Women* (1869) Mill became the most authoritative spokesman for genuine liberal democracy. In *Social Liberty: or the Necessary Limits of Individual Freedom Arising out of the Conditions of our Social Life* (published posthumously) Mill began to build the bridge between liberalism and revisionist socialists who saw in socialism the fulfillment, not the negation, of liberalism – the bridge leading to contemporary social liberalism.

In the twentieth century liberal positions were clarified, and at times reformulated, in the light of new situations and problems. Keeping in mind that any selection is somewhat arbitrary, while limiting the list of works to twenty, the following have been chosen to indicate major lines along which clarification and reformulation have taken place:

Leonard T. Hobhouse, *Liberalism* (New York: Holt, 1911), an excellent and comprehensive essay, reflecting primarily the British experience, but going beyond it.

Walter Rathenau, *The New Society* (London: Williams & Norgate, 1921), first published in German in 1919, the thoughtful position of a German liberal, prominent in private activities and in public service.

James Bryce, *Modern Democracies* (London: Macmillan, 1921), the crowning work of a distinguished Liberal statesman and scholar.

Guido de Ruggiero, *The History of European Liberalism* (published in Italian in 1925, in English, London: Milford, 1927), the work of a philosopher, spurred to write on liberalism by the rapid advance of fascism.

J. Salwyn Schapiro, *Condorcet and the Rise of Liberalism* (New York: Harcourt, Brace, 1934), an American historian presents liberalism through the thought and action of one of its major spokesmen. Also by Schapiro are *Liberalism and the Challenge of Fascism: Social*

Forces in England and France, 1815–1870 (New York: McGraw-Hill, 1949), and the brief but clear and cogent *Liberalism, Its Meaning and History* (Princeton: Van Nostrand, 1957).

Benedetto Croce, *History as the Story of Liberty* (London: Allen & Unwin, 1941), the foremost Italian intellectual of the twentieth century presents history as the product of human creativity.

Salvador de Madariaga, *Spain* (London: Jonathan Cape, 1942), this, and other works, explains the commitment which enabled the Spanish liberal statesman and *homme de lettres* to withstand the bitterness of a forty-year exile (1936–76).

Karl R. Popper, *The Open Society and its Enemies* (London: Routledge, 1945), a masterful attack against advocates of dictatorial systems, whatever the colour of their ideological armour.

Frederick M. Watkins, *The Political Tradition of the West; A Study in the Development of Modern Liberalism* (Harvard University Press, 1948), an excellent synthesis of what liberalism is and how it developed.

Arthur Schlesinger Jr, *The Vital Center; The Politics of Freedom* (Boston; Houghton Mifflin, 1949), an argument for liberal principles and the institutions needed to avoid the disastrous results of polarisation and extremism.

Friedrich Meinecke, *The German Catastrophe; Reflections and Recollections* (Harvard University Press, 1950), the reflections of a liberal historian which apply to all nations at all times.

Adlai E. Stevenson, *Major Campaign Speeches, 1952* (New York: Random House, 1953), the faith of the major spokesman for recent American liberalism.

Joseph Grimond, *The Liberal Future* (London: Faber & Faber, 1959), the leader for over ten years of the British Liberal party speaks to his fellow-liberals in the United Kingdom and elsewhere.

Harry K. Girvetz, *The Evolution of Liberalism*, rev. edn (New York: Collier, 1963), a thoughtful treatise written mainly from the viewpoint of liberalism in the United States.

Kenneth R. Minogue, *The Liberal Mind* (London: Methuen, 1963), a book more far-ranging in space and time than that of Girvetz.

Robert D. Cumming, *Human Nature and History: A Study in the Development of Liberal Political Thought* (Chicago University Press, 1969), a comprehensive, perceptive and informative treatise focused primarily on a discussion of John Stuart Mill.

Jean-Jacques Servan-Schreiber, *The Radical Alternative* (New York: Norton, 1971), lively advocacy of liberal policies by a brilliant writer and influential French politician.

Ralf Dahrendorf, *Class and Class Conflict in Industrial Society*, rev. edn (Stanford University Press, 1973), a foremost cosmopolitan academician and international public servant analyses widely held misconceptions concerning the role of conflict in society.

A concise statement of the post-1945 liberal position is contained in *The Liberal Manifesto* (London: The Liberal International), drawn up at the International Liberal Conference held in Oxford, England, in April 1947, and in resolutions approved in successive Congresses of the Liberal International.

Among books on freedom by concerned writers who lived through the crises of the Second World War and during the difficult post-1945 period, are the following: Dorothy Fosdick, *What is Liberty? A Study in Political Thought* (London: Harper, 1939); Isaiah Berlin, *Two Concepts of Liberty* (Oxford: Clarendon Press, 1958), also *Four Essays on Liberty*, (Oxford University Press, 1969); Mortimer J. Adler, *The Idea of Freedom* (New York: Doubleday, 1958); Herbert J. Muller, *Issues of Freedom; Paradoxes and Promises* (New York: Harper, 1960), also *Freedom in the Ancient World* (New York: Harper, 1961), and *Freedom in the Western World* (New York: Harper & Row, 1963); Oscar and Mary Handlin, *The Dimensions of Liberty* (Harvard University Press, 1961); Carl J. Friedrich (ed.), *Liberty* (New York: Atherton, 1962); Bruce F. Harris, (ed.) *Freedom as a Political Ideal* (University of Auckland, 1964); David Spitz, *Essays on the Liberal Idea of Freedom* (University of Arizona Press, 1964). John B. Bury, *A History of Freedom of Thought* (London: Williams & Norgate, 1913) is the classical treatise on its subject. Glenn Tinder, *Tolerance, Toward a new Civility* (University of Massachusetts Press, 1976) is the reasoned answer to the advocates of the 'new' intolerance. Deeply felt humanistic commitment saves some moderates from joining the ranks of conservatives: Walter Lippmann, *An Inquiry into the Principles of the Good Society* (Boston: Little, Brown, 1937); Wilhelm Röpke, *Civitas Humana, a Humane Order of Society* (London: Hodge, 1948); Friedrich A. von Hayek, *The Constitution of Liberty* (London: Routledge, 1960). Constitutionalism can be the ante-room to liberalism: Aristotle's *Politics* and Cicero's *Republic* and *Laws* are as timely today as they were when free institutions were being obliterated in ancient Greece and Rome; among modern and contemporary writers on constitutionalism are: Walter Bagehot, *The English Constitution* (London: Chapman & Hall, 1967); James Bryce, *Constitutions* (Oxford University Press, 1905);

Charles H. McIlwain, *Constitutionalism, ancient and Modern* (Cornell University Press, 1940); Carl J. Friedrich, *Constitutional Government and Democracy: Theory and Practice in Europe and America* (Boston: Little, Brown, 1950).

In the economic field, Ricardo, his disciples, and the 'Manchester School' never held a monopoly of liberal thinking. There were different and sounder liberal voices, particularly in the United States, starting with statements (and policies) of Thomas Jefferson and Andrew Jackson, and with treatises written early in the nineteenth century: Mathew Carey, *Essays in Political Economy* (1819); Daniel Raymond, *Thoughts on Political Economy* (1820); John Roe, *Principles of Political Economy* (1834). Having considerable impact on American economic thinking and policies in the twentieth century are the works of Adolf A. Berle and Gardiner C. Means, *The Modern Corporation and Private Property* (New York: Macmillan, 1933); Alvin H. Hansen, *Economic Policy and Full Employment* (New York: McGraw-Hill, 1947); Paul Douglas, *Economy in the National Government* (Chicago University Press, 1952); Adolf A. Berle, *The Twentieth Century Capitalist Revolution* (New York: Harcourt, Brace, 1954). In Great Britain, already Bentham in his *Manual of Political Economy* differentiated himself from dogmatic free enter-prisers. However, the main innovator in liberal economic thought was John Maynard Keynes, whose writings include *The Economic Consequences of the Peace* (London: Macmillan, 1919), *The End of Laissez-faire* (London: Hogarth Press, 1926), *The General Theory of Employment, Interest, and Money* (London: Macmillan, 1936). Works by William Beveridge, such as *Social Insurance and Allied Services* (London: H.M.S.O., 1944) — the so-called 'Beveridge Report' — and *Full Employment in a Free Society* (London: Allen & Unwin, 1945), provided main guidelines for social reforms in Great Britain introduced by the Labour party, and most of them confirmed by the Conservative party. Dealing with neo-liberal economic policies in the post-1945 period were: Walt W. Rostow, *The Economics of Take-off into Sustained Growth* (New York: St Martin's Press, 1964); Jean-Jacques Servan-Schreiber, *The American Challenge* (New York: Atheneum, 1968); Ralf Dahrendorf, *The New Liberty: Survival and Justice in a Changing World* (Stanford University Press, 1975).

Among interesting post-1945 publications on liberalism in specific countries are: Louis Hartz, *The Liberal Tradition in America, An Interpretation of American Political Thought since the Revolution* (New York: Harcourt, Brace, 1955); Leonard Krieger, *The German Idea of Freedom* (Boston: Beacon Press, 1957); George Fischer, *Russian Liberalism, From Gentry to Intelligentsia* (Harvard

University Press, 1958); Donald G. Rohr, *The Origins of Social Liberalism in Germany* (University of Chicago Press, 1963); Ivor Bulmer-Thomas, *The Growth of the British Party System* (London: Baker, 1965); Wilfred H. Calcott, *Liberalism in Mexico, 1857–1929* (Hamden, Connecticut: Anchor Books, 1965); Leopold Marquard, *Liberalism in South Africa* (Johannesburg: South African Institute of Race Relations, 1965); Tatsuo Arima, *The Failure of Freedom; a Portrait of Modern Japanese Intellectuals* (Harvard University Press, 1969); Hao Chang, *Liang Ch'i Ch'ao and Intellectual Transition in China* (Harvard University Press, 1971); Jean F. Revel, *Without Marx or Jesus; The New American Revolution has Begun* (New York: Doubleday, 1971); William G. Rosenberg, *Liberals in the Russian Revolution, The Constitutional Democratic Party, 1917–1921* (Princeton University Press, 1974); Chris Cook, *A Short History of the Liberal Party* (London: Macmillan, 1976).

Among documents embodying liberal principles and making of them the foundation of institutional orders, are the following: the *Mayflower Compact* (1620) of 'Pilgrims' settling in New England; the English *Petition of Rights* (1627), *Habeas Corpus Act* (1640) and *Habeas Corpus Amendment Act* (1679), *Bill of Rights* (1689) and *Act of Toleration* (1689); the American *Declaration of Independence* (1776), the U.S. *Constitution* (1787) and its first *Ten Amendments* (1791); the French *Declaration of the Rights of Man and the Citizen* (1789) and *Constitution* of 1791 (and also the *Constitutions* of the Second and Fourth Republic); among other liberal constitutions, the Spanish one of 1812 served as rallying point for continental and Latin American liberals, the German one of 1919, that of Japan (1947) and that of India (1949) are well thought out; the *Covenant of the League of Nations* (1919) was the first attempt to institutionalise the liberal political process on a global level; the *Universal Declaration of the Rights of Man* (1948) is the testimonial to the world liberals hoped to create: it was drafted by René Cassin, P. C. Chang, F. Dehousse, John P. Humphrey, Charles Malik, Eleanor Roosevelt and Hernan Santa Cruz.

Historical works focusing on the role of liberty, whatever the time and place of events, have been important carriers of liberal convictions. Some of the most influential were not written by academic or professional historians. Widely diffused at the time when French culture set the tone on the Continent and its overseas dependencies, and its influence was felt in English-speaking communities, were Montesquieu's *Considerations on the Causes of the Greatness and Decline of the Romans* (1734), Voltaire's *Essay on the Manners and Spirit of Nations* (1756) and histories of the times of Charles XII of Sweden (1731), and Louis XIV of France (1751), and the *Sketch for a Historical Picture of the Progress of the Human Mind* (1795), a posthumously published work of Condorcet. The conservative Gibbon's interpretation of *The Decline and Fall of the Roman Empire* (1776—88) in the West was accepted by progressive members of the intelligentsia and rejected by traditionalists.

Selecting among the many distinguished and influential liberal historians of the nineteenth century, a list of twelve could include the following: the Swiss Simonde de Sismondi (also an economist who dissented profoundly from the prevailing *laissez-faire* school), author of the *History of the Italian Medieval Republics* (1807—24); the German Karl von Rotteck, author of a *History of the World: from the Creation to the Present Time; Containing a General History of the Rise, Progress, Revolutions, Wars, Events, etc. of All the Nations of the Earth* (1807—24, continued by C. J. Peterson and published in New York in 1875); George Bancroft, whose *History of the United States from the Discovery of America* (1834—74) is a ten-volume revolutionary hymn, and his contemporary William H. Prescott, whose heroes and villains were Spanish monarchs and *conquistadores*; the German Friedrich C. Dahlmann, a major figure in the revolution of 1848—9, made liberal propaganda through a *History of the English Revolution* (1844) and a *History of the French Revolution* (1845); Great Britain and the French revolution fascinated the Frenchman François Guizot (a prominent liberal until fear of the mob caused him to join conservative ranks), who wrote a *History of the English Revolution* (1826—8), Augustin Thierry, author of *The History of the Norman Conquest of England* (1825), Adolphe Thiers, whose many-volume *History of the French Revolution* (1823—7) and *History of the Consulate and the Empire* (1840—55) were written during interludes between periods of intense political activity; the British George Grote wrote about ancient Greece in his *History of Greece* (1847—56); Thomas B. Macaulay sang the praises of the Whig revolution in his *History of England* (1848—61), a best-seller in Great Britain and in the United States; also enjoying considerable popularity were John R. Green, author of a *Short History of the English People* (1874), and John D. Acton, whose *Lectures on Modern History* and *History of Freedom and Other Essays* were published posthumously in 1906 and 1907 respectively. The liberal temper shows in the pre-1914 edition of the *Cambridge Modern History*.

Among twentieth-century authors whose histories had liberty as focal points are: the Frenchman François Aulard, who wrote the *Political History of the French Revolution* (1905); the Czech Thomas G. Masaryk, first President of Czechoslovakia and author of *The Spirit of Russia: Studies in History, Literature and Philosophy* (1913); the German Friedrich Meinecke, who published in 1908 a

Study on the Origin of the German State, the Russian Paul Miliukov, among whose works are *Russia, To-day and To-morrow* (1922) and *History of Russia* (1968–9); the Italian Benedetto Croce, who criticised despotism in *A History of Italy, 1871–1915* (1929) and in the *History of Europe in the Nineteenth Century* (1933); the Spaniard Salvador de Madariaga, whose *Bolivar* (London: Hollis & Carter, 1952) is one of his many works on Spanish and Latin American history; the American Robert R. Palmer, author of, among many other works, *The Age of the Democratic Revolutions: A Political History of Europe and America, 1760–1800* (Princeton University Press, 1959–64). Comprehensive general histories are those of the British H. A. L. Fisher, *A History of Europe, Part Three, The Liberal Experiment* (London: Eyre & Spottiswood, 1935) and the eleven-volume *The Story of Civilization* (London: Angus & Robertson, 1935–75) by Will Durant.

Authoritative enemies of liberalism are legion. Whatever the phraseology, the statements made dogmatically by authors relying on intuition and tradition, the arguments developed by authors relying on reason, their works justify institutional systems which enforce authoritarianism and conformity. A major reasoned argument for absolutism was developed in Thomas Hobbes's *Leviathan* (1651), a book more popular perhaps in the post-1945 period than in previous generations. Sir Robert Filmer's *Patriarcha* (1680) is an example of commitment to absolutism founded on arational thinking. For several generations Roman catholic thinkers were in the fore-front of the opposition to liberalism. They range from the French de Bonald to the Canadian Paquet, the Italian Tacchi-Venturi, whose position like that of thousands of others was synthesised in encyclicals, from *Mirari Vos* (1832) to *Quanta Cura* (1864), *Pascendi Gregis* (1907) and more recent ones. Two major currents of illiberal thought have appealed to the twentieth-century intelligentsia. Liberal principles, values and institutions were frankly rejected by those whose spokesmen have been the French Barrès, the Anglo-German Houston S. Chamberlain, and other integral nationalists and racists, and those whose authority was the unfortunate Nietzche, a perceptive *littérateur* on the brink of insanity as political and social thinker. In this category, the most popular book has been Adolf Hitler's *My Struggle*, published in German in 1924 and in English translation by Hurst & Blackett in London and by the Stackpole Press in New York in 1939. Liberal institutions were denied in the name of the liberals' aspirations (and at times of liberal principles also) by Jacobins, Hegelians and Marxists, whose relationship to Rousseau, Hegel and Marx is no closer than is that of a majority of Christians to Christ. They share the common feature of being unable to conceive spontaneity, and of reducing the liberty of all (equal or unequal) to their own liberty. In this category the thinker (and doer) who fascinated most people has been Lenin, whose *What is to be Done?* (1902), *Imperialism, the Highest Stage of Capitalism* (1917), *State and Revolution* (1918) and other essays have been meditated upon by millions. Particularly influential in the post-1945 period has been Mao Tse-tung, whose aphorisms published in millions of copies of a small book with a red cover have been the equivalent of holy scriptures. Helping to crystallise ideas and providing a guide to action have been the works (in alphabetical order, and among many others) of: Régis Debray, Frantz Fanon, 'Che' Guevara, Herbert Marcuse, Kwame Nkrumah, J.-P. Sartre — each of them expounding his brand of, theoretically, libertarian communalism, each a committed supporter of totalitarian regimes (one a dictator himself, another a dictator's right-hand man).

SELECTIVE INDEX- GLOSSARY

Many of the names mentioned in the book are not listed in the Index—Glossary; for the better known names only basic dates are given. Topics are included in so far as they are important for liberalism.

European continent   *see* Continent, the
expression, freedom of (one of liberals'
  two essential liberties)   75f., 187—9,
  206—9, *passim*; the Achilles' heel of
  liberalism   206—9

Fabianism   *see* socialism, democratic
Fair Deal: rallying motto for U.S. Democrats
  during Truman's Presidencies 1945—53
  50, 103, 107
fanaticism (incompatible with liberalism)
  14, 119, 125—30, 178, 201
Far East   *see* Asia, eastern
Fascism   *see* national socialism
Faure, Edgar (1908—   ): French liberal
  statesman   53
Federalist party, U.S.: right-of-centre wing
  of revolutionary constitutional liberalism
  (and forerunner of the Republican party)
  34, 97
Fethy Bey (Okyar): Turkish national liberal
  statesman, founder of Liberal Republican
  party in 1930s   169
Feuillants, France: right-of-centre wing of
  revolutionary constitutional liberalism
  (and forerunner of the party of Independent Republicans)   34, 124, 126
Finland   143
Forward from Liberalism (1937) by
  S. Spender   5
four freedoms: of speech and expression, of
  conscience, from want, from fear — enunciated 6 Jan 1941 by F. D. Roosevelt
  152, 187
Fourier, Charles (1772—1837): early French
  socialist   20
Fox, Charles (1749—1806): for several
  decades leading progressive Whig   14
Fox, George (1624—1691): British Quaker
  and abolitionist   11
France   121—35, 138, 148, *passim*
Frankfurt School: of German intellectuals
  opposed to liberalism   40, 150
'Free and Equal': liberal slogan of American
  revolutionaries   xii, 26, 45, 59, 61, 96
Free Democratic party: German post-World
  War II liberal party   xiv, 147
Free Masons: eighteenth-century carriers of
  liberal ideas and aspirations   20f., 196
'Free Trade': for too long a war-cry of
  British Liberals   21, 56, 58
freedom of conscience   *see* conscience,
  freedom of, and tolerance
freedom of expression   *see* expression,
  freedom of
freedom of the individual   *see* liberty
freedom, political   *see* liberalism, and
  liberty, political

freedom of the press   *see* expression,
  freedom of
Friderichs, Hans (1931—   ): German
  liberal statesman   14
Friends of the People: early 1790s British
  Whigs in sympathy with French revolutionaries   34
Froebel, Friedrich (1782—1852): German
  progressive educator   52, 188
Frondizi, Arturo (1908—   ): Argentinian
  progressive liberal statesman   160
Fuller Ossoli, Sarah M. (1810—1850):
  American writer and advocate of women's
  rights   195
Fuzukawa Yukichi: Japanese educator, in
  1882 co-founder of the Reform party
  173

Gaitán, Jorge (1902—1948): Colombian
  liberal leader   19, 158, 161
Gallegos, Romulo (1884—1969): Venezuelan
  author and liberal statesman   158
Gambetta, Léon (1838—1882): French progressive liberal statesman   34, 135
Gandhi, Indira (1917—   )   4, 176f.
Gandhi, Mohandas (1869—1948)   175f.,
  179
Garibaldi, Giuseppe (1807—1882): Italian
  national democrat in the Jacobin tradition   128
Gaulle, Charles de (1890—1970)   151
Gaullism: post-World War II French conservative movement leaning towards
  authoritarianism   3, 35, 147, 153, 217
Germany (pre-1871 also the Germanies):
  passim; during the Reformation   70—2;
  and the socialist movement   138; liberals
  in post-Napoleonic period   132ff.; post-
  World War I   146f.; post-World War II
  East Germany   57, 143, 146, 186;
  post-World War II West Germany   4, 57,
  146, 153, 186
Giolitti, Giovanni (1842—1928): Italian
  liberal statesman   116, 135
Girondists, France: left-of-centre (democratic) wing of revolutionary French
  liberalism (and forerunner of Radical and
  Radical Socialist parties)   34, 41, 81,
  124f.
Gladstone, William (1809—1898)   87
Gobetti, Piero (1900—1926): Italian progressive liberal   116
Gokhale, Gopal K. (1866—1915): Indian
  national liberal   19, 175f.
Gomez, José (1858—1921): Cuban liberal
  statesman   158
government, constitutional   *see* constitutionalism, and liberalism, constitutional

movement leading to the revolutions of 1688, 1776, 1789   xii, 218; major steps   ch. 3

liberation movement, women's   *see* women, emancipation of

liberation movements (are not necessarily liberal)   xiii

libéristes: dogmatic advocates of integral capitalism   17, 58; indifferent to equality, they join conservatism   58

Libertas (1888): papal encyclical   30

liberties, too many indifferent to   60; medieval in Great Britain   75

liberty   22, 24, *passim*; increases awareness 88; a burden for most   60; a capacity for choice   1, 9, 11, 20, 23, 31, and as spontaneity   23, 62, cannot be proved or disproved   23; erodes conservatism 216f.; the source of creativity   24; definition   23; the source of dynamism 187–91; breeds diversity   24; breeds tensions   61; equal, is liberalism's central concept   25, 97, 210, 213, 215; its revolutionary impact   183; and richness of life   23; and self-discipline *see* ethics; divides socialists   138; striving for   xi; and survival   1, 13, 217; the highest value   27

'Liberty, equality, fraternity'   xii, 26, 163

Lib–Lab: merging of progressive liberalism and revisionist socialism in social liberalism and/or liberal socialism (Lib–Lab is the position of many Labour and Social Democratic parties) 91

Liebknecht, Karl (1871–1919): German authoritarian socialist, co-founder of the German Communist party   138

Lin Yü-t'ang (1895–1976): Chinese author and advocate of freedom of expression 171

Lincoln, Abraham (1809–1865)   13, 127, 196

'Live and let live': basic Whig attitude   55, 83f.

Lloyd George, David (1863–1945)   19, 56, 93, 135, 175

Locke, John (1632–1704)   9, 13, 20, 23, 55, 79, 81, 96, 117, 120, 217

Lopez Michelsen, Alfonso (1913–   ): Colombian liberal statesman   5, 161

Lorimer, James (1818–1890): Scottish jurist and internationalist   14

Löwe, Wilhelm (1814–1886): German democrat, later liberal leader   135

Luxembourg, Rosa (1871–1919): Polish authoritarian socialist, co-founder of the

German Communist party   20, 138

Lvov, George (1861–1925): Russian liberal, head of the revolutionary Provisional Government March–July 1917   19, 165

Lyon, Mary (1797–1855): American educator   195

Macaulay, Thomas B. (1800–1859)   91f.

McGovern, George (1922–   ): U.S. liberal political leader   98

Mackenzie, Alexander (1822–1892): Scottish-born Canadian liberal statesman 111

Madariaga, Salvador de (1886–   ): Spanish liberal spokesman   14

Madero, Francisco (1873–1913): Mexican liberal statesman   19, 157

Maher, Ali (1882–1960): Egyptian national constitutional statesman   179

Maklakov, Vasilii (1870–1957): Russian liberal   165

Malaya, and Malaysia   17, 177f.

Malik, Charles (1906–   ): Lebanese educator and liberal statesman   19, 179

Manin, Daniele (1804–1857): Italian liberal democrat   135

Mann, Horace (1796–1859): U.S. progressive educator   14

Mao Tse-tung (1893–1976)   5, 17, 170

market economy (use and remuneration of economic agents largely influenced by supply and demand   *see also* capitalism, *dirigisme*, economy, *libéristes*)   55, 59, 189ff., *passim*; one of four cornerstones of liberalism   2

Marshall, John (1755–1835): chief justice of the U.S. Supreme Court   97

Marshall Plan: of U.S. aid to European nations (after George Marshall)   109

Marx, Karl (1818–1883)   56, 89, 136, 138, 149

Marxism   *see* socialism, authoritarian

Masani, Minoo (1905–   ): Indian liberal spokesman   14

Masaryk, Jan (1886–1948): Czech liberal statesman   19

Masaryk, Thomas (1850–1937): Czech national liberal statesman   19

Mason, George (1725–1792): U.S. progressive statesman   97

massimalisti: majority faction in the pre-World War II Italian socialist movement 144; *see also* socialism, centrist

Mavros, George (1909–   ): Greek liberal leader   5

maximum: the counter-productive integra-